DISCARDED

DETROIT 1985

DETROIT 1985

Donald MacDonald

1980
Doubleday & Company, Inc.
Garden City, New York

ISBN: 0-385-11538-5
Library of Congress Catalog Card Number 76-23776

COPYRIGHT © 1980 BY DONALD MACDONALD
ALL RIGHTS RESERVED
PRINTED IN THE UNITED STATES OF AMERICA
FIRST EDITION

This book is dedicated to the memory of the late Jack D. M. White, a sensitive man and automotive writer, who died on June 4, 1972, after a long struggle with complications resulting from being run over by the automobile industry. His fate could have been mine.

ACKNOWLEDGMENTS

My main debt is to the anonymous authors of press releases, speeches, and statistics that unceasingly flow from the public relations departments of the automobile industry here and abroad, most particularly the statisticians whose calculations could be turned to sometimes prove the opposite of what was intended. I thank them.

James C. Jones, an old friend and Detroit Bureau Chief for *Newsweek* magazine, was most helpful in refreshing my memory of events long past, as was Tom Kleene, Automotive Writer for the Detroit *Free Press*, and Dave Smith, Editor of *Ward's Auto World*. And certainly I should thank Ralph Nader, whom I've never met, for writing his book *Unsafe at Any Speed*. It prompted General Motors to hire private detectives, and their bumbling attempts to discredit Nader indisputably led to the formation of the vast bureaucracies which now regulate the automobile industry and the cars we buy. Without this unnecessary expansion of government I would have no cause and, thus, no book.

I suppose, too, I should thank *Motor Trend* magazine and *McGraw-Hill World News* for paying me those twenty-odd years in and around Detroit while I unknowingly researched what is in this book, for exposing me to the industry so I, in turn, could expose it.

Lastly, I must thank Doubleday & Company, Inc., and my editor there, Susan Schwartz, for their patience while this manuscript slowly unfolded. The delay was not my fault or theirs. I could not keep pace with my characters. For example, Lee A. Iacocca, a key individual herein, changed jobs three times in those three years.

FOREWORD

My belief that there weren't and still aren't enough automobile manufacturers in the United States dates even prior to 1954 when I was elected president and chairman of the newly formed American Motors Corporation upon George W. Mason's untimely and unexpected death in October of that year. At the time Packard and Studebaker could still be considered major producers of passenger cars, along with AMC, Chrysler, Ford, and General Motors. Today only the last four remain, so the case for divestiture—economic birth as well as death—would seem stronger than ever.

American Motors was formed by the merger of two troubled "independents," Nash-Kelvinator and Hudson Motor Car Company, and for a while Mr. Mason envisioned that Packard Motor Car Company would join the new combine. Many advantages could be foreseen, obvious among them being economies resulting from reduced tooling costs, volume purchasing, future commonality of major components, and the pooling of talent. An additional purpose in effecting the merger was to ameliorate distribution problems.

The "Big Three" monopolized distribution by the simple tactic of discouraging their dealers from dualing; that is, selling a noncompetitive make from outside the "family" in the same showroom. During most of the first decade following World War II, the prohibition (which in effect it was) mattered little because the American public was starved for transportation. People lined up and begged for cars of any make, type, or style. By 1954, though, this demand had been satisfied. Dealers had to compete for sales once again and the independents, including AMC, simply did not have enough dealers in enough locations. Nor were dealers easily recruited in competition with the more lucrative Big Three franchises so readily available in those days.

A Nash or Hudson deal in 1954 was an attractive proposition for a dealer already franchised for one of the Big Three nameplates. A little later, a newly rationalized AMC franchise was even more attractive but we were effectively excluded by the tactic I have mentioned, a tactic that was later abandoned because of its dubious legality. And by that time, a flood of imports had entered in the competition for representation.

American Motors alone among the domestic independents survived, solely because we concentrated on producing sensible transportation in an age of automotive dinosaurs. Don MacDonald well remembers that bleak winter morning in 1956 when, in conjunction with the annual New York Automobile Show, AMC hosted a press breakfast at the Hotel Plaza. Our line of compact cars had not yet turned the corner and I even thought some of the press might be aligned against us. I pleaded with my audience—yes, with tears in my eyes—to help us put our concept across. Some writers reported the breakfast as a "cut-rate wake for the compact" but they were wrong. AMC did return to modest prosperity with its sensibly sized 1956 models, and it was a few years before our major competition could catch up.

I mention the incident because it illustrates another, more permanent, legacy of bigness; namely, its tendency to be arbitrary and insensitive. The Big Three, for example, had conditioned the market to demand extravagance, and that emphasis in their model mix was not significantly changed until Corporate Average Fuel Economy (CAFE) standards became effective with the 1977 model year. Where were smaller Chrysler, Ford, and GM cars in 1973 when the OPEC nations first began restricting our petroleum import? No manufacturer or group of manufacturers should possess the power to dictate public taste.

Don MacDonald capitalizes the word "Bigness" in this book and rightly so. He suggests that an intense sense of power is generated by corporate success, power that permeates down to individuals as well as committees, and I agree. He theorizes that the proliferation of government regulatory agencies might never have happened had General Motors not made the mistake of hiring private detectives to shadow Ralph Nader. That is possible although I suggest that had not this incident occurred, there would have been many other excuses of sufficient magnitude. Excessive power misapplied begets control and, with it, the inevitable multiplication of bureaucracies to administer this control. No observer of Detroit today can disagree. It is a multi-billion-dollar fact, an intolerable burden on both industry and taxpayers.

There are indeed too few automobile manufacturers in this country. The United Automobile Workers is a monopolistic organization that is too powerful. Our government should cease its day-to-day regulation of industry. It should adopt laws that will vest ultimate power in consumers in the marketplace just as ultimate political power is vested in citizens through the ballot box. This will require a national economic policy that results in the birth as well as the death of competitive enterprises and an end to the basic conflict between the antitrust policy of competition and the collective bargaining policy that fosters monopoly on the part of employers and unions. Good judgment and, with it, equity for all, tend to evaporate in an atmosphere of either excessive public or private power. We should take away rather than give the power to control.

George W. Romney
Bloomfield Hills, Michigan
July 1979

CONTENTS

INTRODUCTION   15
1 The Case Against Bigness   21
2 Idiot Lights and Sacroiliacs   37
3 How Clean Is Clean?   56
4 The Well Runs Dry   69
5 Protect Us for We Know Not   84
6 Not Invented Here   100
7 Behind the Styling Curtain   115
8 Tedium Besets Arthur Z.   129
9 Fall from the Pinnacle   140
10 Vice-President, Sales   155
11 The Take-Over House   170
12 The Pitchmen   185
13 "Call Us Toll-Free"   198
14 The Experimental Affordable Vehicle   213
15 The Solution   228

INTRODUCTION

There are perhaps a hundred men and women in this country who have spent the major part of their careers interpreting the automobile industry and its products for one or another print media and I am one of them. The roster does change, from death and replacement, but merely departing for more rewarding pursuits, whether emotional or financial, never erases your label as an automotive writer. Big Four press releases will follow wherever you go. For example, the late Ken Purdy was really a fine novelist but he is remembered today as an old car writer and indeed he excelled at that too. I know no other man who could recite from memory the bore and stroke of each significant Bugatti. And there's Ralph Stein, the cartoonist who drew Popeye and then bought the work of others for *This Week*. But he liked old cars, as an avocation, and chanced to write well about them and that was his end, an old car writer. Those of us who wish to escape risk the fate of the fish which was caught early in the day, unhooked and placed upon the dock to die. It flapped and flapped, for hours, and then by chance fell back over the edge into the water and drowned.

I know but one who did escape. His name is Johnny Williams who, while Detroit Bureau Chief for *The Wall Street Journal* back in the 1950s, became fascinated by the secrecy surrounding the introduction of new cars and the sin that was attached to breaking a release date. He knew as we all did that the embargo was self-serving, that the auto companies wished to protect themselves, not from competition but from their untested conviction that premature pictures of forthcoming cars would ruin the sales of those leftover in the showrooms. So Johnny determined to get his own pictures. He never, of course, divulged just how he did but I suspect he went around to the makers of those exact scale, plastic promotional models which used to appear on toy store shelves simultaneously with the real thing. From them he got blueprints and from those, he had drawings made, the first art aside from political cartoons ever to be used by the staid *Journal*. It was 1955, a year of big change, and the pictures appeared weeks ahead of "when they should." There was consternation in Detroit. Some companies continued to invite Johnny to their press functions and when he appeared they were impolite to him. Others simply removed him from their guest list. At a press luncheon one day, I saw William C. Newberg, then president of Dodge Division, put his arm around Johnny's shoulder and lecture him as would a father on the proper relationship between press and source. And finally, General Motors announced the ultimate punishment; it was canceling its advertising schedule in the *Journal!*

The affair ended happily. GM canceled its cancellation. Leftover 1954 cars got sold. Some auto companies, particularly Ford, began providing the press with early sketches on the grounds that less accurate ones obtained elsewhere were uncomplimentary to the car. All companies began holding "lead-time" previews for publications whose representatives were willing to sign a pledge not to break the release date. Thus, those who didn't sign could engage in a new form of competition, that of being first to print pictures obtained from anywhere except the public relations departments. And Johnny, he escaped. After a face-saving delay, he was transferred by the *Journal* to Boston, given a raise, and promised he would never again be assigned to cover an automotive function.

It was not exactly my intention to "escape" when I began writing this book three years ago. At least not consciously. I'm comfortably stashed on a mountaintop in Southern California and the closest I physically come to the industry's activities is occasionally to see closed and guarded vans unload at some scenic spot nearby, disgorging the secret new models for the photographers from the advertising agencies. It's been 1973 since I've had breakfast, lunch, dinner, or drink on a public relations man, although there were times, due to absorption with this book at the expense of making a living, that I wasn't sure how I would manage the next meal in any other way.

You see, my true thoughts about the industry and its people and products could not surface during the twenty years I wrote for publications that were beholden to their advertisers and, for that matter, while I was beholden to press agents for access to information. I was effectively censored by circumstances if indeed what is in this book was in my head at the time. Those twenty years of captivity were necessary. Johnny Williams' opportunity just came to him a little sooner.

I should thank the U. S. Department of Transportation for moving me to action. Their press releases followed me here to the mountaintop and I read them for the first time. Five billion dollars for our capitol's Metro, $600 million for New York's subways, 1,202 new buses for Los Angeles, four for Keokuk, 18 million Fords recalled, Detroit must reinvent the automobile, where is the socially responsible car? Why? Where is all this money coming from? Those people must hate cars! Who are they? How did they get into government? Who gave them this power?

That is how I came to capitalize the word "Bigness" in this book and how I, normally an apolitical type, remembered a long dormant piece of legislation called the Hart Bill and its call for divestiture. It was General Motors and Ford, and to a lesser extent Chrysler and American Motors, who created the bureaucracies that now torment them. And spend my money and make cars cost more. And then I remembered a line blue-penciled by a worried magazine editor from my copy years ago: "Characteristic of General Motors executives is the conviction that no odor will arise when they go to the toilet." That was why. Smugness, thoughtlessness, ruthlessness, disregard for ecology and conservation, disregard for you and me. What politician could resist the opportunity to punish Bigness? I understood and decided to say something. I was there and that is this book.

Idyllwild, California
April 6, 1979

DETROIT 1985

CHAPTER 1
The Case Against Bigness

Back during the first two decades of this century when the auto industry and its product were chuffing through infancy into childhood and on to adolescence but not, in 1920, quite coming of age, it was feasible and often profitable for an ambitious man to build a few cars, place his name on their radiators, and expect to sell them. Henry Ford, Ransom E. Olds, the Dodge brothers, and David Buick are pioneer medallions that still smash insects in their paths. The Packard and Studebaker brothers, Charles Nash, and, more recently, Henry Kaiser are remembered for having tried, and on a grand scale, too. The factories they erected remain standing and many of their cars still run, driven for the most part by ordinary people who rely on them for daily transport. Owners get from these orphans much the same measure of reliability and comfort as can be found in the latest models from the makers that survive. And there were at least twenty-five hundred other American nameplates that today are relegated to either museums or oblivion. Some of these were very bad cars. Some were just bait trolled by devious promoters. Most, though, represented serious efforts to convert some man's dream into reality. And modest fortune did come to many. I could add the unfortunate Elizabeth Carmichael's name to the list as the one woman I know of, but was the three-wheeled Dale a car and Carmichael a Ms.?

What caused our domestic auto industry to shrink in scope while it grew in volume to where today just two manufacturers prosper, a third profits erratically, and a fourth barely survives? These plus a handful of crossbreeds make the field in a race a thousand times richer than it was when dozens of independent entrants flourished and more dozens managed to exist. The answer is bigness, Big Bigness, big to a degree that deifies mediocrity, manipulates the national economy, robotizes employees, dictates to customers and that still, though more subtly than in the past, purchases politicians. General Motors currently (1978) ranks second in size among U.S. corporations on *Fortune* magazine's list of five hundred, Ford Motor Company is third, Chrysler Corporation tenth and American Motors slogs along in ninety-fourth place, exceeding $2 billion in annual sales very occasionally. Only the tail of the dog, the oil industry, in combination is bigger.

Chrysler remains with its 11.87 percent of the U.S. market, give or take a few points, because neither GM with 47.66 percent nor Ford with 21.78 percent dares become larger except at the expense of each other. Imports with 17.30 percent, while not exactly nurtured, are tolerated here for fear of retribution elsewhere. AMC with its minuscule 1.35 percent share, however, is surreptitiously succored by the Big Two as a living if pallid symbol that competition, in theory if not fact, is sacred. GM in particular knows that AMC's demise of an evening would bring on divestiture proceedings by morning!

My purpose in parroting however briefly what may seem like a monologue against bigness delivered over cocktails by an eager attorney from the Department of Justice is not to condemn or even to question the vertical evolvement of the auto industry. Exactly this path has been followed by the industry in every other country where it exists. And, too, the makers of white goods, brown goods, almost every form of durable goods whose purchase represents a substantial investment by the consumer and thus, of course, an exponentially larger risk in tooling and inventory by the entrepreneurs, inexorably cannibalized each other until only a few are left in each specialty to fill slots once occupied by many. Those facts require no substantiation. Neither does the statement that the lone entrepreneur in our capitalistic society today fares best with something simple and imaginative like Pet Rocks, or perhaps stereo components which are too new and technically volatile to nurture bigness as yet. Polaroid, Pong, and microwave ovens are exceptions, not the rule. Realistically, therefore, my concern with the system is only how it may affect the men and women in the automobile industry, how it sterilizes their thinking and thus the product they are forced to force upon us.

That perceptive though chauvinistic English essayist, John Ruskin (1819–1900), once wrote: "In order for people to be happy in their work, these three things are needed: They must be fit for it: They must not do too much of it: And they must have a sense of success in it." Ruskin spent his energies championing craftsmen in an age when, although machines produced most artifacts, the skill of the individual operating them was critical to quality. Craftsmanship was still essential, demanded by the employer and appreciated by the consumer. Today in the auto industry, however, the craftsman is more likely to be seen maintaining the automated machine. He has little hope of ever being elevated to the boardroom of the company for which he works, much less break away like Walter Chrysler and found his own.

The fourteenth floor of the General Motors Building in Detroit is occupied solely by men and a token few women possessing proven skills in manipulation, coercion, and beguilement, capped by the ability to apply these skills for and against each other in committee. The law is studied for what it will allow and not for intent. Customers are "statistically sound" groupings, not individuals who could ever hope to speak directly to an officer. At Ford, the qualifications are much the same except there's the added complication of a man still around whose name is on the building. Chrysler and AMC, in turn, probably derive efficiencies and certainly economies by being unable to afford management in depth.

So, I might paraphrase Ruskin by saying: "In order for people to be happy making automobiles, these three things are needed: They must be able to fit in: They must not do too much: And they must delegate their success in doing it not to those under but to those above." That last applies whether we speak of a group vice-president or of the last person to be hired on the assembly line. For example, former Ford president Lee Iacocca apparently found time among his other duties personally to design the first Mustang, for he unblinkingly accepts credit for it, giving none to stylist Joe Oros.

"Management in depth" is a super euphemism certain to be employed whenever a GM spokesman is defending his colossus against those suspecting that ten thousand or so individually honest, bonus-level executives might tend to stretch their social consciences when cloaked with the anonymity provided by the committee process. You see the phrase in the transcript of every government hearing on the auto industry. You hear it in justification for the seeming lack of corporate concern when key men, such as Semon Knudsen and John De Lorean, suddenly quit. Those two in fact were victims of management in depth; they were among the handful who, each in his own time, are always being held in reserve for the presidency. The carrot just out of reach is vital to management in depth and there are those independent thinkers, even within GM, who ultimately rebel. And once gone, they flounder, Knudsen lasting nineteen months at Ford and De Lorean not under yet but barely afloat with his dream of building a safety-oriented "DMC-12" sportscar for those twenty thousand buyers a year who (he hopes) have tired of Porsches.

Perhaps the most damaging aspect of management in depth is, to put it politely, the conviction among GM executives that no odor will arise when they go to the toilet. Years have passed but no one expressed it better than Charles E. Wilson, GM's Korean-War-era president on loan to the government, when he said: "What's good for General Motors is good for the country." Thoroughly brainwashed, Wilson was amazed, not dismayed, by the furor that descended. To him, the relationship was as complementary as apple pie and ice cream. Much later, GM ran afoul of a then obscure consumer advocate named Ralph Nader. Nader was questioning the safety of a GM product, the rear-engined Corvair. The first tactic was to ignore Nader with an official "No comment" followed by a private "Who's he?" But Nader persisted, and politicians such as Abraham Ribicoff (D-Conn.) sensed paydirt, as did a covey of lawyers specializing in product liability claims. So, Nader found himself entertaining uninvited guests—private detectives hired by GM. Such investigations are inherently messy when exposed, especially when the only sin that could be substantiated was Nader's boringly celibate single status. However, public sympathy for underdog Nader was mild punishment compared to what befell GM and the rest of the industry as a direct result of this action. It triggered government involvement in automotive safety, the product itself and not just highway standards and driving habits as before. The cost to the industry of this involvement stands at $35 billion to date, a sum which, of course, has all been passed on to you, the consumer.

Nader himself could not have been provided with a more propitious launching of his book *Unsafe at Any Speed*[1] if GM's hundred-man-plus corps of press agents had been working for him. He starred on nation-wide talk shows, the lecture circuit and, most significantly, at congressional hearings. His every comment was given front-page display. Meanwhile, automotive engineers the world over squirmed—those at GM in enforced silence—because while early Corvairs did inherit a certain instability when one rear wheel became entangled with a high shoulder in the road or a rut, an instability common to most inexpensive rear-engined cars then current, the resulting impairment of control was no more and probably less than the reaction of any comparable car such as the Volkswagen with the same so-called "swing-axle" type of rear suspension. Accidents of this nature were primarily caused by driver error, a judgment later upheld in all but the first lawsuit involving the Corvair.[2] Ignored by Nader were advantages of the rear-engine configuration, an important one suggested by the whimsical ad showing snowplow drivers arriving at work in Volkswagens.

Details of the massive government involvement deriving from Nader's technically unsound condemnation of the Corvair are the subject of a later chapter in this book. The point here is that GM's chosen weapon when attacked by the gadfly was silence, not a dignified silence but one based on the assumption that corporately it could do no wrong. With it was the assumption that

[1] Grossman Publishers, New York, 1965.
[2] Plaintiff in the first lawsuit proved a dealership employee had inflated the front and rear tires to incorrect pressures just prior to the accident. The case was settled by GM out of court for $250,000.00. It is true that early Corvairs would handle erratically if any tire were not properly inflated.

the public and its elected representatives would instinctively ignore an individual, any individual, with the temerity to challenge GM's engineering judgment. It was unthinkable for GM to admit an error or, more fairly in this situation, the fact that there are tradeoffs in the design of any car. Instead, reaction was swift and not in GM's favor. Everyman's resentments, however vague, against Bigness that purveyed sometimes shoddy products, tolerated incompetent service departments, and shrugged off complaints, swelled to the surface. Politicians, in turn, found an issue akin to motherhood. Who could be against safer cars?

You'd think GM would have learned by then the benefits to be gained from practicing rigorous corporate honesty in its relationships with the car-buying public, but no. Another major deception came to light during the 1977 model year. This was the long-standing industry practice of interchangeability; that is, commonality of certain major components used by the various car-producing divisions within GM. For example, a replacement windshield bought at a Chevrolet dealer will fit both the standard-size Chevrolet Impala/Caprice and the seemingly larger, certainly more expensive Cadillac De Ville. That fact indicates commonality of key body structures, in this instance the cowl. It makes sense and every automaker does it. In England, the practice is unkindly labeled "badge engineering." Ford Motor Company in turn uses engines in Mercury and Lincoln cars identical to those installed in similarly sized but less expensive Ford Division nameplates. Ford does not, however, attempt to hide the common origin of these engines by labeling one, say, a "Mercury Sizzler" and its twin a "Ford Hurricane." If they're labeled at all, the decal reads "Power by Ford Motor Company."

GM at every level of management was certainly aware that it's illegal as well as immoral to call a shovel a spade even though both will accomplish essentially the same job. Nevertheless, it allowed a large number of engines manufactured by Chevrolet to be used in Oldsmobiles, Pontiacs, and Buicks. Manufacturing convenience dictated the move and all would have been well if these engines had been identified as to their origin. However, buyers were led or, rather, allowed to believe they were getting genuine Oldsmobile, Pontiac, or Buick power in their cars and were not informed of certain internal differences between the genuine engines and the Chevrolet substitutes. What's more, GM neglected to consider future service needs, resulting in the innocent owner of a Chevrolet-powered Buick or whatever being turned away at the dealership where he had bought the car! Items as common as a fan belt were not stocked for the substitute engines except, of course, by Chevrolet dealers.

It actually was a broken fan belt on a '77 Olds that sent a Chicago man from the Chevy dealership where he had to buy the replacement straight to the Illinois attorney general's office to initiate the first of many legal actions involving, at this writing, about a half million owners. Weeks after the first incident, GM came up with an offer to exchange the Chevy-powered cars on an even basis, less eight cents a mile, for new ones that might or might not have the right engines, or, owners could keep their original cars and receive a special 36-month, 36,000-mile warranty. Still later, in a settlement reached with attorney generals of forty-four states, GM added a $200 cash payment to each owner. The exercise of the first two options cannot influence any future litigation, so the initial cost to GM of $60 million may not reflect the ultimate loss due to policy that was soundly based but deceptive as practiced.

GM has yet to issue any form of public apology; instead, after the fact, it ran institutional ads extolling the "GM Family of Engines." The Corporation, unfortunately, is still not big enough in the true sense of the word to gracefully admit an innocent mistake. Why? Because management remains convinced that no mistake was made. There is no need, it seems, for the buyer to know who manufactured the engine in his car even if he must have the package serviced at two different dealerships. And, the affair put GM in the awkward position of having to reassure victims of the switch that Chevrolet engines were every bit as good as the presumably higher quality, more expensive engines built by Oldsmobile, Buick, and Pontiac. Cadillac somehow emerged unscathed even though it uses modified Oldsmobile engines in its gasoline- and diesel-powered Seville models.

What's right for GM is right for the buyer, despite rapidly diminishing credibility in the eyes of government and public alike. Congressional hearings on the subjects of car safety, fuel economy, and emission standards are conducted today in an atmosphere of almost total disbelief in anything the automakers say. The cost to consumers of the ill-founded legislation that results is reflected not only in dollars but in wasted engineering man-hours that might better have been spent on the kind of product improvements you want, which, of course, are the kind that sell cars.

Ford's Iacocca in a 1977 speech cited a report which estimated that simply filling out the forms required by various governmental bureaucracies costs American business $75 billion a year.[3] He went on to say: "Let's face it, some governmental regulation and control are desirable and necessary. What I am saying is that businessmen and businesswomen—in fact, everybody—in this country has got to get busy and put some controls on government or our precious, two-hundred-year-old freedom is going to be nothing more than a collection of interesting documents in the National Archives." Brave words for a man who represents management in an industry that's freewheeled its way downhill to where, according to a mid-1977 Harris Poll, "more people are dissatisfied with car manufacturers and garages than with any other industry or service."

A paradox is at work here. Businesses such as Ford and GM understandably resent government interference in their activities and most strongly of all the imposition of unsolicited aid in the design of their products. But, the increasing degree of intrusion was invited by the simple act of growing big. There is only one car manufacturer I know where if an owner calls he can reasonably expect to speak to the president. That is tiny (three hundred units a year) Avanti Motor Corporation,[4] which follows a policy instituted by its late founder, Nate Altman. The only time Nate wasn't immediately available was when he was out troubleshooting a problem on the assembly line. For better or worse, there is always communication at Avanti. But if you own a Ford or a Chevy, or a Plymouth or a Concord, and want to speak to its

---

[3] A 1979 report by the Center for the Study of American Business estimated government-bred paper work to cost all industry and business $116 billion a year, an amount twenty times the direct cost to the taxpayer of supporting the major regulatory agencies.

[4] Avanti still hand-builds plastic-bodied luxury sports cars to a 1963-vintage design acquired from Studebaker. Nate Altman was a major South Bend, Indiana, Studebaker dealer.

maker, you dial one of the widely publicized "hot lines" established a few years ago and theoretically you could reach "Our Man in Detroit." He, supposedly, is vice-president in charge of consumer relations but, in practice, the voice that answers will belong to an employee much lower in the echelon, one who will record your complaint but who is not authorized to make decisions, particularly decisions favorable to you. About the only improvement over channels available in the past is that now you can call toll-free.

Isolation created by layer upon layer of management has destroyed meaningful communication between car manufacturers and their single most important source of guidance—their customers. So, the always opportunistic politicians and bureaucrats stepped in. If your new Ford or whatever catches fire or loses a wheel, or even if the ashtray squeaks, call Joan Claybrook, head policeperson at the National Highway Traffic Safety Administration, on her hot line (800-424-9393). She may not answer the phone personally but you'll eventually get action. Any delay may be blamed on the same problem; to wit, layer upon layer of management within Ms. Claybrook's own shop.

Such communication as exists between customers and car manufacturers parallels in all but one respect that between voters and politicians. If a brand-new car like the Chevette is placed on the market and only half of projected production is sold the first year, which was what happened, GM will get the message quite quickly. But if you're dissatisfied with your Chevrolet Impala and in frustration trade it on a Plymouth, your action in terms of communication is as voiceless as one vote against a political candidate. It would take thousands of Chevy owners switching in a short period of time to show meaningfully in the ten-day sales reports studied by top management. The dissimilarity is that most politicians do visit with their constituents regularly whereas Detroit relies on its dealers to take the public pulse.

It would be a rare dealer who would risk his franchise to do battle for you. In fact, the omnipresent threat of disenfranchisement inhibits frank, objective communication between dealers and their factories even on matters that don't concern the customer. A Ford franchise for a growing suburb, or a Chevrolet franchise anywhere, is a very valuable, highly liquid commodity that is bestowed upon one among hundreds of eager, qualified applicants. Greed and fear, rather than honesty and courage, govern the industry at the retail level. Thus, the impotency of the National Automobile Dealers Association (NADA) is not surprising. Nor is it surprising that American Motors works the hardest to keep its dealers (and its customers) happy. It has a hard time finding either.

The NADA would lack reason for being were it not for the car manufacturers' own penchant for self-destruction. Past-president Reed T. Draper, second generation owner of two Chevrolet dealerships located in the industry's backyard, says "the franchise is a one-way street marked with a sign that says 'we may and you (the dealer) must.'" Draper also wonders, as do his successors, why the factories continually quibble over claims for warranty work performed; why an established dealer is constantly pressured to increase his equity in facilities while simultaneously the same factory subsidizes the opening of a new dealership barely outside his territory; and, of course, why the factories seem unable to communicate with Washington. NADA presidents are destined to go on asking the same questions for the simple reason that revolutions aren't started by fat cats. Significantly, another industry in which dealers have banded together primarily for self-preservation is oil, where the National Congress of Petroleum Retailers fights with equal ineffectiveness to strengthen fragile franchises. As I've noted, the two industries suffer from the same malady—Bigness.

Valid motives for the constant friction between car manufacturers and their dealers are difficult to find; policy seems deliberately designed to promote unrest. And, certainly, the consumer is the ultimate victim. He was forced to burn his lemons on factory lawns until the government stepped in, and now he pays in the form of taxes for the privilege of complaining.

One would think in a family-run firm, however big, like Ford Motor Company that communication would be more effective, but it's not. Henry Ford II took over a degenerate empire in 1945 at the age of twenty-eight and at first of necessity and later because he liked it became used to the role of dictator. He is a rather benign, sometimes philosophic despot who seems to enjoy stirring unrest in his organization. Wherever derived, Henry II's pattern is to periodically strip the togas from the backs of key executives just when their futures would appear predictable, leaving them naked, confused, but still employed.

Ford Motor Company is known as a tough place to work, at any level, for repercussions from the executive chess game follow all down the line like a freight train stopping. Onetime heir-apparent Lee Iacocca has three times been a victim, once in 1968 when "Bunky" Knudsen was brought in over his head from GM, again when Henry II formed a "troika-at-the-top" in preparation for retirement in 1982, and finally in the summer of 1978 when he (Iacocca) was summarily fired. Power, of course, is the sweet I speak of, not salary, for all of Henry II's vice-presidents become millionaires in their own right thanks to stock options and bonuses.

Henry II had a tough time explaining his troika at the press conference announcing it, not as it showed on paper but how it would operate in practice. Nothing has changed since the beginning of the sixteenth century when Machiavelli wrote: "The world has always been inhabited by human beings who have always had the same passions." So, what makes Henry II think a troika consisting of himself, the driving Iacocca, and an until-now obscure Ford career executive named Philip Caldwell could contribute to the progress of his company? Friction under the pseudonym of checks and balances is inherent in the idea and friction, remember, is Henry II's delight, as it was his grandfather's.

We have a physically and, on occasion, emotionally tired man whose name is on the building, concerned because there's no Ford coming along capable in the immediate future of chairing the enterprise. (Brother Benson died in 1978, William Clay is disinterested, and a son, Edsel II, fails in his father's judgment to qualify as yet.) And then until recently we had the ambitious Iacocca, retaining much of his power even though he reported to a vice-chairman, Caldwell, whenever Henry II was absent, which, by the latter's own statements, was to be more and more frequently. Each of the three was given one-third veto. Such an arrangement would have seemed an exercise in futility for the human beings involved, but actually the status was a variation on quo. Henry II's "one-third" voice was stronger than those of the other two combined, especially if he stewed them in their own juices by abstaining.

Whatever problems management in depth might breed, there is one penalty of Bigness that's peculiar to the automobile among manufacturing industries. Everyone has seen baseball teams suffer when they're bought by owners who have no love for the game. Thus, is it unreasonable to suggest that automobile companies might better be run by men who have gasoline rather than finance or marketing or production in their blood? One doesn't need to be a stove or refrigerator buff to sell white goods successfully, as marketing expert James J. Nance proved when he brought Whirlpool to dramatically sudden prominence in that field. Yet when the same Mr. Nance took over Packard, the company tumbled precipitously down the tube. Score one for the theory. But then, the late Sherwood Egbert, who was an enthusiast, tried with the remnant, Studebaker-Packard, and was equally unsuccessful. Score one against. Today, the only incumbent chief executive officer who can be fairly classified as a car buff is chairman Gerald C. Meyers of American Motors. But AMC is not exactly a blue-chip property, so score two against.

Chrysler hasn't had a true automobile man at the helm since cantankerous K. T. Keller departed in the forties, and K.T. almost over-engineered them into oblivion. At GM there has only been one such in recent times, the late Edward N. Cole. Cole couldn't keep his hands out from under the hood of any car he was driving, but he was ineffectual during his tenure as president of GM. He was honest, outspoken, and product-oriented, and therefore his press agents hid him from public view wherever possible along with his pet project, a vastly improved domestic version of the Wankel rotary engine. Knowledgeable readers might argue a case for the current GM president, Elliott M. "Pete" Estes, because while he headed the Pontiac and then Chevrolet Divisions, he surreptitiously promoted racing despite a long-standing corporate ban on any activity connoting speed and power. That he did, but has the policy changed to one of open support now that he's in a position to change it? The answer is no.

An automobile man in charge *should* result in better, more ex-

THE CASE AGAINST BIGNESS

citing, more salable cars but the record shows that it doesn't and can't, at least today. It should also result in a sincere, prideful concern for the customer but it doesn't, as witness the ever-growing volume of service complaints. More significantly, the record shows the automobile man to be less than successful at corporate infighting, uncomfortable operating through committee, and somehow incapable of ignoring dramatic product innovations that might suddenly obsolete major capital facilities. He therefore is seldom promoted to the top. The result is cars stamped from boringly similar molds, no safer or cleaner than the government requires, and whose fifteen thousand or more parts are unlovingly assembled on an unhappy line. That sterile product is the legacy of Bigness. The admen are the true heroes, skillfully crediting their clients for the government-decreed differences between the old model and the new.

So you want to start a car company? Be Detroit's guest. They'll be glad to sell you engines, transmissions, and other major components on an "as available" basis and if you have cash. Orders on your books generated by displaying your prototype at an auto show are not viewed as cash. You've already investigated materials for your distinctive and safe body design and found the only solution to be laboriously hand-formed fiberglass. That's because you must project a volume of a hundred thousand units a year for at least three years to amortize the cost of tooling for more easily formed steel. You dreamed of incorporating a radical new suspension developed by your tiny engineering team—in fact, it was the feature that brought customers to your stand at the show—but you're scared because it's unproved. It's worked flawlessly on the prototype, leaning in as it was designed to do on corners instead of out, but will it hold up for a hundred thousand miles on all kinds of surfaces? You don't know because you haven't got a proving ground, much less the time and money, for that kind of testing. So, you drop the idea and incorporate a conventional suspension, thus removing the last vestige of uniqueness from your dream car except for its sleek, sporty styling. You had your own ideas on instrumentation, too, but no one would build the digital readouts to your specifications because volume was too low. So, you shape the panel for stock Stewart-

Warner gauges, available in any parts store, and try to cram in off-the-shelf heat and air-conditioning units around them.

You know deep within you that there's nothing really better about your car than the total of the supplied hardware from which it was assembled. You know too, by now, that the hand labor required to mate mismatched components, the high cost of materials purchased in small quantities, and your own need to replenish your dwindling capital at usurious rates have forced the price up to at least $20,000, four times more than a car just as good from Detroit and three times more than the $6,750 you originally had projected. But the gull-wing body with its air doors looks good and you know you can sell a few thousand of them. After all, Bricklin did and so did Carroll Shelby. You realize, finally, that you might, if you're lucky, find a niche in the specialty market big enough in which to survive without creating waves. Don't get any bigger, though, because Detroit might look at your niche and find it attractive. You cringe at that flash of reality. Ford, you remember, moved in and crushed Shelby for no reason more than a whim. And the other day in Palm Springs you passed a row of brand-new, leftover Bricklins gathering dust in a used car lot.

Our saga of the would-be car manufacturer is more truth than fiction. There are at least a dozen men scattered around the United States actively pursuing just such a dream. Most will create "replicars," clothing modern chassis off Detroit's shelf with bodies shaped like the great classics of the past. These range from David Stevens' $30,000 Excalibur cum Mercedes SSK to the $10,000 Glassic, not too accurately molded in the image of a '30 Model A Ford. Glenn Pray's plastic Auburns and Cords belong in that group but not Jim O'Donnell's $65,000 Stutz. That one has thoroughly modern steel coachwork hand-formed in Italy, and the only similarity to the legendary Stutz is the name. Soon, there'll be John De Lorean's DMC-12, also original in concept. And I'll not easily forget Jim Gaylord of bobby-pin wealth who built six professionally designed and bodied Gaylords in a fit of pique, just because his Rolls-Royce leaked incurably.

These small-scale operations do not represent a revival of opportunities that existed in the twenties. The pseudo Stutzes and Auburns, the Glassic and the rest are toys built for an affluent fringe, not as transportation for the masses. The idea of a newcomer building a line of family cars evaporated here with the demise (1955) of Kaiser-Frazer, and in Germany (1961) with Carl Borgward. I speak of complete manufacture, including engines and bodies. No one else has given it a good shot since the middle of the century, with the exceptions of state-subsidized assembly in emerging countries, overseas ventures by established manufacturers, and the occasional effort, such as Daf in Holland, of a firm already prominent in an allied field. The only successes since World War II have been Volkswagen and the Japanese, each of whom shared the common starting point of total devastation. And sometimes, unlimited capital and resources are no guarantee, as witness the $250 million Henry Ford II purportedly dropped on the Edsel.

The closest Detroit has come to "total devastation," and with it a chance for independents to emerge from the ashes, was the abortive Industrial Reorganization Act written and championed by the late Senator Philip Hart (D-Mich.). The impact of the Hart Bill, as it is more commonly called, was not lessened by its failure to ever emerge from committee, as there are at least thirty-four similar divestiture bills pending before the current (96th) Congress. The original proposed to outlaw "mere possession of monopoly power" as defined in any one or more of three ways. At least 140 giants in seven different industries would ultimately have been studied for possible divestiture, but the automotive industry had top priority on the basis that a shared monopoly exists when any four corporations account for 50 percent or more of sales for a similar product in any year of the most recent three prior to filing of a complaint. (The other two grounds for complaint, a return on net worth exceeding 15 percent and lack of substantial price competition, didn't and still do not apply to existing domestic carmakers.) Market penetration figures I've already cited show that GM in combination with either Ford or Chrysler qualifies for the carving board without even counting "little" American Motors.

The bearded, soft-spoken Hart believed that monopolies inherently tend, however benign and cautious they may be, to regulate prices, stifle competition, cause drastic fluctuations in employment, and to a great degree smother innovation. And many

Democrats still agree. The language and intent of the Industrial Reorganization Act was in essence incorporated into the Party's platform for the 1972 election year. More significantly, although neither Democrats nor Republicans are likely to publicly risk the admission, monopolies tend to spawn vast bureaucracies specifically created for their control. So if Bigness doesn't smother innovation, the Civil Service will.

Senator Hart himself never speculated on the specifics of divestiture but economists have written books on the subject as applied to the automobile industry. Lawrence J. White of Princeton University, for example, suggests spinning off the Big Three into eight new companies. Stanley E. Boyle of Virginia Polytechnic Institute proposes that each present plant be made an independent producer. Of the two, White's idea is the more realistic but both ignore the economies effected by parts interchangeability. We do know that as the industry presently operates, an auto company must turn out at least 250,000 passenger cars a year to break even, for that is the figure around which AMC hovers year after year, despite the sometimes self-defeating but necessary policy of retaining the same body designs for periods more than twice as long as the industry average.

My own thought, unsubstantiated by any official industry estimate, is that if the standard-size Chevrolet with its three-year cycle between major changes and its current 500,000-unit annual production was spun off as an independent, an Impala that costs $6,000 today would double in price tomorrow. One reason: the new firm presumably would no longer have access to GM's catalogue of common parts such as bodies by Fisher for which three of the other four divisions have shared the tooling costs. Another reason: the doors of GM's vast research and development organization would bang shut. And one more of considerable importance: an independent Chevrolet could hardly match GM's present financial resources, so great that borrowing money for capital improvement is seldom necessary. However, these negatives are premised on carrying the old way of thinking into the newly independent operation. Given some fresh ideas on management, or even reverting back to the initiative extant before Alfred P. Sloan created the brain-logged monster that is GM today, we might see a vastly improved $5,000 Impala!

CHAPTER 2

Idiot Lights and Sacroiliacs

Burt Stickshift, domestic car product planning director, leaned back and contemplated the schematic of his company's new "L" car reflected full size on the screen. For once, he mused on that dreary winter day in 1977, we've got something all to ourselves. His eyes fondled the front-drive mechanism of the neat little five-door minicar that would be in Chrysler showrooms by January. Every line and dimension in the drawing was etched on his mind, including maybe five thousand detail changes in the original of four long years ago which, he knew so well, was but the Americanization of a design inherited when Chrysler acquired controlling interest in its onetime French affiliate, Simca. Scrub as he might, more than a touch of Gallic remained, much like the persistence of rancid oil oozing from a well-seasoned salad bowl.

That, though, he could rationalize. The competitive Chevette and Fiesta were "international" cars, stripped of character by GM's and Ford's attempts to attract customers in all nations. He had been pleased by the clumsy pig-German language in the introductory Fiesta ads, Ford's way of implying German standards of quality in a car containing major components manufactured in three other countries. No, he wasn't out in left field; his "L" car *really* looked like it came from Europe despite assembly in Belvidere, Illinois.

Best of all, and Burt knew these circumstances to be irreversible for at least a year, he had a five-door sedan in front-drive format at a time when Chevette had the doors but not the drive and Fiesta the drive but not the doors. That's what comes from waiting, he could say, but he knew better. Indecision born of corporate poverty had lucked out. That "L" car could have been on the roads here two years ago, and then he would have had five doors to Chevette's three and no Fiesta of any kind to worry about.

Burt Stickshift is a composite of several real people employed by Chrysler. I chose that company as a loose model of how product planning works in the automobile industry, or should work, because the function there at the operating level stands separate and equal to engineering, as well as purchasing and an office of vehicle safety and reliability, the latter like in all the companies being a post-Nader creation. Styling at Chrysler reports to product planning rather than dictating to it or operating on a cloud by itself. All the functions mentioned so far answer to a single group vice-president who, in turn, has direct access to the president and chief operating officer.

At GM and Ford, product planning as such does not appear in the title of any vice-president. GM still buries it at the divisional level where it is coordinated by a corporate staff whose head is not a vice-president. At Ford the apex is labeled "advanced vehicle development" which connotes primary interest in futuristic concepts rather than designs being detailed for production. Obviously, product planning gets done at GM and Ford; it's just that Chrysler seems to have found the easier way, on paper at least.

So, let's examine Burt Stickshift's qualifications for his vital, dual role. It's dual because he must (or should) put what he thinks you will buy four or five years hence into a package that's within the capabilities of his company to produce at that future time. Within that generalized frame, his problems become multifaceted. His two immediate superiors at this writing, product planning and development vice-president George Butts[1] and

[1] Illustrating another of the hazards facing Burt Stickshift, the one-year interval between writing the page above and proofreading it saw Lee Iacocca replace Cafiero as Chrysler's president, with the consequences that Cafiero

IDIOT LIGHTS AND SACROILIACS   39

group vice-president for engineering, product development, and purchasing, Dick Vining,[1] have dominant backgrounds in truck engineering and general manufacturing, respectively. Neither may be accurately labeled a car buff so whatever package Burt proposes must have obvious appeal for a broad market segment; put another way, his best chance is a "safe" proposal.

And it better be producible in existing plants because on up the ladder sits president Gene Cafiero,[1] another manufacturing man, and chairman John Riccardo, an exceptionally sharp-eyed and bad-tempered accountant. Burt knows those backgrounds to be a mixed blessing because while there have been no major product successes or failures of their own to prejudice these men, both relatively new in their jobs, there'll be a parallel reluctance to experiment in unknown areas. He'll get quick decisions, though, for Cafiero and Riccardo dominate the Operating Committee, which collectively is God. And once in work, there won't be a procession of outside directors, Italian designers and New York marketing consultants bending his ear and possibly the shape of the car at every stage of the project as had often been his experience at Chrysler in the past. He also remembers one of Cafiero's first pronouncements as president: "We've got to build a reputation for Chrysler of doing what is right for Chrysler and not just a knee-jerk reaction to what Ford and General Motors are doing."

Burt, now in his early fifties, has made a career of Chrysler's ups and downs, having worked nowhere else in the twenty-six years since he graduated from prestigious Chrysler Institute with a master's in automotive engineering.[2] But back in 1951, with the ink not yet dry on his diploma, the future seemed more bleak than usual. A new series of "Keller-era" cars[3] with their chair-height seats (Chrysler body engineers in those days were still under orders to wrap every concept around the measurements of

---

was fired and Butts and Vining were moved over to other jobs. Burt's new boss, Harold K. Sperlich, is a car buff.

[2] For many years Chrysler Institute was the only industry-sponsored institution accredited to award advanced academic degrees.

[3] K. T. Keller and Fred Zeder, both engineers, designed the first Chrysler car in 1924 which was advanced for its time. Keller rose to the top after Walter P. Chrysler's death in 1940 but his thinking failed to keep pace with the industry. The equally conservative Zeder became chief engineer and in charge of such styling as was attempted.

chairman K. T. Keller seated at the wheel wearing his Homburg hat) was committed to production and these looked more archaic, relative to competition, than the stodgy designs about to be retired along with K.T. himself.

The period for Burt was a practical postgraduate course in how not to run an automobile company, with or without Keller. But changes were in the offing. The new president, a flamboyant attorney named Lester Lum "Tex" Colbert, did create a styling studio (Chrysler's first) and placed a talented outsider, Virgil Exner, in complete charge. There followed in rapid succession Exner's all-new "Forward Look" of 1955 and the even more all-new "Wedge Shape" of 1957. The latter models were nearly a foot lower than anything Chrysler had produced before, spectacular to look at but plagued with mechanical problems bred by the rush to market. About the only parts that could be counted on to follow those 1957 offerings down the road without coming unglued were the awesome fins atop each rear fender. By 1958 Chrysler was $34 million in the red, losing both its money and its reputation for engineering excellence in simultaneous debacles. Burt somehow survived, although the engineering staff was chopped nearly in half during the five-year corporate depression that followed.

There was product planning of a sort at Chrysler in those hard days. Each of the four producing divisions extant at the time had a chief engineer whose job was to give *his* car individuality despite corporate sharing of major components such as engines, transmissions, and bodies. The function of the division engineer was a peculiar blend of styling, engineering, and marketing; that is, exactly what product planning is today. And if there were excesses, they were in the area of marketing.

Burt will long remember a purple and violet 1956 Dodge convertible variant called "La Femme" for which he "engineered" a vanity case complete with pop-out lipstick along with holsters in each door to hold matching parasols, all standard equipment with this model.[4] At the same time he was beefing up Dodges in sedan form to attract the taxicab and police markets. And week-

[4] Never explained was the improbability of *two* female occupants, each wearing costumes that matched the purple parasols.

ends he disappeared into the Carolinas to curry the make's performance image on stock car racing circuits. The product planner then was victim of Detroit's urge to be all things to all buyers and if the bread-and-butter family cars lacked such essentials as comfort and reliability because of the diversions, so be it. Almost anybody with a screwdriver, pliers, and a couple of hours to spare could turn a Dodge into a Plymouth, or vice versa, simply by transposing the interchangeable brightwork. Yet if you read the ads for both, they were unique and different from each other and, of course, from their predecessors, each model year.

Product planning finally acquired vitally needed stature when it was moved from a division to a corporate function in varying degree at all the major domestic producers. This wasn't a voluntary or timely move; Americans in significant number were "thinking small" and Detroit belatedly was gearing to meet that market. Cars that came to be known as "compacts" were scheduled for introduction as 1960 offerings. These of course were in their preliminary design stage at GM, Ford, and Chrysler as early as 1957, the downsizing being prompted by a number of factors. An immediate influence was the growing consumer revolt against excess bulk; particularly, heavy and useless sheet metal overhanging each set of wheels, attenuated by widths that barely scraped by the state of Vermont's 80-inch limit for passenger cars. The "Dollar Grin" with its flamboyant front grilles and excess of chrome had already been a target of industry critics, one such being John Keats, whose widely read book, *The Insolent Chariots*,[5] effectively attacked Detroit's products on grounds of both waste and taste.

But then in fairness I must note that throughout this period (1955–61), the more obscenely garish the design, the better it sold, with the epitome of poor taste generally conceded to have been reached with the industry's 1959 models. One exception that year was a reasonably esthetic standard-size Ford which outsold Chevrolet's equivalent by a slight margin for the first time in twenty-four years. Early in the model run before the sales pattern was predictable, a worried Ford Motor Company, thinking its conservative design was out of tune with the times,

[5] J. B. Lippincott Company, Philadelphia, 1958.

had anonymously sent press-ready cartoons to newspapers everywhere. The nastiest showed a child approaching the family garage from which protruded the fearsome, gull-winged tail of what was unmistakably a 1959 Chevrolet. "Mama," the child cried, "something's eating my bicycle!"

More prodding came from import sales statistics. These totals had risen from a mere 12,251 in 1949 to 614,131 ten years later, a fiftyfold increase despite poor distribution and poorer service. Most of these were economy models and it finally dawned on Detroit executives, including product planners, that not very many were being sold to customers who just wanted to be different. Fewer still were sold on the premise that anything imported, like French wines or Danish pornography, was superior in quality to the domestic product. And even though some Volkswagen owners persisted in beeping at each other as late as 1959, the "in" factor associated with driving an import had long been lost in the numbers. Nor was the import buyer a car buff; more likely, he was the type who begrudged every dollar he spent on transportation.

Contemporary experience with homegrown compacts had been confusing. On the one hand George Romney had after a long struggle dredged American Motors from a sinkhole of losses with a line of relatively small cars. He stumped the country with more fervor than he later exhibited while campaigning for various political offices, extolling the civic as well as mechanical virtues of practical-sized transportation and coining the term "compact car" in the process. Romney's definition of a compact as "anything under two hundred inches" was accepted; his suggestion that anything larger was a "dinosaur in the driveway" met with less favor. Anyhow, after 1956 modest profits replaced red ink in AMC's ledger.

In conflict was the fact that "dinosaurs" still accounted for the overwhelming majority (at least 85 percent) of sales. And against the imports and Romney could be weighed Studebaker's notable lack of success with its small Lark as well as the earlier failures of Kaiser, Willys, and Hudson which had each tried to stave off disaster with compacts tooled in blood.[6] I say "could"

[6] Even in those days, an all-new car required a minimum $50 million investment for special tooling and facilities.

because nothing the independents did had any influence on Big Three product planning, then or now. Mercedes yes, Volkswagen yes, Toyota maybe, but not AMC. Then, and we're still in the late fifties, Ford showed its defiance of evolution by creating a dinosaur called the Edsel. And to further lull industry and buyers alike, the first of our energy crises was fifteen years away from stirring under the burnouses of the Arab oil moguls.

In other words, Big Three product planners finalizing in 1958–59 details of new generation compacts to bow in 1960 were not under pressure to save their nation, or their industry, or even their company. In fact, the most clearly stated guideline from management was that the compacts were to be priced low enough to attract young adults buying their first car or established families buying an additional car. The late-model used car then dominated both of those growing market segments, which meant that the new compacts must retail at a price close to the average paid for a one-year-old Chevrolet, the traditional leader in used car value.

No attempt was made to compete price-wise with the economy imports, then selling complete with ashtray for around $1,800. Thus, for approximately $2,000, a buyer in the fall of 1959 could choose between a new Chevrolet Corvair, Ford Falcon, and Plymouth Valiant or, of course, the existing AMC Rambler and Studebaker Lark. For this he was assured reasonable durability with adequate performance and comfort in an atmosphere of minimal luxury. Or he could continue to buy the used, year-old standard package with its then considerable degree of luxury and performance, risking only unknown but certainly higher costs of maintenance and operation.

The first Big Three compacts as they finally appeared presented interesting contrasts. The 1960 Corvair with its engine mounted at the rear was unique and different from anything theretofore marketed by a domestic producer. That came about, not from product planning, but from the dynamic persistence of one man, Edward N. Cole, who had pushed the rear-engine concept within GM for ten years, first at Cadillac and then as chief engineer and finally general manager of Chevrolet. The Corvair's very existence was an amazing fluke when looked at within the framework of GM's corporate attitude toward innovation. The

Corvair represented a triumph of engineering imposed on unwilling management and, as it turned out, an equally unwilling public. Ford's Falcon and Plymouth's Valiant, on the other hand, were conventional and therefore "safe," the Falcon wholly so and the Valiant in all but its slanted engine and European styling. Of the three, as might be guessed, the Falcon was by far the most successful.

GM's brief excursion from orthodoxy (the studiously conventional Chevy II was there to backstop the Corvair within a year) had an unfortunately negative effect on the emerging function of product planning. The "I told you so" types everywhere in the industry gained strength at the expense of innovation, just as they had years ago when Chrysler attempted and failed with the then revolutionary Airflow.[7] Product planners henceforward thought in terms of sameness because it was safe. If management wanted a small car, the planners would shrink it in the image of a larger one. If it were to be a "personal" car, such as the first Mustang of 1964, a pseudo-sporty body was grafted onto existing running gear. No really original compact, no totally new design, was to be tried until Chrysler's "L" cars, known in final format as the Plymouth Horizon and Dodge Omni, appeared late in 1977 to break the utter monotony of the domestic offerings.

The Omni and Horizon, as I've stated, owe much to European precedent. The ads omit mentioning that the engine was designed by and, for the first year at least, will be built by Volkswagen. The touted transverse engine and front-drive layout is commonplace in a variety of European as well as Japanese economy models. The industry in every nation but ours had been thinking small since before World War II. Lots of expertise existed everywhere but here in fitting four adults into minimal, wheeled boxes.

Admittedly, however, I'm writing this in 1978 and not 1959, the year in which the then record 614,131 imports were sold. By 1962, import sales plummeted to 339,160. Reason: None but Volkswagen among the economy types at that time could cope mechanically with high average speeds maintained over long distances, a deficiency compounded by the typically casual

[7] It was the Airflow's failure that turned Chrysler's K. T. Keller and Fred Zeder into fear-ridden conservatives for the remainder of their careers.

attitude of American car owners toward maintenance. Those tiny engines in the imports, reciprocating at twice the rate of the big "Detroit Iron" just to keep up with traffic flow, wore out in a matter of months, not years.

Enthusiasts willing to spend each weekend tinkering with their imports proved to be in short supply. Much to Detroit's surprise, those first compacts of 1960 were snapped up by disillusioned import owners. Excepting again the ubiquitous Volkswagen Beetle, which was seemingly indestructible, it took six years, numerous casualties, and extensive redesign of the survivors for the import makes to recapture their accustomed 15 percent share of the marketplace. Detroit at the time could easily have pushed the imports into the sea but instead management chose to gussy up their originally austere compacts, adding power with each increase in weight to where soon all semblance of economy, both in pricing and operating costs, was lost. And as a further step away from practical transportation, second-generation compacts such as the Pontiac Tempest and Olds F-85 of 1961 were actually large enough to start a new size category called intermediate. Obviously with the minimum two-year lead time required to design a car, these along with Ford's Fairlane were in the works long before any trends could be apparent.

What was management's motive in ignoring public demand, in twisting sales statistics to justify a return to dinosaurs and the status quo? The answer is simple. Cars in those days sold for about $1 per pound so it was (and still is) more profitable to add than subtract weight. Product planning was indeed off to an inauspicious start, for it was management that dictated the outlines of a new car, not the buyer.

One would think, too, that product planning would be the logical source of decisions involving type and specification for the materials to be used in a new car, but this was not always so in the industry and particularly at Chrysler, at least in the years and months before July 1961. That was when a dissident, substantial, and highly vocal Chrysler stockholder named Sol Dann forced the Corporation to acknowledge that there might be serious conflicts of interest at the highest managerial level. The sacrificial offering, to quiet Dann, proved to be none other than president William C. Newberg, who was genuinely surprised to be chosen. Once fired and free to express his indignation, Bill Newberg cornered his former friend and boss, chairman Colbert, in the locker room of the Bloomfield Hills Country Club and emerged the victor by a technical knockout in the first round.

The practice of those with the power to influence purchasing decisions of accepting favors, ranging from television sets at Christmas to stock in supplier corporations, was so widespread as to seem moral. About the only difference between the situation at Chrysler and Ford or GM was the degree. It was a way of corporate life in the auto industry, the reason for the Detroit Athletic Club's existence, a perquisite so entrenched that a gift refused rather than one accepted was cause for comment. No one knew these facts better than Lester Lum "Tex" Colbert, which was why he got punched out. Influence peddling was closer to the surface at Chrysler because bonuses to management-level employees were skipped more often than paid and, too, salaries for equivalent jobs were lower than at GM or Ford. In a very real sense, unofficially condoned payola had been a form of compensation at Chrysler, an inducement for key people to stick with the company through the frequent lean years.

Newberg's precipitant removal (he had been president for only two months) was a visible enough action to temporarily mollify most angry shareholders and soon thereafter Colbert was banished across the Detroit River to the sinecure presidency of Chrysler Canada, where, to his credit, he did a good job. At a lower level the ongoing reduction among white collar forces took care of the junior offenders, including one engineer of my acquaintance who built his own Imperial at home (Chrysler's largest, most expensive model at the time) using parts he had liberated one by one from factory bins. However, if every guilty executive had been fired, the Corporation could not have continued to function. GM and Ford, in turn, reacted to the scandal with pious assertions that nothing more than a free lunch was ever accepted by their buyers, probably true if you ignored the fact that these lunches were served at hunting lodges in Montana, beach resorts in the Bahamas, golf clubs in Georgia, or wherever.

It was many months before reps working Detroit adjusted to the quaint idea that price, service, and quality—in that priority—

would win them their order in the sterile new atmosphere. Coffee in offices replaced dry martinis at the London Chop House.[8] The creakily exclusive Detroit Club started accepting vice-presidents as members; the less selective DAC opened its doors to anyone with the initiation fee; and uptown at the Recess, waiters began asking luncheon guests if they wished separate checks. Cobwebs grew on the phones of call girls. Nightlife in Detroit, if it ever could have been called that, disappeared into the suburbs. Two major hotels were converted to condominiums and taxi drivers starved. But cars still got made and product planners still planned; now, though, with more substance to their recommendations.

The product planner is above all else a coordinator and perforce a diplomat. Aside from all-new cars, which are in the works at all times, the instrument panel presents him with a routine and oft-recurring challenge. The complete package, consisting of the instruments themselves, the cluster face and housing, and the structural panel stretching across in front of you (which also must contain provisions for a storage compartment and ventilating outlets as well as accessories, such as any of a variety of radios, a clock, and an ashtray), is at least as complicated a design exercise as a household refrigerator. And where basic body shells for a line of cars may be retained essentially unchanged for from three to eight years, the instrument panel is extensively redesigned every two years, sometimes annually. Reason: interior styling will influence more buying decisions, particularly late model trades of the same make, than changes on the outside simply because the owner will spend more time inside the car than he will admiring it standing in his driveway. To pursue the obvious, you can't see the outside while you're driving.

Although a new panel would seem to be a matter that could be decided between stylists and engineers, a wide variety of specialists become involved and Burt Stickshift must keep the peace. Using Chrysler's full-sized "R" bodies to illustrate, there is first of all shared usage of these among Dodge and

---

[8] The Chop House, a Detroit bistro considered by many to be one of the ten best (and most expensive) restaurants in the United States, was the scene of more million-dollar business decisions than most banks.

Chrysler nameplates. The Chrysler design must at least seem more expensive than that of the Dodge. Then, a key cost-cutting consideration is that as many hidden components as possible be interchangeable among all the corporate offerings for the year, including light trucks. Save a dollar per car that way and it parlays to a million or more for the season. A warning light, even though not hidden, is one such interchangeable component.

Enter now the marketing people. There is a stable of these bright young men employed by each Division. Some are car buffs, some are not, and that mix is deliberate. Those who are not read compilations of the latest survey taken at random among well-dressed persons, aged twenty-five to thirty-five, in exact proportion to the whites, blacks, and miscellaneous ethnic backgrounds of both sexes[9] that lived in that "typical" suburb, one of maybe six similar ones across the country. Respondents are assumed to be people in the market for a new car tomorrow, which is mistake No. 1.[10] The question is: "Would you prefer warning lights or gauges in the instrument panel of your next car?" A question unasked is: "If gauges, should they be round and precisely calibrated or square and vague?" Asked no questions at all are the kids of driving age, who are assumed to be hot rodders, and those thirty-six or older whose opinions no longer set any trends. The erroneous nature of this selection is apparent; even the most liberated female or militant black might not know the true and rather important difference in function between a warning light and a gauge.

The product planner, being an engineer with a keen sense of esthetics and an active conscience, is acutely aware of this difference. Management justifies warning lights on the premise that the average driver seldom looks at the gauges while operating the car and wouldn't understand what they indicated if he (or she) did. Warning lights are called "idiot lights" in the trade, a label I interpret as an insult. The fact is that warning lights are less expensive than gauges.

---

[9] Ford once surveyed blacks to determine their buying habits. The surprising, to Ford, finding was that blacks had the same preferences and expectations as whites.

[10] One such survey was taken in the presumedly wealthy suburb of Palos Verdes Peninsula, California. The area is known locally as "Hamburger Hill."

Let's give an example of how $5 invested by the factory for gauges could easily save the owner $1,000 or more for engine repairs, not to mention the inconvenience and danger of a roadside breakdown. When a so-called "fan belt" begins to slip, a reasonably knowledgeable driver will notice a slight drop in the charge rate shown on the ammeter and a slight rise in the temperature shown by the heat indicator. That is because this belt drives not only the fan but also the coolant pump and the alternator. Slippage of the belt often precedes breakage, but there would be no indication of this from the two warning lights involved. Only *after* the belt had failed would you see the light telling you, not warning you in advance, that the charging system had also ceased to function. Sometime later, if you continued to drive, the temperature light would come on to tell you that the engine *was* overheated. That's not a warning.

Odds are by then, particularly after you had struggled on to the nearest service station, that the damage would be done. Gauges, on the other hand, would have shown you the sudden switch to discharge when the belt broke, and then the progressive rise in temperature. You would have had time to seek help *before* risking damage to the engine. But management, justifying the savings from installing lights instead of gauges, says this simple sequence of a typical and expensive breakdown, usually miles from home, is too complicated for you to understand. By implication, you haven't the intelligence to read gauges. Oddly, gauges are least likely to be found in luxury cars where they could be best afforded and where presumably owners intelligent enough to make the money to buy these cars would be best able to read them.

A compromise is then reached between the marketing, styling, engineering, and planning people involved, and this compromise pleases management. Gauges are made standard equipment on only a few premium-priced, performance-oriented models in the line. You can also buy an "instrument package" for some lesser models at a considerable extra outlay because the package involves many more items than just the gauges. Whatever preferences the survey may have shown are ignored. Management is pleased because the recurrent controversy has been resolved in a way that adds to rather than subtracts from corporate profits.

For the short term, at least. But the average customer, sitting by the side of the road with idiot lights glaring and the engine smoking ominously, may have a few unkind words to pass on about that make to his friends, neighbors, business acquaintances, and relatives. Then when the car is towed in, it is seen by countless more people who may have been thinking about buying one like it.

To Chrysler's and Burt Stickshift's credit, it must be said that the Corporation is generally loyal to gauges even though more often than not these have been square and vague. The luxury Imperial for a few years before its demise even sported a full complement of gauges with a warning light for each to forestall any possible criticism. This effort failed to make the slightest dent in Cadillac sales but it does, though, illustrate a peculiar form of nostalgia which afflicts management, particularly at Chrysler and Ford.

Any automobile buff will tell you that the "golden age of motorcars" spanned the decade between 1929 and 1939. It was a period when a baker's dozen of makes here and more abroad were built almost without regard to cost. Long hoods filled with gargantuan straight-eight engines, and later V12s and V16s, framed by sweeping "clamshell" fenders and graceful, vee'd radiators was the setting provided by these select car manufacturers for gorgeously proportioned and appointed coachwork from a stable of custom builders. Sinuous and lean, the cars fitted around their passengers as tightly as a leotard. They breathed power and excitement as perhaps epitomized by the "Twenty-Grand" Duesenberg sedan displayed at the 1933 Chicago World's Fair. These cars all, of course, were doomed to failure as commercial ventures because their availability coincided with the Great Depression but odd bits and pieces of the format linger incongruously today. Example: The phony spare wheel bulges in the trunks of current Lincoln Continentals and Chrysler Le Barons. Another: Wheel covers that imitate the once predominant but highly impractical wire wheel. So-called "classic" memorabilia burdens just about every design presently in production and each item I can think of adds to rather than subtracts from the cost of manufacturing the car. Oddly, it's not the stylists or the planners but the marketing people who insist on these anachronistic touches.

Put another way, eliminating the simulated wood trim on instrument panels would pay for gauges.

Stylists and planners would prefer to showcase modern materials and concepts. The wheel again provides an example. The industry standard today consists of a stamped-steel center welded to a safety rim. These wheels are light and very strong but no attempt is made to "design" them. They are roughly finished and cursorily painted, often not even the same color as the car. Also, no attempt is made to spruce up the nuts and studs attaching the wheels to the car as these will be hidden by hubcaps or at extra cost to you, full wheel covers like the wire variety mentioned above. The standard wheel is beloved by management because it is cheap to produce and becomes a profit center when buyers pay to hide the crude appearance behind decorative trim.

Esthetics aside, it is quite surprising that wheel covers and, to a lesser extent, hubcaps haven't been noticed by those who write the government safety regulations. A typical wheel cover, weighing about two pounds, is potentially more lethal than fixed radiator ornaments or protruding door handles, which were both legislated out of existence years ago. Any freeway clean-up crew (or insurance company for that matter) will tell you that wheel covers, while maybe not as common as empty Coors cans, account for a substantial tonnage of the litter collected. And most weren't left behind by forgetful motorists who have just changed a tire. They fly off a speeding car when the driver changes direction suddenly. Any wheel will bend slightly under this stress and the flex may be enough to loosen the cover. And once airborne at fifty-five or more miles per hour, these covers can and do cause accidents.

A wheel, being perhaps the most purely functional shape in existence, can be made in an infinite variety of stunning designs. In fact, the aftermarket "mag" wheel is big business, accounting for about 60 percent of the $5 billion annual volume of a specialty equipment industry that has prospered by filling voids in the choices catalogued by automakers. Styled wheels like these could be mass produced for a cost at least equal to an ordinary wheel with its decorative cover but until recently only a few imports such as Honda have them as standard equipment. Those belatedly offered by Detroit in the past few years have been high-ticket options.

Burt Stickshift and his ilk could argue with some justification that a designer wheel, however esthetic, would lose its appeal if it were made standard. The same argument could be applied against the most blatant anachronism of all, the padded vinyl top coverings that from motivation attributed to nostalgia for the now extinct convertible, are ordered by an overwhelming number of new car buyers. It costs an average of $150 extra to have one of these heavy covers glued to an already painted steel roof where, especially if dark in color, it imposes a severe load on the air conditioning system and therefore markedly increases fuel consumption. The reason is the same as why people don't wear top coats in the summer. The covers are relatively hard to clean and age more rapidly than a painted surface. They serve no practical purpose whatever. If given the opportunity, stylists could create a similar effect in steel but that of necessity would be a standardized design and the profit center created by the option would be lost. Or perhaps, people would then pay extra for a newly exclusive cover that would simulate the old-style painted roof.

No one, of course, should fault Detroit for cataloguing options, however ridiculous, that sell in profitable quantities. It is the new car buyer who perpetuates the folly. However, the antisocial character of some items offered makes the industry highly vulnerable to criticism from those whose goal would seem to be eventual elimination of the automobile. There are such people and they make influential noises in inverse proportion to their numbers. They have found a home in government bureaus, in publishing houses, and at universities. Those temporarily without jobs mount crusades which in turn lead to consulting assignments and the lecture circuit.

This phenomenon more properly awaits study in later chapters dealing with safety, air cleanliness, and fuel economy, but it can be seen that the product planner is in a unique position to either mollify or irritate these critics. The problem is that almost anything which makes cars more salable is an irritation. Performance per se, for example, is considered dangerous even though proper use of extra horsepower on tap can save lives in a variety of situations where brakes offer no solution. Typical would be realizing you've misjudged the speed of an approaching vehicle after you're committed to a passing maneuver on a two-lane road.

Ideally, the route to higher performance should be a reduction in the weight-to-power ratio. This approach, taken by all manufacturers with a true racing heritage, avoids much of the criticism leveled at Detroit's method of accomplishing the same goal. That is until recently, stuffing an oversized engine into a car essentially designed to provide sedate, comfortable family transportation. The long-lived Porsche 911 series, for example, has never to my knowledge been seriously labeled by the Nader types as dangerous even though in its most sophisticated form it will outperform domestic machines with twice the power. Why? Because the Porsche weighs less than half as much. And too, while the Porsche is not likely to win economy contests, it uses far less fuel than, say, a Chevrolet Corvette, which is the closest to a total performance machine ever to be built in any quantity in this country.

The two-passenger Porsche, of course, is far too expensive and limited in its usefulness to be the way to go. The fact is, however, that if the least sophisticated of the 911 models were built in the quantities to which Detroit is accustomed, its price would probably be within reach of the average buyer. That is almost but not quite true already of certain useful, albeit compact, family sedans such as have been offered here by BMW and Alfa-Romeo.

All of this is just as obvious to Burt Stickshift and his management as it is to you, the reader. Also, the design and manufacture of such a car is perfectly within the capabilities of any of the extant Detroit producers, complete with the handling agility one associates with any of the makes mentioned. Even the Japanese have done it with their Datsun Z-cars. Why, then, are Detroit's still persistent efforts at packaging high performance typified by such cumbersome, energy-wasteful bombs as Chevrolet's Camaro Z-28, its counterpart from Pontiac called Trans-Am, and Dodge's Magnum, to name a few?

Answers to the technical aspects of the question are complex but the economic and marketing reasons are not. Even though the buyer will pay a substantial premium, it costs very little to increase the displacement and thus the power of an existing engine, the same as in more docile form is used for the larger family cars in the line. Add a larger carburetor, fiddle with the ignition and valve timing, and you have a machine that will burn rubber with each change of gears, reaching 55 mph from a standstill in seven seconds or so despite handicaps imposed by today's arbitrarily low compression ratios and strangling emission controls. Such a car will go very fast in a straight line only, so to give the illusion of handling, again at minimal cost to the manufacturer but considerable to the buyer, stiffer springs and shock absorbers are added. Toss in plastic spoilers front and rear which actually are functional and candy paint jobs which are not and you have a package which commands a $2,000 premium. At least two thirds of that amount is net profit for the manufacturer, although he will claim that inconvenience on the assembly line justifies the surcharge.

Why do some Americans stand in line to buy cars like these? Despite sociological theories that assign reasons ranging from sexual gratification to Babbittry, I think it's simply because among those more than casually interested in cars, a far larger number attend or follow drag and stock car racing events than are attracted by the less exciting contests for sports cars. Indianapolis-type racing and the growing number of Grand Prix being staged here are not a factor because those esoteric machines bear no resemblance to anything that can be licensed for highway use.

In any case, performance Detroit-style is doomed, not by its many critics from both social and purist camps but by newly enacted fuel economy regulations. Each manufacturer's fleet, excluding captive imports, must average 27½ miles per gallon by the 1985 model year and that requirement leaves no room for the so-called "muscle car" with its ravenous appetite for fuel. The obvious alternative, optionally turbocharging smaller engines to gain power with little or no sacrifice in economy, has already appeared on some Buick and Ford models. The $1,000 or so extra for one of these is justified in terms of both efficiency and performance. Add a chassis to match and Detroit would have machines that might bear comparison with Europe's best for the minority who desire them, but that is an unlikely millennium.

If you are confused or possibly disillusioned by these examples of problems confronting the product planner and actions taken to solve them, then so too is Burt Stickshift. It is impossible for him to fulfill his mandate. He cannot respond to the conflicting demands of government, management, and the buying public without painful compromise. Over all hangs the specter of costly failures, the most recent being Lincoln's compact but luxurious Versailles. Why should it fail when the similar Cadillac Seville succeeded? Perhaps it's because as one industry observer said years ago: "A million Kaisers a year would have been sold if General Motors had made them."

CHAPTER 3

How Clean Is Clean?

Back in 1966 when the only piece of mandated emission control hardware to be found on most new cars was a $5 positive crankcase ventilation (PCV) device,[1] the trade publication *Automotive News* printed a series of articles entitled "The Billion Dollar Smog Hoax." Joe Callahan, the author and one of the paper's editors at the time, smarted under accusations of gross exaggeration and disregard for fact. Today, thirteen years later, if a similar article were published, it could be factually titled "The $20 Billion Smog Hoax." What's more, that figure could mean just what's already been spent on cleaning up cars, or, it could be used with equal accuracy to indicate what hopefully will be the minimum spent, by you and me, in only the next five years. And alas, to the eye of the average resident of the Los Angeles Basin where the phenomenon was first observed twenty-five years ago, it seems as smoggy as ever. The ominous pall has spread north to Santa Barbara; to the southeast, it even taints that mecca for sunworshippers, Palm Springs.

Air purity is another issue akin to motherhood. No politician, except perhaps those elected by Detroit and its satellite auto manufacturing centers, can fail to espouse it. No publications other than industry trade magazines dare suggest that perhaps the automobile is not the only culprit. Yet, most Americans, watching the service station attendant groping for the dipstick

[1] 1967 models sold in California, the first to be tightly regulated, were equipped with $50–$75 worth of emission control equipment.

hidden under the maze of emission control plumbing in a typical modern car, will curse the price of tune-ups, bewail the loss in performance, and complain about fuel economy.

The public is entitled to bitch. The cost in increased fuel consumption is not even included in the vast expenditures cited above. That loss is a whopping 25 percent from the 1970 norm (the year of the second and stiffest of the Clean Air Acts), caused about equally by emission controls and the arbitrary lowering of compression ratios to permit the use of relatively low-octane, lead-free fuels.[2] Then, high fuel consumption is further aggravated by impatient owners stepping harder on the accelerator pedals of their sluggish new cars. And finally, tune-ups not only cost more but with annoying frequency are less than successful due to the complexity of the emission controlling mechanisms. A professional mechanic risks a $50,000 fine if he removes or disconnects any part of the emission control system but there are those who will do it, just to get the car running and out of the shop. And that action, in turn, may cause more harm than good, as new cars aren't designed to operate without the hardware.

When Professor Arlie Haagen-Smit of the University of Southern California identified what the people of Los Angeles call "smog" as a reaction between sunlight and certain chemicals, such as hydrocarbons and oxides of nitrogen, that occurs mainly in trapped, inverted air masses, he did not single out the automobile for the entire blame. What, in effect, he said at the time was that the automobile was a major, identifiable source of these emissions, along with other obvious sources such as jet aircraft, industrial plants, public utilities, incinerators, and even the natural emissions of plant life, cultivated or wild.[3] It was many years before scientists came to general agreement that the automobile,

[2] Though tetraethyllead used as a fuel additive is extremely toxic, no one has yet proved that lead oxides emitted to the atmosphere are detrimental to health. In any case, elimination of lead was later necessary to prevent fouling of catalytic converters. A further blow to conservation is the fact that each gallon of lead-free fuel requires a significantly greater amount of crude to manufacture than its leaded equivalent.

[3] The Great Smoky Mountains of Appalachia were named for the omnipresent deep blue haze now known to be caused by natural emissions from the indigenous turpentine-producing yellow pine.

before controls were applied, could be blamed for about 30 percent of the smog-causing emissions in Los Angeles, not necessarily elsewhere. And no one has yet proved that smog of this type has been the direct cause for the demise of a single human being. It may, however, aggravate existing respiratory diseases, particularly among the very old and very young segments of the population.[4]

Smog of the photochemical variety is still visible more days than not over most urban centers in the nation. It is ugly at worst, unpleasant at best, but vast improvement is evident in recent years. Generally, if air quality over all of these cities except Los Angeles were to be rated on a scale from "clear" to "murky," a count made for 1977 would be almost the reverse of one in 1967; that is, there are as many clear days now as there were murky ones ten years ago. Then as now, the majority of days fall somewhere between but the same reversal of degree is evident. Then, considering that the number of motor vehicles on the road has risen from 103.5 million in 1969 to an estimated 139 million currently, it would seem that we are winning the battle for cleaner air. However, how clean is clean?

When smog first became a national issue in 1965, give or take a year, the auto industry refused to admit even partial guilt. Whatever might emerge from exhaust pipes that could be considered noxious was due directly, it was claimed, to improper maintenance. Unfortunately for Detroit, as it turned out, visible exhaust emissions or "smoke" of the type caused by worn or improperly tuned engines, though unpleasant to those in the vicinity, were proved to have little to do with the formation of photochemical smog.

More unfortunately, auto industry spokesmen chose dubious weapons for their counterattack. A Chrysler engineer named Charles Heinen, addressing a Chicago audience on the subject of smog, reminded his listeners of how it was in the days of Mrs. O'Leary's cow when the streets were paved with dung, the alleys with human slops, and the air a mixture of effluents from these

---

[4] Back when cars were a rarity, a writer in *Appleton's Magazine* estimated that twenty thousand New Yorkers died annually from "maladies that fly in the dust."

and coal smoke.[5] His intentions were good but his approach caused a stink of another variety. As Charlie Heinen, who was and is a good guy and who is now in charge of Chrysler's emission control efforts, learned, one had best not throw dung when outnumbered by the teary-eyed, coughing, righteously indignant citizenry of Chicago or any other community.

By this time, of course, politicians sensing paydirt had joined the fray. Oddly, one who emerged a leader among those who would illogically require emissions from auto exhausts to be purer than the air ingested through the carburetor was Democratic Senator Edmund Muskie whose home state of Maine can boast perhaps the cleanest, if dampest, air in the nation. Muskie himself has admitted that it was not conditions there but the fumes hovering over Secaucus, New Jersey, through which he frequently passed while motoring back and forth between the nation's capitol and his constituency that first drew his attention to the problem. Ironically for Charlie Heinen, the principal activity in Secaucus is raising hogs; any contribution of auto exhausts to its atmosphere is incidental.

Far-off California also exerted a strong influence on the thinking among lawmakers in Washington. What expertise there was on the subject of smog existed in Los Angeles County, which had already created its own Air Pollution Control Board. This Board recommended laws that were dutifully passed by the County Board of Supervisors complete with teeth for enforcement. The area in the early sixties was desperate for relief. Inspectors were everywhere, chasing down motorists with smoking cars, delaying long-distance truckers, fining ship's captains in the harbor for prolonging by even a few seconds the necessary operation of "blowing stacks," shutting down industrial plants and power companies, banning trash burning and even, for a while, the seemingly innocuous and pleasant fire in the hearth at home. Early on, California was exempted from federal clean air statutes so that it could apply stiffer standards of its own. Automakers squirmed and protested but caved in when meaningfully threatened with a ban on new car sales. California was their biggest

---

[5] In 1908 there were an estimated hundred thousand horses active in Chicago, each contributing twenty-two pounds of solid and a gallon of liquid waste to the streets every working day.

single market, usually accounting for about 10 percent of all cars sold.

For some years the technically ignorant clean air strategists in Washington would filch California's standards intact for application one or two years later in the rest of the states. Automakers, for their part, continued to claim that each new set of standards was "impossible" to meet even though they were already meeting them, increment by increment, on vehicles destined for sale in California. Admittedly these standards, wherever their source, were more often arbitrary than not. They were chosen and applied with little regard to the dollar cost of the benefits that could be expected and with no regard whatever for the effect on fuel consumption of the various control devices required. Nobody had any idea at which stage of cleanliness the population would see visible improvement in the air, so the push was for an Ivory Soap degree of purity. In fact, measuring techniques for both the pollutor and the polluted were of dubious accuracy.

As matters stood in 1966–67 with the first of the Clean Air Acts under consideration in Congress, it is quite probable that if automakers had faced reality and had suggested an equally arbitrary goal of, say, 70 percent purity, credibility would have been established and the lawmakers would have acceded to a reasonable timetable for achievement of the goal. But no. Detroit pursued its indefensible protests with fresh vigor by appointing vice-presidents to carry on the war against Washington. And also at the same time, of course, a war of even greater magnitude, financially, was being waged on the safety front complete with its own vice-presidents. In most cases men chosen for these thankless tasks were executives whose careers had already been sidetracked by internal politics at their home offices. One told me that he would rather be lobbying on behalf of tobacco, sugar, or Carter's Little Liver Pills because at least those harassed products might swing a few vested votes.

The lack of communication then and now has its roots in basic conflict between business, or "free enterprise," and a federal bureaucracy nurtured on injustices allegedly perpetrated in the name of free enterprise. Whatever amount the Jay Goulds, the Rockefellers, the Vanderbilts, and the rest of the early "robber barons" may have bilked years ago from gullible investors and intimidated workers, it was trivial when compared to the cost of the mistrust generated since in an economic system that has been only occasionally abused. It's you and I who are really to blame. We guarantee General Motors its constitutional right to exist and then snipe at the fiber of its being. We who are, or who are free to be, shareholders in General Motors demand that it be managed by skunks who will serve our greed and then look askance when another specie of skunk whom we elect to Congress squares off for what can only be described as a pissing contest between skunks. I do not wonder that the industry's men in Washington are confused, frightened, and powerless. They cannot even play their hole card, which is that we all walk!

I think it odd, if not unfair, that the sum total of the action taken against the industry by our government should not be that each new car bear a readily visible label. You've guessed it. That label would read: "Congress Has Determined That This Automobile Is Dangerous to Your Health." You could then choose for yourself whether to drive one or not, as today you can choose whether to smoke cigarettes or not.

But Senator Muskie, intent on riding through the White House doors on a blanket of smog, was not through with Detroit yet. He spearheaded passage by Congress in 1970 of the second Clean Air Act, generally known as the Muskie Bill. You'll remember I speculated earlier in this chapter that if Detroit going in had volunteered to achieve a 70 percent improvement in emissions, the industry would have been allowed to proceed on a timetable pretty much of its own making. Instead, no action at all was volunteered. Painfully prodded each percentage point of the way, Detroit had indeed achieved 70 percent purity with its 1970 models and at this point in time was hit by Muskie's oxides of nitrogen bomb. The Act called for a reduction by 1976 models to 10 percent in the *then extant* (1970) levels of all exhaust pollutants. This meant achieving a 93 percent degree of purity, a level considerably higher than the air we (or cars) breathe at street level in any city!

These percentages actually fail to illustrate the full degree of difficulty. Ask any housewife. She'll tell you that while 70 percent cleanliness could be achieved and maintained most of the time in her home, 93 percent would be improbable even if she devoted her entire day, every day, to the task. To get to the 99.9 percent level found in the so-called "clean rooms" used in some industrial processes requires a vast expenditure for special air-filtering and sanitizing equipment. The equipment needed for such a room usually occupies more space than the room itself. In other words, cost rises exponentially as perfection is approached.

One reason in the case of automobile exhausts is that the three smog-producing constituents so far isolated—unburned hydrocarbons (HC), carbon monoxide (CO), and oxides of nitrogen (NO_x)—tend to interact. The first two are products of incomplete combustion and therefore can be reduced by improving the efficiency of the engine. (That's efficiency in terms of complete combustion, which is not necessarily translated to improved performance or better fuel economy.) However, as combustion becomes more complete, the quantity of NO_x emitted tends to rise. For example, diesel engines which are just now being made available in domestic passenger cars are inherently clean in terms of HC and CO emissions, but the NO_x content in their exhaust is high compared to a gasoline engine of the same power.

In fact, the theory behind the formation of smog raises serious doubts about the approach we are taking to eliminate it. It is, as I've said, generally accepted that smog in a stagnant air mass results from the reaction of either unburned HC, or CO, or both with NO_x in the presence of sunlight. The troublesome fact is that in all presently feasible types of internal combustion engines, minimum levels of unburned HC can only be achieved at air-fuel ratios which tend to produce maximum levels of NO_x. As the air-fuel ratio is leaned to reduce the NO_x, engineers face the dual problem of maintaining combustion while HC emissions, because of the marginal combustion, rise once again to unacceptable levels. Carbon monoxide, fortunately, can be reduced to acceptable levels within the useful range of air-fuel ratios and does not rise as the mixture is further leaned.

Squinting through the complex technology, it would seem unnecessary to fiddle with NO_x emissions at all if both HC and CO were reduced to their practical minimums because, according to the theory, it requires one or the other of these *plus* the NO_x to form smog. To belabor the obvious, a fire requires a combustible substance in the presence of oxygen or, in practice, air. Eliminate either the combustible substance or the air, and there can be no fire.

At some point in this sad tale of governmental and industrial ineptitude, I must use numbers because they are the name of the emission control game. And it might as well be now because each of the seemingly inconsequential decimals to be cited represents *billions* of your and my dollars. These are the numbers created out of thin if impure air, evolved from exasperation, by Senator Muskie and his Clean Air Committee back in 1970, simply because Detroit wailed "impossible" once too often. Tempers triggered perhaps the most costly regulatory reaction in history. There was certainly no basis in reason or science for what resulted!

The Clean Air or Muskie Bill of 1970 as originally written projected the millennium in cleanliness to be attained with then far-off 1978 models. Actually, these weren't as far off as it seemed because in the gestation of any car, engineering in every detail should be finalized and parts ordered from suppliers within a period of between twenty-four and twelve months before the start of car assembly. Congress couldn't, or wouldn't, and still won't, comprehend this fact of industrial life. Any compression of timing tends to add exponentially to the cost of the effort. Any serious delay could prevent the scheduled start of production which, in turn, could make shutting down some or all plants the least expensive of two evils. So, when I speak of 1978 models or whatever, remember to subtract the absolutely vital lead time required.

I've already stated that an astonishing 93 percent of purity was reached with 1977 models. In terms of grams of emissions per mile, the figures that brought this about were HC, 1.5 gpm; CO, 15 gpm; and NO_x, 2.0 gpm. But the 1978 requirements as they originally stood were the backbreakers. These were HC, 0.41 gpm; CO, 3.4 gpm; and NO_x, 0.40 gpm. Together they would bring us to something like 95 percent purity and for once Detroit had justifiable reasons to wail. Although only outspoken Henry Ford II actually threatened to shut down his plants, the others would have had to as well, so Congress was prodded into reluctant, hair-breadth postponements during calendar years 1976 and 1977 which permitted production of 1978 and 1979 models. Even

Congress this time could realize what could happen if it did not act, albeit at the very last moment. The nation and then the Free World would have been plunged into an economic recession unlike any that had come before, costing perhaps a million autoworkers their jobs immediately, and soon thereafter the livelihoods of one out of every five workers in this country. Such would be the chain reaction should auto industry purchases dry up. And, of course, I should note that each of the 1.4 million or so cars imported annually would have had to meet the standards or be withdrawn from the U.S. market. The importers employ 127,000 persons here who receive nearly $1.5 billion annually in wages.

Tens of thousands of new cars were produced at the beginning of the 1978 model run with no assurance whatever from Washington that they could be legally sold. Also, General Motors had spent about $100 million to develop a diesel engine option for some of its larger 1978 Oldsmobile and Cadillac models, as well as Chevrolet and GMC light trucks, which, unless the NO_x standard remained at 2.0 gpm, could not legally be sold. The diesel, as I will clarify in the next chapter, is about the only path GM or any other manufacturer with a predominance of large cars in its model mix can follow to meet fuel economy standards also mandated by Congress—not so much the 17.5 miles per gallon fleet average required in 1978 but future, higher averages en route to the legislated peak of 27.5 mpg for 1985 models. Scheduling low volume field testing of the diesel in the hands of actual buyers for 1978 was a necessary preliminary to uncover problems, if any, prior to large-scale use.

The decision to go ahead and produce cars with their legal status in doubt was part powerplay, part calculated risk but, really, should it be necessary to play games with jobs? Meaningful, rational dialog still does not exist between Detroit, Congress, and personnel of the Environmental Protection Agency (EPA) whose tough but fair deputy administrator for air and water pollution, Eric O. Stork, was recently fired for being "too soft on the industry." Mr. Stork's sin was not softness, as any of his adversaries in Detroit will attest; it was his willingness, rare at EPA, to be guided by reality. Specifically, he came to agree on purely technical grounds that the 1978 standards cited above, which have now been postponed until 1981, are impossible to achieve within the present state of the art. He had come to understand after eight years of combat the complex relationship between emissions, fuel economy, the toxic as versus esthetic quality of the atmosphere, and the overall cost to U.S. taxpayers, whether they buy cars or not.[6]

Aside from technical feasibility, Stork knew, as does Detroit, and as should you and I, that the Clean Air Act Amendment of 1977 which postponed the original 1978 standards until 1981 merely postponed an industry, and thus consumer, expenditure estimated at *$15 billion annually*. That's the price for 95 percent purity. Consider this price in light of the fact that as far back as 1970 the automobile accounted for only 4 percent of the total *toxic* air pollutants hovering over this country! Consider it also in light of recorded proceedings that the Amendment was adopted only after an impassioned appeal by a newcomer to Washington, former Governor Wendell Anderson of Minnesota who had appointed himself to Vice-President Mondale's vacant Senate seat. Anderson cried out at a crucial moment during the Committee debate that "carbon monoxide from the gas guzzlers obscures our view of the Washington Monument . . ." Carbon monoxide is an invisible gas, despite Mr. Anderson's imagination. The haze over Washington, D.C., according to the Bureau of Naval Research, is mostly caused by decaying vegetation in the woodlands surrounding the city, not by cars. But Mr. Anderson has yet to atone for his falsehood by chopping down a single cherry tree.

Mr. Stork, in turn, should be thankful he has been separated from this grievously expensive, scientifically ridiculous charade. More and more responsible persons in each camp now wish that some face-saving way could be found to live with the status quo; namely, existing 1977–79 standards in perpetuity. In that way we could rely on the normal cycle of thirteen years from showroom to junkyard to eliminate, at no further cost to anyone, older, less stringently controlled cars from the highways. Only in that way can we even determine with any degree of accuracy what, if

[6] Buyers ultimately pay for cleaning up their new cars; taxpayers support EPA's multibillion-dollar annual budget.

anything, has been accomplished so far. By 1983 the vast majority of cars and light trucks in use would be 70 percent clean; by 1990, 93 percent cleanliness would be the norm, and the fraction of toxic pollutants caused by motor vehicles would be infinitesimal. Simple arithmetic shows that $15 billion spent annually for a dubious improvement in air quality translates to approximately $1,000 added onto the already inflated base price of each car sold. There may be many who would refuse to pay such a premium, who would prefer to keep their old cars and thus prolong the alleged pollution.

The oddest fact of all is, for the past year at least, Detroit has had access to positive proof that the ultimate emission goals decreed by Congress (HC, 0.41 gpm; CO, 3.4 gpm; NO_x, 0.40 gpm) are impossible to meet in the foreseeable future. This proof exists in tangible form. Its credentials are impeccable. Its development was an eleven-year, international effort. It is a research project that succeeded because it failed. It is known in the industry as the $32 million Granada.

Ford currently builds a car called the Granada and that's what this proof looks like on the outside and why it is so named. The familiar shape, however, hides under its hood the best, cost-be-damned joint effort of eleven corporations whose trademarks are known in every corner of the world to create *one* car that could comply with the final stage of the Clean Air Act as it is written today. It can, for just 4,000 miles of operation, at which point it must undergo an extensive overhaul to achieve another 4,000 clean miles. Unfortunately, though, the law stipulates that emissions must meet standards for at least 50,000 miles before *any* service to the mechanisms involved is required. Therefore, the $32 million Granada cannot be legally sold in 1981, the year in which the standards cited above must be met, even if it were producible at something approaching a reasonable cost, which apparently it is not.

Was the project deliberately pointed down a path toward failure? I think not, and to my knowledge no one in government has voiced that suspicion. There were too many prestigious names involved in the project, some outside the auto industry. Begun in 1967 with the official title "Inter-Industry Emission Control," known for short as IIEC-1, the research was jointly sponsored by

Ford Motor Company and Mobil Oil Corporation. In 1968 automakers Fiat, Mitsubishi (Colt and Arrow), Nissan (Datsun), and Toyo Kogyo (Mazda) joined the group along with Amoco Oil, Atlantic-Richfield, Marathon Oil, Standard Oil (Ohio), and Sun Oil. In 1974 the project became known as IIEC-2 with Toyota joining the group and Fiat, Toyo Kogyo, and Sun Oil dropping out. The self-policing nature of the effort may be assumed, for certainly the oil companies involved would keep the automakers honest. The latter have already tried blaming emission problems on the quality of fuels available.

The prototype clean car was shown to the press in February 1978. It represented, according to its sponsors, the largest and heaviest (4,000 pounds) car that could be expected from assembly lines during the early 1980s. Under the hood was an experimental and very sophisticated fuel injection system, extensive and equally sophisticated computerized electronic control systems, and no less than five catalytic converters. It was a mechanic's (and owner's) nightmare. The oversized battery was so overworked running all the computers that a separate cooling system had to be installed for it. Project coordinator and Ford's research vice-president, Dr. W. Dale Compton, stated flatly that the electronic fuel control system alone was so complex that "there is no way I know of to put it into production."

Dr. Compton was understandably cautious when it came to committing his sponsors, who included, of course, his employer. The most he would say was "it is going to be extremely difficult, and maybe impossible, to meet the emission requirements on a 'heavy' car." Left unsaid was the fact that it would be extremely difficult, and maybe impossible, to entice customers into buying such a car even if it were producible.

The subject of communications, or the lack of them, seems to be the recurring theme of this chapter. Sponsors of the $32 million Granada have made no attempt since the press presentation to show the car to congressmen or EPA officials. A project spokesman explained: "Ford is not an 'I told you so' company." So, sometime in calendar 1979, Detroit once again faces a fight with Congress to force further postponement of emission standards already on the statute books, a fight that has not been resolved at this writing.

I can lead you to no conclusions on the subject of automotive emissions and their control. "I'll be judge, I'll be jury," said cunning old Fury; "I'll try the whole cause, and condemn you to death."[7]

[7] Lewis Carroll's *Alice's Adventures in Wonderland,* Chapter 3.

CHAPTER 4

The Well Runs Dry

I've long delayed the writing of this chapter. I've been waiting for the world to run out of oil as, during the "energy crisis" of 1973-74, they told me it would. I remember the service station where I lined up on alternate days for my allotted few gallons of gasoline. I remember that billions of ration coupons were printed should they be needed. I remember realizing that even my Permatex trousers were created from hydrocarbons, as was the electricity for ironing them. I was awed by the thought of life without oil—the immense stillness, the chilling darkness, people immobile, crops rotting in the fields, Dodger Stadium deserted. Chagrined and humble, I stood accused as the kind of wastrel that had brought all this to pass. I stood willing to pay the piper. I sang shorter songs in the shower, froze in the winter, sweltered in the summer, wiped my own windshield and, most patriotically of all, traded my Detroit-built Chrysler on a Japanese economy car. Three successive Presidents of the United States have beamed approval of my actions.

I got screwed. The facts today are that the world's proven, recoverable reserve of petroleum stands at an all-time high of over 660 billion barrels,[1] which is a thirty-four-year inventory at the present rate of consumption. I further have learned that more oil is discovered each year than is used, and that more has been discovered in recent years than ever before. I found out

[1] A "barrel" of petroleum equals forty-two gallons.

that 90 percent of all the oil and gas wells ever drilled in the world have been drilled right here in the United States and that only a few thousand of these have gone deeper than 15,000 feet despite existing technology which permits drilling to twice that depth. The rest of the land surface of the globe, I'm told, is virtually undrilled, as are the seas and polar ice caps, which cover 80 percent of the earth's crust.

I hear a lot which I don't understand about how, if petroleum prices here were free instead of fixed, there would be the incentive to drill for more oil. Yet, what counts faster these days than the dollar-and-cents dial of a self-serve gas pump? True, a petroleum-heavy imbalance of our trade deficit disappears into the pockets of politically volatile sheiks and princes; enough, in fact, for them to buy General Motors with two weeks' income. But I know of no better way to frustrate Communism, for one can't yet acquire Cadillacs with rubles. Those Arabs are wearing grins wider than the radiator grilles of their new limousines. But really, they're no more self-seeking than our own Texans. Why drill a glory hole in the lobby of Dallas's Hyatt-Regency Hotel when there's already enough oil at hand to fuel cars and heat homes for the next several decades?

It just needs to be brought to market in usable form. With that the United States has a problem. Much of the petroleum gallonage imported is already refined, simply because we do not presently possess enough capacity to process all the crude oil needed. We couldn't even build these facilities if we wished because the handful of firms worldwide capable of designing and constructing a major refinery are committed to foreign customers far into the future. And this again is a dilemma created by an industry so big it recognized no boundaries and acknowledged no political aspirations in others, certainly not the docile Arabs ever wishing to emerge from vassalhood. Thus it was that the free world's most modern, largest refineries have been built where it was cheapest to build and operate them—adjacent to the remote oil fields rather than near the civilizations which they serve.

Now, of course, we no longer control many of these fields and refineries. They were taken from us in the same ruthless manner as we, years ago, walked in and appropriated the precious resource that is their reason for being. Paradoxically like the beggar pitying himself because he had no shoes till he saw the man with no legs, we today find ourselves putting the Arabs on wheels in return for their oil.

But once again we have an issue as holy as motherhood. Although we all do it every hour we're awake, and also while we sleep, who when asked would advocate wasting an essential resource? Of course you wouldn't, even if supplies were inexhaustible. If nothing else, waste costs money and that is not inexhaustible. And there are those among us who object to littering the countryside with Chicken Delight containers, aluminum (especially) beverage cans, old tires, and even old cars. Fitting somewhere between are the realists, who advocate biodegradable litter. I found out where I fit the day my son requested money to pay his citation for an "open container" found in the family car while it was occupied by him and some friends. They had, he claimed, consumed the wine while parked and, rather than litter, they saved the bottle for later disposal in a suitable receptacle. That argument impressed me no more than it did the cop making a routine stop-and-search accorded all cars containing long-haired kids on the street after midnight back in the flower-child era.

Americans consume over 4 billion tons of goods and materials each year. That's approximately 200 million trailer loads, or if they were shipped by rail, the train hauling our annual needs would stretch nearly seventy-five times around the earth's circumference at the equator. From those roundhouse figures one can gain an idea of the litter created by just one civilized country and its peoples, for matter cannot be destroyed. It returns to whence it came, sooner or later, and mostly in unusable form. Even the cartons and crates used for shipping much of this stuff would fill a train almost as long if they were all returned for reuse.

Thus, industry carefully weighs the economics of recycling these containers against giving them away, the time and cost involved in reuse versus the convenience, however seemingly wasteful, of onetime use. In California where I live the once common return-for-deposit beer and pop bottles are limited to a few brands. The nickle you get back is of interest only to kids and pensioners. There will always be glass, for the silica from which it is made is the most ubiquitous substance on earth, but the furnaces in which the glass is fired burn oil or natural gas. To molt aluminum from its ore requires vast amounts of electricity, and power companies prefer to generate with oil. And then there is plastic, the most pernicious of litter, which is all but immune from destruction by the elements. Much of it is formed from hydrocarbon molecules that, if rearranged, could have been gasoline for your car. So it is not only cars to be blamed for our alleged shortage of petroleum. Cars, in fact, account for only 30 percent of our gasoline consumption and only 13 percent of our petroleum consumption.

Those involved with these matters, whether officially or self-appointed, have somehow failed to grasp the commonality of those twin national goals—conservation and cleanliness. Common sense should tell us that if we stop manufacturing throw-away containers, then we will no longer have to pick them up and, in turn, we will save the energy required for their manufacture. Recycling the raw materials from which the containers are made is but a partial solution, first because reprocessing consumes energy and secondly because human nature being what it is, only a fraction of these materials will be returned. The $2 per hundredweight now being paid for empty aluminum cans attracts less than 1 percent of the quantity manufactured. The rest are tossed. Recycling is a public relations gesture except when applied to industrial wastes. Better we go back to fetching our beer in a pail.

Unlikely, you say? Perhaps not. However lamentable the lack of foresight, industrial and political, that was its cause, our energy crisis is very real. But if mankind could just make a modest effort to minimize waste, many of our actual and potential shortages would evaporate. So too would much of our pollution.

Let's boggle our minds for the moment with a day in Mother's life come the new age of waste-free distribution, just taking that ninety minutes or so she spends shopping for groceries. In her cupboard are rows of sturdy, clearly labeled containers of various, standardized capacities. She already has or there is available a suitable container for every grocery item she could conceivably want that does not come prewrapped like a banana by nature. She loads those that need refilling into her Cadillac and is off to the supermarket, where wheeled baskets await her in the parking lot. I've already anticipated some of your objections. After all, if we've managed to put men on the moon, we certainly can invent reusable containers for products that must be vacuum-sealed at the time they're packed. So if you want some "canned" asparagus or sardines, or anything that demands an odd-shaped container, be sure to bring back the empty or be prepared to pay a stiff premium for a new one. Most foods, though, will fit comfortably into any size or shape receptacle so these could be interchanged at will. Just as, I might remind you, our ancestors did with the mason jar. And what's to stop the packager from fresh-freezing the contents of these containers if that's your preference?

Some foods, of course, might never be adapted to the new system. But do we really need aerosol dessert toppings, liquid cheese in tubes, biscuit dough in a cylinder, or lemon juice in a plastic lemon? TV dinners, if they're what's bothering you, could be packed with real tableware which could be either collected or returned. Imagine TV China as the successor to Depression Glass at the yard sales of the future!

Wrapping would not be entirely eliminated, as I don't know, for example, of a better way to keep flies off fresh meat. We could, though, dispense with the paper sacks in which they put all this stuff at the check-out counter. Sturdy, stylized shopping bags with handles, like Grandmother used again and again, would be one solution. And too, I don't have a ready answer to compliance with truth-in-labeling laws under the new system, as there would be very few, if any, labels other than generic identification on the reusable containers. But then, there would be fewer cancer scares. Or, a reference book could be compiled if you insist on knowing that dried whey and disodium succinate are among the ingredients that help make Tuna Helper so tasty.

I anticipate resistance to this proposal. The food industry's considerable investment in brand names would be wiped out overnight but as Gertrude Stein might have written had she been aware of them, a Fig Newton is a Fig Newton, etc. There would be chaos on Madison Avenue for a while until the agencies switched from promoting one or another brand of corn flakes as best to a campaign plugging any corn flake as better for any kid than any wheat flake. This, of course, would generate a counter campaign by the wheat interest, with Kellogg and Post cheerfully footing their shares of the bills for both. And the supermarkets themselves might expect to lose their considerable income from the impulse buyer. Sales of Vienna sausages and mandarin oranges would certainly plummet if the customer were forced to decide before going to market. But people would be thinner, and healthier.

Before you dismiss these imaginings as not pertinent, or too costly, or too much trouble, realize that Mother in the foreseeable future *might* have to *walk* to the store or, at the least, drive there in a vehicle somewhat less comfortable and commodious than her Cadillac, something, say, like a closed version of an electric golf cart, if petroleum production and distribution problems remain unsolved. Or, if our government has its way, she would take the bus. Realize, too, that automobiles which consume only 13 percent of our petroleum are receiving practically all the blame for both waste and pollution. And on the subject of costs, realize that General Motors alone must spend *$1 billion* to reduce the average fuel consumption of its fleet[2] for a given model year by just *one half mile per gallon!* Congress has already decreed that this average must reach 27.5 mpg by 1985. We started with 17.5 in 1978, so that's 20 halves or $20 billion. Since GM accounts for somewhat less than half of production, the total bill for the industry could be rounded off at $40 billion. Actually it's your bill, for this is just another item that will be added incrementally to the sticker prices of future cars. Now is it too much trouble to fetch beer in a pail?

Then there is the cost of all the regulation being poured on the auto industry. The infant Department of Energy which now consolidates all functions of the Federal Power Commission, Federal Energy Administration, and the Energy Research and Development Agency already employs nearly 20,000 people and was granted a budget for fiscal 1978 of $10.6 billion. Industry sources won't disclose the average cost of drilling an oil well, but DOE's budget represents $266,871 for each of the 39,763 wells sunk in 1976. Even if the average well costs $1 million, which I doubt,

[2] "Fleet" here is a trade term meaning model mix.

DOE might serve us better by drilling 10,600 additional wells each year instead of holes in the national economy. As it is, we're putting out 4 cents toward supporting DOE every time we buy a gallon of gasoline or home heating oil, or 42 cubic feet of natural gas. Actually, it's much more because industry must pay the same share on each gallon of its much larger petroleum consumption and, of course, this added cost is passed directly on to the consumer.

I mentioned in a previous chapter an estimate that paperwork generated by government costs industry $116 billion annually. To put that sum in perspective, the combined net profits of all U.S. nonfinancial corporations in 1978, a very good year, was only $61.5 billion. Determining fleet economy averages is too new for statistics to be compiled but the cost of testing programs for exhaust emission certification is well documented. In one year GM drove 284 prototypes (114 costing $55,000 each) a total of 5,200,000 miles at a cost of $24 million. If all the attendant paperwork required of GM were gathered together, it would create a pile 200 feet high. Ford counted differently, figuring 2,476,000 pages of documentation for the same project. "Little" Chrysler got by with 2,000,000 miles of testing, burning only 125,000 gallons of gasoline in the process.

Certification costs of various kinds, however impressive, account for only a small portion of the overall bill imposed on the auto industry as it marches toward the 27.5 mpg fleet average required for 1985 models. The reason is the same as why some of us enrich Jack LaLanne and the growers of alfalfa sprouts—we want to get slim and stay that way. Each individual's list of motives may vary but vanity is always one of them. The gamin look, however, has not been considered beautiful in cars. Historically, most of us have dreamed of owning obese Cadillacs and have bought Chevrolets almost as large until we could fulfill our dream. Our auto industry catered to this vanity. It gave us what we wanted and profited in the process because, you'll remember, cars with few exceptions were priced by the pound. A technically minded buyer still can find little real difference between a top-line Chevrolet and a Cadillac except that the latter weighs more and therefore costs more, and thus is more profitable to its maker. He also would know he could expect to pay a penalty of about seven gallons of gasoline every 10,000 miles to cart each 100 pounds of this extra weight around.

I truly doubt that any significant slimming of our domestic cars would have occurred were it not for government regulations. Automakers disagree, saying that market demand would have brought this about although, admittedly, at a slower, more digestible pace. My doubt exists because I'm aware of the industry's track record, but the 1973–74 energy crisis intervened so the argument will never be resolved. We were denied a chance to see whether $1.00-per-gallon gasoline would cause a majority of us to insist on lighter, more economical cars,[3] as it did in Europe and Japan years ago—and whether the industry would respond comprehensively and voluntarily.

Of course there were other pressures too. Mercedes each year puts a bigger but as yet not significant dent in the snob appeal of Cadillacs. And for this reason alone and not to save gas, Cadillac marketed its luxury compact called Seville. Then there is the parking problem, but I don't find lot operators offering a discount to minicar owners. Nor have cities so far seen fit to set aside a preferential freeway lane for small cars, just lanes for mostly large cars carrying three or more people which are used so lightly that traffic would actually be expedited if all lanes were opened to all users. So much for the other pressures; they fail the vanity test. Emerge from a plush restaurant side by side with a Cadillac owner and see whose car is brought up first by the attendant.

Miracle carburetors, fuel homogenizers, and super spark plugs that claim to double your gasoline mileage may exist in advertisements but not in reality. No oil company has ever been foolish enough to buy up and hide away in its vault the formula for a pellet that when dropped in water will form gasoline. No such pellet has ever been invented nor, likely, will it be. There is no magic to propelling a car down the road; it takes energy and the heavier the car the more energy that is required. Thus, the most practical approach at the design level to obtain better fuel economy is to remove weight.

---

[3] Gasoline reached $1.00 per gallon in some sections of the country in 1979 but cars started to shrink in 1977.

One method is to make cars smaller both inside and out. General Motors with its Chevette was the first in the United States to take this step and if nothing but 38-mpg Chevettes were offered by that firm, it would have no difficulty meeting fuel economy regulations now or in the future. However, other problems would arise, the main one being bankruptcy. Chevette, now entering its third year of production, accounts for barely 5 percent of GM's passenger car sales on a unit basis, and still less in terms of dollars. Obviously, the minicar or subcompact is not yet a sustaining item for U.S. manufacturers; in fact, GM until recently lost money on the Chevette. Ford has avoided a heavy commitment to the minicar field by importing the Fiesta rather than building it here as was originally planned. Chrysler, in turn, has achieved modest success with its Omni and Horizon twins but the volume isn't great by industry standards, just relatively so for that company. A majority of Americans persist in buying larger cars despite energy crises, real or concocted. Perhaps they understand the mathematics of fuel economy. If you drive 10,000 miles a year, for example, you can save $167 by switching from a car that gets 15 mpg to one that gets 20 mpg. But if your car already gets 25 mpg, you save only $67 a year by switching to a car that gets 30 mpg.[4]

Another way of removing weight, and the one which inspired GM's estimate of $1 billion for each one-half mpg gained, is to take the typical "family" car, whether intermediate or full-size, and shrink the outside while retaining essentially the same interior dimensions. Further parameters are no loss of safety or performance. Shrinking the outside wasn't difficult, oversized behemoths such as pre-1977 Cadillac De Villes or even Chevy's Impalas being wonderfully suited to such surgery, though actually a computer rather than an axe was used.

To maximize the visible reduction, however, requires the complete redesign of hundreds of hidden parts. Why? Because savings can be doubled if weight is removed in the design stage. In these days of the 55-mph speed limit, not to mention the goal of more economical operation, there is no sense for example in installing the same, heavy, 250-horsepower engine in a model from

---

[4] Based on gasoline at $1.00 per gallon.

which 450 pounds or so of avoirdupois has been stripped. Then, a new, smaller engine can be mated with an equally new, smaller transmission and less beefy driving axle, and so on down to the lowly bolts which attach the springs to that axle. It's this total redesign effort, along with the opportunity thereby afforded to pioneer new, lighter materials and structures, that costs the kind of money GM is talking about. Thus we find the all-new 1979 Olds Toronado is 22 inches shorter, nearly 9 inches slimmer, and approximately 900 pounds lighter than any of its predecessors without sacrificing a single inch of passenger or luggage space. Or, for that matter, a single item of the luxury equipment for which this model is noted. Each of the Big Three U.S. automakers is well embarked on such total redesign programs, line by line, as the 1979 model season opens. Yet, again using the gasoline-engined Toronado as an example, all that was accomplished by the multimillion-dollar effort lavished on it was a three-mile-per-gallon improvement (to 16 mpg) over the average fuel consumption of 1978 Toronados. That's far short of the 27.5 mpg fleet average required by 1985, so Oldsmobile, or rather GM corporately, has some stepping to do if the likes of Toronados are to remain in production.

Then, preferably after weight has been minimized, alternate power plants can be considered. I would like to be able to state that the energy crisis had brought such exciting prospects as the gas turbine, or a revival of steam, or even a practical electric car closer to reality but it hasn't for a variety of reasons complex enough to warrant a separate chapter in this book. And, enveloping engineers in a murky cloud of cross-purpose are the existing and incompatible requirements for cleaner as well as more economical engines. Keep in mind if you're buying a used car that 1975 models, produced a whole year after the Arab oil embargo, burned an average 25 percent more gasoline than their counterparts of 1967, the last year for engines without emission controls and, not too incidentally, the last year of the great horsepower race. Detroit did not face up to the dual problem until 1976 when emission requirements were met despite a slight improvement in economy. Though seemingly illogical, the unfortunate technical facts are that gas misers are inherently dirty and, conversely, clean burning engines consume more fuel. Attempts to improve both characteristics simultaneously produce results frustratingly similar to the antics of the dodo bird, an Australian species that purportedly flies around in increasingly smaller concentric circles until it disappears up its own you know what.

The incompatibility of the Clean Air Act and the Energy Policy and Conservation Act also inhibits the development and use of alternate power plants. The diesel engine offered as an option in the 1979 Toronado mentioned above, as well as in some other recent model cars and light trucks, *could* make it possible for Detroit to continue building family-sized cars in unrestricted quantity past 1985, for the same Toronado that now gets 16 mpg with gasoline power will do 21 mpg with the optional diesel. However, the diesel's superior fuel economy makes it dirty. Oldsmobile is hard-pressed to meet current NO_x standards of 2.0 gpm with it, much less the 1.0 gpm demanded by 1981 and beyond. Consequently, a federal waiver was reluctantly granted to allow 1.5 gpm in 1981 through 1984 for cars powered by "innovative technology." Somehow the diesel was deemed "innovative" even though it was patented by its inventor, Rudolf Diesel, in 1892 and first put to practical use by the American brewer Adolphus Busch as early as 1898.

Despite Oldsmobile's glowing description of their performance, diesel engines at best are no more than an interim solution to the problem of meeting future economy standards with cars of a size to which Americans are accustomed. Fuel in the diesel cycle is ignited by compression rather than by a spark. Compression ignition is explosive, which accounts for the pockety-pock clatter a diesel makes while it's running. And the diesel's innards must be extremely strong to withstand the forces generated by these explosions. Long-distance truckers like diesels for their economy and durability and are willing to put up with the noise and vibration. A well-designed diesel truck engine will run 250,000 miles or more between major overhauls, but it costs $2,000–$3,000 more than a gasoline engine of similar power. Oldsmobile's costs only $900 more and therefore is not claimed to be any more durable than its gasoline-powered counterpart. The owner of a diesel Olds would have to drive about 47,000 miles to recoup his extra investment from the greater mileage and cheaper fuel; at the 100,000-mile point when both types of cars are presumably worn out, the diesel owner will have saved $1,350.[5]

But throughout that 47,000 or 100,000 miles he would have to search out sources of fuel. There are only 13,500 stations that sell diesel oil in the country at this time and most of them are located on major trucking routes which may or may not be near his home or place of work. You certainly won't find them on Park Avenue or in Beverly Hills. Restricted fuel availability, the higher noise level, poorer performance, slower starting, and premium cost of the diesel have heretofore been tolerated only by a small cult of Mercedes and Peugeot owners. Whether ordinary folk who buy Oldsmobiles and Cadillacs at one extreme and Volkswagen Rabbits at the other will wax enthusiastic (and patriotic) remains to be seen. The ultimate diesel for the cultist, of course, is the $25,000 Mercedes 300SD which will perform on a par with any of the five gasoline-powered 8-cylinder Chevy Malibus or Ford Granadas you could have bought instead for about the same money.

It is true that some though not many of DOE's millions have gone to support research on new and different power plants. Unfortunately, though, most of this relative pittance has been poured into that old turkey, the electric car. Back in 1915 a Baker or a Rausch & Lang electric victoria would convey your great aunt Patience about 30 miles at a maximum speed of 30 miles per hour and then it had to be laid up overnight to recharge its batteries. Aunt P. liked her electric's silent, fume-free operation and it did suffice for short, sedate jaunts about the neighborhood. The best of today's electrics can do about 50 miles at 30 mph. So progress in this field is not very electrifying, mainly because nobody but the National Aeronautics and Space Administration has been able to significantly improve upon the familiar lead-acid storage battery.[6] NASA's esoteric space batteries, however, cost about $10,000 each. The only customer attracted to the electric in recent times has been the U. S. Post

---

[5] Based on the diesel's 21 mpg versus the gasoline's 16 mpg, at average fuel costs of $.84 and $1.00 per gallon respectively.

[6] GM's prototype Electrovette, a modified Chevrolet Chevette, requires 20 batteries weighing 920 pounds. They occupy the entire rear of the passenger compartment.

Office, which operates 268 of them, and which may be why it takes two days for a letter to be delivered across town.

I would be less inclined toward harshness in reviewing our government's witless efforts in the area of fuel conservation if even a modicum of attention had been paid to driving habits. True, a national speed limit of 55 mph was decreed in the wake of the 1973–74 energy crisis and it is fairly rigidly enforced, under penalty of individually lax states losing their 90 percent share of federal highway funds. And it is also true that should rationing be imposed, most of us would learn real quickly how to get the most from each drop of gasoline. However, rationing would unseat the administration that attempted it and the 55 mph limit has no effect on 80 percent of our driving, that vast majority part we spend stuck in freeway jams or creeping from one traffic light to another.

The national goal as first enunciated by President Ford and not enlarged by anyone since is to reduce automotive fuel consumption by 25 percent.[7] This goal could be met in its entirety, easily and without significant expenditure of federal funds, if each of us would 1) learn or, if you already know, practice how to drive properly, and 2) maintain our existing cars in peak condition. That 25 percent is considerably less than the difference in fuel consumption of two identical cars, one driven by an abjectly careless driver and the other by a reasonably skilled driver. The expert can do far better, relatively, and proper maintenance would be a bonus or a balance.

Why hasn't some kind of national driver education program been proposed, or even an appropriate textbook on the subject issued by the Government Printing Office? There is no evidence in official utterings that anything of this nature has been suggested, much less studied. The only effort remotely related is a proposed series of regional economy contests to be conducted by the Sports Car Club of America to which the Department of Transportation has lent its tacit approval. I don't, though, think that contests are the most practical approach to the great mass who consider driving a chore.

[7] President Carter wants gasoline consumption kept at 1978 levels through 1985, a much more modest goal even when benefits from the 55 mph speed limit and more small cars in operation are taken into account.

Sure to thwart any effort aimed at transforming Americans into a nation of featherfoot drivers is lack of incentive. Warnings and pleadings issued in an atmosphere of plentiful supplies are less than realistic. Nor, of course, would it be wise to create a temporary, artificial shortage, for we no longer believe what our leaders say, and they know it. And then there is the issue of individual freedom which, as I will detail in the next chapter, reaches the ultimate in absurdity as we face the prospect of paying $200 for passive restraints (air bags) in our new cars because politicians feel it would be unpopular and maybe unconstitutional to pass a national law forcing us all to wear our existing seat belts at all times.[8] Thus it's within the law to zoom away from a stop sign as long as you first obey it, or to idle the engine while a train passes, or to never turn off the air conditioner, or to practice any other of a long list of ingrained bad driving habits that together waste the 25 percent of our fuel supply we all wish to save.

In Los Angeles citizens responded to pleas to conserve water during the 1977–78 drought so conscientiously that the municipally owned water company nearly went broke. Why? People were made aware of the need by effective, honest publicity and there wasn't even much of an outcry when everybody ended up paying more for less water. Gas and electric utilities have met a similar, positive response across the nation to their low key, quite effective campaigns to conserve energy. Why? Because the need was clearly stated and then backed by equally clear information on how each customer could contribute.

Oddly, our bureaucrats and elected representatives in Washington treat us like a race of Geminis. We are considered capable of turning off the lights when we leave our houses, of turning down the thermostat, and waiting until the dishwasher is fully loaded, but they seem not to believe that our other personality behind the wheel of a car is capable of being educated. Or capable of responding to reason properly presented. I wonder at the nation's reaction if a law were passed restricting us to building two-room minihouses because bigger ones required too much

[8] France, Australia, New Zealand, Sweden, Norway, Denmark, the Netherlands, Luxembourg, Switzerland, Spain, Belgium, Czechoslovakia, Israel, Austria, Finland, and two provinces of Canada have mandatory belt laws.

fuel to heat. Or that we must move to communes. Don't be overly complacent. Washington for some time has been buying buses by the thousands, giving them to our cities at a discount of 90 percent off list and then subsidizing their operation. What is a bus but a mobile commune? What happens when an unneeded, government-sponsored bus remains nearly empty? It's an embarrassment, that's what, so ways will be found to fill it.

Those whose goal is to harass private automobiles from city streets on grounds of inefficiency perhaps should remember from whence we came, via the automobile. I'll let a recognized authority state the case:

"The horse," said Thomas Alva Edison in 1910, "is the poorest motor ever made. He consumes ten pounds of fuel for every hour he works, yet his thermal efficiency is only two percent." At the time Edison said this, 88 million acres of American farmland were used exclusively to provide food for horses and mules, and most of this was recycled in short order onto our streets.

Urban mass transportation has its place in certain cities, notably New York, Philadelphia, and Boston. And it has limited application practically everywhere. However, to stuff buses or subways down the throats of people who neither want nor need them, which is the present, publicly stated aim of Secretary Brock Adams and his Department of Transportation, is sanctioning a "motor" only slightly more efficient than the horse. Strings of fifty-two-passenger buses, each occupied by three or four people plus the driver as can be seen clogging the streets of Los Angeles most times of the day or night, use a lot more fuel, dirty a lot more air, and take up a lot more space than an equivalent number of compact cars each occupied only by its driver.

CHAPTER 5

Protect Us for We Know Not

No topic lends itself less to rational and objective exploration than safety, whether the area discussed be automobiles or coal mines. In fact, in one of the more improbable contexts where it is always a consideration, war, exaggerated emphasis on safety has been abandoned. Aggressive action is considered "safer" than defense. In the overall, it is safer to risk the exposure of attacking than to await enemy initiative in the temporary safety of a supposedly impregnable fortified line. In other words, the safest way of conducting a war is to win it.

Military commanders and their civilian superiors coolly and constantly assess risking 130 or whatever lives to gain a specified objective. "Risking" is perhaps the wrong word; there's a certainty born of experience that a calculable number of lives will be lost in any specific military action, on the average, and regardless of the outcome of that isolated action. But once peace is declared, the value of a single human life becomes inestimable.

I did not pick the number, 130, at random. It happens to be the average daily count of traffic fatalities in the United States during 1977. And I can play around with that bare statistic and twist it to fit any thesis I select. If I were Joan Claybrook of the National Highway Traffic Safety Agency, I would point to a 4.7 percent increase over the number of people killed in 1976 to bolster my view that there has been no real progress in making cars safer, or that people are no longer obeying the 55 mph national speed limit. If I were the spokesman for a car manufacturer, I would recompute the statistic in terms of deaths per 100 million miles traveled to show that the fatality rate was 3.25 in 1977, only 0.02 off the all-time low reached in 1976. Also I might note, were I beholden to automotive interests, that the rate back in 1925 was nearly 18 deaths per 100 million miles and thus prove there had been some voluntary progress in automotive safety between then and 1967, the last model year before federal standards applied when the rate was 5.60.[1] Or I could cite some suspect data (because it is a projection of localized statistics) that if only the four out of five people who presently refuse to use seat belts already in their cars would buckle up, then 16,000 lives would be saved annually. And lastly, were I a state highway engineer, proud of my most recent freeway project, I could show that if all arterial roads were rebuilt to freeway standards, the fatality rate on them would fall to 1.3 per 100 million miles because that is the rate on existing freeways.

But the fact is, and will always remain, that there is an element of risk to yourself, and others, whenever you get behind the wheel of your car. If you think about it at all, you feel that the 20 million to one chance of being killed during your planned five-mile round trip to play bridge with friends is the kind of odds you're willing to accept in preference to walking or staying home. I should add, too, that I purposely drew the seemingly irrelevant comparison with war because others do so. Safety authorities are constantly telling us that almost as many people are killed on our highways each year than the total of U.S. battle deaths in World War I or the seven years of our involvement in Vietnam.

We all laughed, perhaps bitterly, when we read about the government's Consumer Product Safety Commission spending $140,000 on a three-year study of the hazards in taking a bath. This study concluded in part: "Slips and falls are by far the most frequent type of bathtub accident and these frequently occur while entering or leaving the tub, or while changing between a

---

[1] Fatalities per 100 million miles (1973) in other industrialized countries ranged from a low of 5.2 in Great Britain to 17.4 in Belgium.

sitting and a standing position." If $140,000 makes us laugh, how about the $2 billion we spend annually to pay for government mandated safety equipment on our new cars, equipment that includes headrests and dent-proof bumpers which no one can prove have saved a single life? Laugh yourself sick because by 1982, those buying full-size cars will pay an additional $200 for the controversial air bag, a device that some experts think may cost as many lives as it saves. And the air bag won't work at all for the four out of five who will probably continue not to use seat belts.

I suspect a majority of people in this nation might be willing to go to war should a foreign power somehow threaten our right to own and drive automobiles. It's not the automobile we cherish but the freedom it represents, the freedom to go any place at any time we choose. I could add, to go in privacy, but public transportation alone could never fulfill the first two conditions. Yet, just this right was threatened in a preliminary, tentative way by a spokesman for our own Carter Administration quite recently. Secretary of Transportation Brock Adams, speaking at a National Press Club luncheon in Washington on February 8, 1978, spelled out DOT's goals and two out of the five dealt with so-called alternate transportation *to be provided at your expense whether you want it or not*. Then there was a third, which is sort of an alternate to the alternate. Specifically, these were:

1). ". . . to provide alternate transportation—whether bus, light rail system, vanpool, jitney or taxi service—to many Americans who now must either depend on private automobiles or who have no cars."
2). " 'Sell' public transit to commuters by demonstrating that it can get them to their jobs quickly and cheaply."
3). "Push for the 'socially responsible' car—one that is safe, economical and non-polluting."

Mr. Adams enlivened his recitation of goals with some comments, such as: "We can start right now to conserve fuel and create some alternates to the automobile, or we can wait for the tidal wave to hit us—and swim like hell." Also: "We all know that the automobile is choking our cities," Adams opined. "When New York City sends up a cloud of exhaust fumes, people cough in Connecticut." Thus, he will "encourage a demonstration of free public transit in a major city as a means of luring drivers from their cars—at least for part of their daily driving."

I don't remember the nation's press returning from the luncheon and writing headlines about our freedom being threatened. The smooth-talking Mr. Adams enlisted the holy cows of safety, conservation, and pollution, and made it all seem innocuous, inevitable, and right. The august Hartford *Courant* didn't even, to my knowledge, protest the slur to the atmosphere over its state, as it well should have. In winter prevailing winds over Connecticut blow out of the northwest, in the summer out of the southwest, only the second direction being from New York City.

A native of the state of Washington might be pardoned for not knowing wind patterns over Connecticut but Mr. Adams is just as loose with the time-honored concept that fuel tax revenues should be reserved for projects of benefit to highway users; specifically, highway construction and maintenance. The sanctity of these funds had been violated before Adams' arrival at DOT but he is accelerating the rape. He has sent to Congress along with his $15.8 billion FY 1979 budget a proposal for legislation to "redirect" highway and public transportation programs. Included is authority to:

* "narrow the difference between the operation of highway and public transportation programs, allowing states and localities to evaluate the relative merits of these alternative forms of transportation;
* "adopt uniform federal matching shares for highway and public transportation—90 percent for all Interstate projects and highway and public transportation projects substituted for Interstate segments and 80 percent for all other highway and public transportation projects;
* "consolidate federal highway and public transportation planning assistance programs;"
* and, "to expand public transportation formula grants to include facilities grants for modernization of rail and bus facilities and routine bus and rail rolling stock replacements . . ."

Again, it all sounds innocuous, particularly the authority, not listed above, "to accelerate completion of the Interstate highway system by concentrating available resources on constructing essential unbuilt segments, and by requiring states to decide by 1982 either to build uncompleted sections or to remove them from the system." What pol at the local level could resist that last one? Let's revitalize Watts with shopping malls and monorails (voters there number 10,000 per square mile and they're mostly black) and forget about completing I-15E between San Bernardino and Sun City (voter density, 1,000, and mostly retired rednecks).

However meritorious this imaginary Watts project might be, it seems unreasonable to ask taxpayers on, say, Long Island, to help fund it because not many are likely to shop in Watts during their lifetimes. On the other hand, why should Watts residents help pay $134.5 million to extend three very real urban transit lines on Long Island, a project recently approved by rail buff Adams? Or for that matter, the $583 million that has been given New York City to maintain public transit since President Carter took office? Or, the $5 billion committed to construct Washington, D.C.'s hundred-mile-long Metrorail? I-15E, at least, would serve anyone from anywhere en route to San Diego. Scattered projects of benefit only to the urban areas in which they are located might be rationalized as trade-offs but we'd run out of money long before each hamlet in the country got its fingers in the pie. Spending public monies for the benefit of the concentrated many is not necessarily fair to the scattered few, who add up to more than the many.

What has all this to do with automotive safety? The answer to that question traces back to 1966 and Ralph Nader, the investigation of his private life by General Motors,[2] and the publication of his book *Unsafe at Any Speed*. A hitherto unknown lawyer, an inept invasion of his privacy, and a technically unsound book enabled an auto-hating politician, Senator Abraham Ribicoff (D-Conn.), to parlay passage of the Highway Safety and Traffic Safety Acts of 1966. The latter Act created a new bureaucracy empowered to order the removal of, or to prohibit the installation of, any component of a car that in its judgment created an unreasonable risk of injury either to occupants or to anyone in

---

[2] Nader sued GM, who settled out of court for $250,000. This sum was crucial in enabling Nader to staff his investigations into automotive safety, the organization that resulted being known as "Nader's Raiders."

the vicinity. This purview was soon broadened to include installation of devices that the National Highway Traffic Safety Agency (NHTSA), as it came to be named, deemed desirable to *prevent* unreasonable risk of injury. In essence, NHTSA was given a mandate to design automobiles although any such intention has been and still is vigorously denied.[3] The Highway Safety Act, in turn, gave bureaucrats the right to withhold the federal 90 percent share of highway funds from states that are lax in enforcing applicable regulations that might be issued by NHTSA.

One result, to which it is difficult to raise moral objection, is that federal highway monies are being siphoned off to state and local traffic enforcement agencies, particularly to expand programs aimed at catching and convicting drunk drivers. The problem here is not intent but method. Alcoholism and drug addiction are diseases, officially recognized as such in 1967 by the American Medical Association, and arresting the driver does not arrest his or her disease. Many authorities recognize this fact but as it's activity that counts at funding renewal time, not progress, the "culprits" are thrown in the drunk tank, fined and released in a repetitive cycle that has only a one-sixteenth chance[4] of ending before the alcoholic or addict causes death to himself and, often, to others. And, of course, the majority incidence of injury accidents related to driver impairment furnishes a strong argument, however inherently specious, for government intervention into the design of motor vehicles. Thus, cars that are "safe" in a 30-mph head-on crash into a barrier have been regulated into being, and 50 mph is being bruited about by NHTSA's Joan Claybrook. Much above that and we'll all be driving tanks! Protect us for we know not.

This brings us to the "socially responsible" car called for by Brock Adams in his speech to the nation's press. One form of socially responsible car that has been around for years is the

[3] A trivial example is a standard prohibiting protruding wheel hubs which effectively eliminated the eminently safe spin-off hub design beloved by sports car enthusiasts. The intent, actually, was to eliminate wheel covers imitative of the spin-off design.

[4] Statistics indicate there are 16 million "practicing" alcoholics among the U.S. population and that only 1 million of these "recover" for prolonged periods.

"Dodge-Em," beloved by sadistic kids and their parents, that can be found operating in a caged-in, speed-limited environment at most any amusement park. They go only fast enough to jar your teeth in a full side collision, head-on contact being against the rules. All Dodge-Ems are alike and reasonably safe. Being electric, there is no gasoline to spill. They weigh the same, no one is any faster or slower than another, and their glass-free structure is surrounded by a massive rubber bumper. Faces grim, drivers hunch tensely over the wheel and as soon as the current is turned on, they aim squarely at each other. There is no "dodging."

A parallel of sorts may be drawn between the Dodge-Em and the kind of car NHTSA wants us all to own someday in the not too distant future. There is also more than a slight similarity between NHTSA's conception of us as real-life drivers on the nation's highways and the way we act in the fantasyland of amusement parks.

Let's analyze NHTSA's thoughts on the latter subject first for they are the most rankling. Risking oversimplification, it could be said that while we are alive and driving, it is assumed we will act with total disregard for the safety of ourselves and others. We are irresponsible, the vehicle we command is a weapon of destruction, we will flaunt traffic laws whenever we think we can get away with it and beyond certain bare minimums, we are considered untrainable. However, once a predictable number of us accomplish the inevitable and get ourselves killed in a crash, the life we lost suddenly becomes of incalculable value.[5]

Thus, the thrust of NHTSA's regulating authority is directed at the car and not its driver or the highway on which he is driving. From 1967 models on, automakers were required to incorporate a constantly accumulating number of safety features as well as to remove or modify a number of items that were decreed unsafe. In essence, the goal was and is to protect occupants from the consequences of their own or others' carelessness. The latest models are "crushable" on the outside and padded inside, the crushability to minimize the impact of what is called the "first

[5] Our collective worth, oddly, is calculable, the sum lost to highway accidents being estimated at $47 billion annually. I've never been able to determine the method used to arrive at that figure.

collision" and the padding to cushion occupants during the potentially more dangerous "second collision," that wherein their bodies want to keep going after the car has stopped. This much is fine and in fact represents a school of engineering thought developed by Volvo and Mercedes in particular somewhat before NHTSA's birth. We find here the basis for NHTSA's definition of a "safe" car; indeed, the concept describes most of what is "new" about the bevy of experimental safety vehicles (ESVs) built under NHTSA auspices with a lavish expenditure of taxpayer dollars.[6] However, the ESVs built so far share two characteristics which combined or separately make them impractical as prototypes for the future. They are far too heavy to be powered by an engine that would meet federal fuel economy standards and they would be impossibly expensive to mass-produce. The fact that they are ugly and might not sell at any price is academic.

General Motors estimated in 1977 that safety and damageability features required by the government added an average of $350 to the cost of each car it produced. The figure, of course, has been inflated and added to each year since, although the cost is countered to some extent by incorporating into newer designs items, such as side impact bars, that were once add-ons. Then, too, the air bag when it becomes mandatory in 1982 will boost the bill for certain popular models by a further $200 in today's currency. My contention is that this total of $550, or at least most of it, could have been much more advantageously spent on features that *prevent accidents from happening*.

Until NHTSA came along, the commonly accepted definition of a "safe" car was one which had superior handling characteristics, a state-of-the-art braking system, a high degree of traction, and a power-to-weight ratio high enough to make use of the resulting agility. Such a car is called safe because it is quite forgiving of occasional driver error. Cars that meet this definition have been and are available within a wide price range but unfortunately they are primarily appreciated by enthusiasts, and en-

[6] Some years ago General Motors, Ford, Volkswagen, and Fiat donated prototype ESVs to the government. But these efforts were considered suspect so, more recently, prototypes are built by obscure, presumably inexperienced research firms to the tune of about $4 million each.

thusiasts, in turn, tend to be better drivers than the average of us who consider it a chore to be behind the wheel. Also, unfortunately, Detroit is not noted for producing cars of this type; most that qualify are imports.

However, it was neither the marshmallow ride of a Buick nor the nimbleness of a Porsche that influenced NHTSA's thinking in any way. The Agency reached out to Detroit for its original staff of engineers and picked up the malcontent and jobless. These people have been supervised by professional bureaucrats and, more recently, Naderites, whose knowledge of the fifteen thousand parts that make up a typical car is minimal. Over all as administrators have been a succession of abolitionists whose interest in automobiles and the industry which builds them is entirely negative. How else could it be? Recognition of industry problems is labeled softness. Any hint of compromise is deemed a sell-out. By whom? The pressures are applied, in order of influence, by Ralph Nader, the Congress, and the incumbent Administration. All claim to act on behalf of the car-owning public and the net result after twelve years is that new cars cost upward of $1,000 more than they would if NHTSA, EPA, and DOE had never been created. That figure is on top of the $30-billion-plus combined annual budget of these organizations which you pay directly or indirectly.

What have we gotten for our money? Cars are already "clean" to the maximum practical degree and that could be a plus if EPA would consider its job in this area finished. Cars are becoming more economical to operate, though it's a question whether regulation by DOE and its predecessors was essential to accomplish this turn-around; those who say it was are debasing the time-proven principle of demand and supply. But addressing ourselves to the last portion of the question, are cars really any safer today than they would be if industry progressed at its own pace? Let's look at the record, and keep in mind as we do so that it was the issue of safety that opened the door for Ralph Nader, who in turn drove the wagon upon which numerous politicians jumped. The latter in their turn created NHTSA, the agency which set the precedent for direct federal involvement in the design, manufacture, and marketing of a major consumer product.[7] The climate was then ripe for EPA and the forerunners of DOE to proceed against their segments of the auto industry's alleged shortcomings.

If industry in 1966 had moved with assurance to defend its own record, and if General Motors had not made the mistake of investigating Ralph Nader's private life, NHTSA very probably would never have existed. True, the industry at that time was in the midst of a horsepower race. Power and speed were thematic in advertising. Car models bore the names of wild animals, violent storms, and famous auto racing events. Youth and sex were climactic at 140 mph despite the handicaps of bucket seats and intervening floor shifts. But object as you might, it sold more cars than pictures of belted dummies impacting their instrumented, plastic foreheads on a padded dashboard in a crash test.

You see, automakers were running crash tests long before our government got into the act. I shall never forget one gory film shown to the press of research being conducted under industry auspices at Wayne State University in Detroit. Apparently in the effort to fabricate crash dummies that would react more realistically, information was needed as to precisely what happened to the human head at the moment of impact. Extensive damage precluded fruitful study after the fact. So, unclaimed cadavers were obtained from the morgue, the heads were severed therefrom and then dropped from the top of an enclosed tower, borrowed from a nearby fire station, that was normally used for drying long lengths of hose. Slow motion movies were made of these heads as they fell to their second doom. The actual splat was captured in Technicolor for the researchers to study and the dummies, presumably, were modified accordingly.

The first government safety czar was William G. Haddon, Jr., a physician with a political bent who had been associated with Ralph Nader. Dr. Haddon was appointed on October 15, 1966, and had until January 31, 1967, to set before Congress a suggested list of standards. He was a working czar, for he had no staff at the beginning, nor was he hampered by knowing anything about the industry and the lead-time required to make de-

[7] An exception to this statement perhaps is aircraft, which, for reasons that can hardly be argued, have been regulated from the beginning.

sign changes. Nevertheless, he produced a list of twenty proposed standards for incorporation in 1968 models and took credit for them as all his own ideas. In actual fact, and quite fortunately due to the lack of lead-time allowed, the list was an amalgamation of standards already set by the General Services Administration,[8] the Society of Automotive Engineers, and various other industry and supplier groups. Fifteen out of the twenty were catalogued as standard or optional equipment in 1967 models already on the road.

That was Detroit's last chance to forestall the take-over, to squash the multibillion-dollar worm. Long before this, the auto manufacturers should have brought their road show to Washington and paraded it before the assembled Congress rather than hide the considerable progress being made behind the locked gates of their proving grounds. Instead, and this is hard to believe in retrospect, the industry didn't even protest the ridiculousness—or fight the precedent—of government ordering future installation of features that were already a part of cars then being sold. The industry totally failed to recognize the danger and, to an extent, so too did I as editor of *Motor Trend* magazine at the time. To quote the February 1967 issue, "automakers were privately relieved"!

I remember, though, composing an editorial shortly thereafter suggesting that Dr. Haddon direct his attention to the driver. Perhaps, I wrote, the time had come when we should institute a licensing system that would recognize expertise, patterned if need be after procedures still used in aviation. There, as is well known, the individual pilot progresses in stages via rigorous testing and accumulating experience from student to the ultimate airline transport rating. Then, to keep that rating, he must undergo periodic proficiency checks. *MT*'s owner and publisher, Bob Petersen, promptly blue-penciled this thought in its entirety and, again in retrospect, I know why. He also published *Guns & Ammo* magazine and was spending an inordinate amount of his time defending the American citizen's right to own firearms without registering them. He was for no regulations at all, any-

---

[8] GSA is a government purchasing agency responsible for the federal vehicle fleet.

where within his publishing domain! But the incident illustrates the lethargic blindness of those who had a very real stake in what was about to happen. *Guns & Ammo* (circ. 90,000) was promoting a somewhat dubious, or at least disputable, cause whereas *Motor Trend*, *Hot Rod*, and *Car Craft* (combined circ. 1,000,000) in the same publishing house were being threatened with a catastrophic loss of advertising revenue heretofore showered on them by a performance-oriented industry and its suppliers. And lose it Petersen did for a few bad years along with many readers who could find nothing of interest in Detroit's safe new products. Unlike the vociferous and highly effective National Rifle Association, car owners didn't and still don't have a spokesman. The American Automobile Association long ago lost its voice by default, that default being conflict of interest in the sale of insurance.

Since the beginning of the automobile, performance has always been the most effective tool in the adman's kit. It appealed to youth, of course; but on a more mature level, performance was synonymous with durability and innovation. The list of contributions to safety by auto manufacturers and suppliers that have been actively involved in racing is much longer than the list from those that have abstained. Hydraulic brakes, safety glass, various ride control devices, and even the rearview mirror all originated within the first group. Contributions to durability, which is an aspect of safety, were even more impressive. The early manufacturers who exposed their stock products under factory banners to the rigors of the Indianapolis 500 race and at the dirt and board tracks scattered around the country staked their reputations, or attempted to gain one, before large and knowledgeable audiences. Back home, the race fan was the man on the block to whom neighbors turned for advice on which car to buy. Even today, auto racing in terms of paid admissions is the second-most popular spectator sport in this country. Horses remain first, thanks to the pari-mutuel windows.

We'd be decades behind in tire technology were it not for auto racing. Firestone and later Goodyear in the United States and Michelin, Pirelli, and Dunlop in Europe unhesitatingly credit the racetrack with being their primary proving grounds, particularly in the days before we could take a 25,000-mile passenger car tire for granted. As with cars, today's racing tires bear little outward resemblance to those which you and I buy, but radial construction, high-strength cord materials, versatile tread patterns, and long-wearing rubber compounds that will also stop you in the rain—all were first tried and proven on the track. So, too, hundreds of thousands of people bought Ford Mavericks and Plymouth Valiants, correctly assuming that the racing experience of the manufacturer would rub off on even the most mundane model offered. Nevertheless, there is periodic sentiment in Congress to ban the sport.

Mention of Firestone brings me to the most flagrant of NHTSA's harassments and I must state going in that, in my opinion, the industry once again dug the pit in which it finds itself. This is NHTSA's legislated right to order mass recalls of cars or components thereof for alleged safety-related defects. And since even a sticky ashtray could be considered safety-related, there is little if any limit to NHTSA's authority.

The Firestone Tire & Rubber Company is currently and literally fighting for its corporate life because of safety-related defects alleged to exist in the company's Firestone 500 Steel Belted Radial tires. More than 1.5 million of these tires have already been voluntarily adjusted (meaning replaced) by the company but a further 15 million are estimated to be still in use. Of these, NHTSA has ordered the recall and replacement of 7.5 million and refund of one half the current retail selling price of another 7.5 million. The company estimates that the program will cost in excess of $200 million. NHTSA claims it has more than 6,000 reports from consumers alleging more than 14,000 individual tire failures, 29 deaths, more than 50 injuries, and hundreds of property damage accidents. Those figures were as of July 9, 1978. The investigation was begun in February of that year because of more than 500 reports from consumers charging blowouts, tread separations and chunking, sidewall blisters and cracks, and out-of-round condition. The difference in these figures is, of course, due to the widespread publicity initiated by NHTSA; initiated, incidentally, before Firestone or the public was officially given any opportunity to present testimony, data, or information relating to the defects. Also, incidentally, the tire in question as well as private brand versions marketed by Montgomery Ward and

Shell passed all tests required by NHTSA before *any* new tire can be marketed. At worst, Firestone's reputation has been damaged irreparably; at best, NHTSA's testing methods cry for review.

About 23 million of these now discontinued tires were manufactured, so failures reported to NHTSA so far represent a minuscule 0.0065 percent of the total. Claims adjusted by Firestone itself, which were not necessarily failures, total a more damaging 7.2 percent. It's a bad scene and Firestone, its stockholders, and its 115,000 employees worldwide have suffered grievous economic harm. The 29 deaths and 50 injuries are impossible for NHTSA to hide and for the press to ignore, even if they were so inclined. Can one weigh these lives and injuries against the welfare of 115,000 employees? No. Then, what might have been the action taken had NHTSA not existed? Who is to say, except that the tire industry had an excellent record for voluntarily honoring legitimate claims. It wasn't altruism; rather, it was stiff competition between 19 U.S. manufacturers and their 200 brand names. And it should be remembered that NHTSA publicized its charges based on consumer allegations and an "analysis" of their reports. The Agency has not claimed to have conducted additional tests, if only to determine why its own initial tests failed to reveal the alleged defects. In other words, Firestone has been judged guilty without trial by NHTSA and the judgment has been accepted by the press.

Firestone's woes are mild compared with those faced by Ford Motor Company in 1978. The year saw 4,018,656 Ford-made vehicles recalled for safety or emission complaints, and an astonishing 14,144,000 additional Ford nameplates are under "probe" by NHTSA and EPA. The word "probe" means that recall procedure has been started by the agency involved which could end in the charge being dropped, or the company voluntarily recalling the affected vehicles, or being ordered to do so after appeals have failed. The largest probe, encompassing about 9,000,000 Ford cars and light trucks dating back to 1970, was prompted by reports of 777 accidents, 259 injuries, and 23 fatalities allegedly caused by automatic transmissions jumping from "Park" into "Reverse" gear. That could be disconcerting if you've left the car momentarily with the engine running to, say, open the garage door.

The most damaging of the Ford recalls, however, involved 1.5 million 1971-76 Ford Pintos and 30,000 Mercury Bobcats of 1975-76 vintage to modify gas tanks that were prone to rupture and catch fire when these models were hit from the rear. It wasn't the $10 per unit cost of the fix that damaged Ford. It was a $128 million judgment won by a young man named Richard Grimshaw who was severely burned when the Pinto in which he was riding was smacked from the rear and caught fire. The punitive damages awarded of $125 million was the largest amount ever granted by a jury. And the sum was not derived from whim, either, as a confidential company memo was introduced into evidence proving that Ford was aware of the hazard even before the Pinto was introduced. Basing figures on projected volume over the Pinto's life-span, the memo estimated that 180 people were likely to be burned to death and another 180 severely injured. This, the author of the memo calculated, would cost society $49.5 million compared to the $137 million it would cost Ford to incorporate the fix immediately. The writer concluded that the modifications would not be "cost effective"! The jury based its award on knowing that Ford had saved $100 million by not installing safer gas tanks until the 1977 model year.

Who, after hearing these widely reported facts, could ever trust Ford Motor Company and its products again? Most everyone, it seems. Pinto sales actually increased in 1978 even though the jury's action was made known on February 9 of that year, and sales of the car continue strong today. Also, the appellate court is not too concerned, for on March 30, 1978, a judge ruled on Ford's appeal that $3.8 million was punitive enough.

Chairman Henry Ford II, however, appears to have found president Lee Iacocca less than cost effective for he was summarily fired immediately after the company's July 12, 1978, board meeting. It is doubtful, though, if the massive recalls facing the company triggered Iacocca's departure. The confidential memo referred to above reflects policies of which Henry II had to be aware. And these policies, obviously, constitute a devastating justification for the existence of NHTSA and Joan Claybrook, who measures her performance as head of the Agency by the number of cars recalled. They do not, on the other hand, support arguments that private automobiles should be harassed out of all resemblance to their present useful form, or be banned from cities, or be denied credit for the fact that the vast majority of cars on the road, of any make, give their three successive owners reasonably trouble-free service for their 125,000-mile average lifetimes.

It must be remembered that the typical car contains about fifteen thousand parts and that the individual failure of at least half of these would be safety-related. There is statistically an absolute certainty that a few of these parts will fail sometime during the car's usage. The manufacturer's policies and attitudes in the past, before NHTSA, were policed by the probability that a lawsuit based on product liability would follow any such failure. Dealers were instructed via a steady flow of service bulletins to look for specific defects whenever cars were brought to them for routine maintenance. The average customer appreciated the concern shown and seldom complained. And there was no publicity. Thus, lawyers specializing in product liability claims had to do their digging for clues and trends.

Before NHTSA, a 0.01 percent failure rate would have gone unnoticed by the general public and that figure is somewhat higher than 777 defective transmissions found so far among the 9 million Ford vehicles. Instead, NHTSA points to the tragedies and, of course, one is too many. Not mentioned or even thought of, as far as I know, is that statistically the probability of improper repairs among the 9 million vehicles recalled will cause as many new defects as were corrected. Even space launches, with millions of dollars spent to reduce even slight probabilities, can't count on perfection. Just what does NHTSA expect?

CHAPTER 6

Not Invented Here

Frank Brisko and Joachim Kolby live two thousand miles apart, have never been formally introduced, but each would undoubtedly know the other by sight. That is because each has spent countless hours in Detroit, waiting in the same lobbies of the same engineering buildings on similarly unsuccessful missions. They are both inventors, that lonely breed of men who devote their lives to an idea that seldom if ever sees any light other than the one over the bench in their basement workshops.

Brisko and Kolby are professionals in the sense that each in his own way has managed to eke out a living from his inventions, Brisko by mail-ordering a simple but effective "Mileage Minder" and Kolby by attracting an occasional investor to his much more elaborate "Curved-Bank" suspension system. Each holds numerous patents. Neither has ever been suckered by those firms which, for a fee, will "evaluate and market your invention." Neither is afraid to sign the auto manufacturers' formidably worded "disclosure" form, demanded from all who approach Detroit with an idea *before* that idea is disclosed. And both Brisko and Kolby are qualified to, and will, speak at length with you about that peculiar Detroit syndrome known as the "NIH Factor." NIH stands for "Not Invented Here."

How many thousands more there are who trudge the same dreary path as Brisko and Kolby is anybody's guess. No record is kept of them in Detroit because they are not wanted. They aren't wanted because somewhere behind the locked doors of the research labs and engineering centers, chances are the same idea already exists. Or, if it doesn't exist, someone is sure to catch hell for its not existing. Tens of thousands of salaried engineers from all disciplines must protect their jobs, and their supervisors, in turn, must justify the size of their staffs. It's a matter of survival, not discrimination.

In another league but with problems akin to those of Brisko and Kolby are the big supplier firms like Rockwell International, Eaton, Dana, and TRW. Companies like these maintain research laboratories of their own and employ people who know exactly which door in which automobile factory to enter with a given idea. Detroit expects ideas from its suppliers and often adopts their ideas, but there is no permanency to the deal, no loyalty offered in return for exclusivity. One can, to be sure, sell Detroit a better mousetrap and perhaps be the sole supplier of this trap for a year. After that, however, if Detroit finds it convenient to manufacture your mousetrap in its factories, it will. Or if your competitor offers to make them for less, he will get the business. What's more, you may be asked to lend your expertise to help set up these alternate sources. You're safe as long as no one wants to, or can, manufacture your mousetrap. Failure to cooperate, insistence on anything substantial in the way of licensing fees, and you'll not be considered when a mousetrap better than yours comes along.

Inside the auto company, an engineer can spend a highly paid lifetime in the continuing development of a single component or system. I could say without fear of refutation that there is not an engineer currently in the employ of General Motors, Ford, Chrysler, or American Motors who has ever had the opportunity to singly design a complete automobile. Automotive history, however, is studded with such individual contributions; examples being Sir Henry Royce with the Rolls, W. O. Bentley, Ferdinand Porsche and his Volkswagen, Ettore Bugatti, DelMar G. Roos and the World War II Jeep and even, at the beginning, Henry Ford. An engineer friend of mine named Victor G. Raviolo who enjoyed a meteoric if short career with Ford and AMC liked to brag that there was no part of a car that at one time or another he had not laid out on his drafting board and that there was no machine tool in the plants that he had not operated. But

Vic Raviolo was an anachronistic genius who never became president of anything other than his own consulting firm. Cars today are designed by committee. And I was at the bar in the Dearborn Inn[1] one night long after dinner should have been served when a frustrated Ford engineer first spoke those words which have since become an industry cliche, that "a camel is a horse designed by committee."

The small team of engineers charged with spark plug selection (spark plug design and manufacture is a separate industry) must report to the ignition committee, which in turn is represented on the engine committee, which forms part of the power train group. After coordination with the chassis and body groups, any decisions involving money must be passed on by the operating committee, which first must obtain approval from the finance committee. You and I, or our mechanics, choose spark plugs from a catalog as did W. O. Bentley and a dozen others whose names are legend in automotive design.

It is therefore little wonder that most cars produced today, whether in Detroit, Wolfsburg, Coventry, Turin, or Nagoya, lack "character," a trait definable for better or worse as the stamp of the car's designer. No committee could have given the pre-World War II Packard its characteristic whine in second gear, Rolls-Royce its obsolete though still current grille shape, or the Model T its cantankerous, pedal-operated transmission. Step blindfolded into any current car and you have no way of telling the make in which you're riding.[2] There's a committee-bred sameness to them all.

Each of the four major U.S. automakers receive about eight thousand unsolicited "suggestions" from the general public each year. These range from a casual idea, such as optionally replacing the cigarette lighter with a lipstick, contained in a letter on another subject, to a full-size working model of a complex inven-

[1] The Dearborn Inn, located conveniently near Ford Motor Company's main office complex and research center, is a favorite listening post for reporters covering the auto industry. One can also photograph new models months ahead of introduction from rooms in the Inn that overlook Ford's test track.

[2] Ford Motor Company once twisted this fact to its advantage by running TV commercials showing people riding blindfolded in the back of a Ford and then in a Rolls-Royce. The actors purportedly "couldn't tell the difference."

tion which is usually accompanied by the inventor in person. But however informal the presentation, all automakers follow a standard procedure, presumedly instituted for the protection of everyone concerned. All incoming mail is screened by personnel who provedly have no technical training. If the correspondence contains even a hint of a suggestion, the sender is promptly informed that his letter has not been read by a qualified official and will not be until the sender signs the enclosed "Request to Consider Submission." This is the disclosure form I mentioned above.

The form is purposely negative in tone. It is intended to discourage and most, as a result, remain unsigned, the would-be inventor fearing he would "give away" his rights with little if any promise of reward. The form and an accompanying booklet point out that only a tiny fraction of the ideas submitted have any merit and, chances are, the idea has already been thought of by the automaker's own development staff. And even if your idea has been patented by you and is accepted for study, the form goes on to say, the automaker will specifically retain the right to prove your patent invalid.

As a point of law this bark is worse than the bite. The disclosure signed by you merely gives legal substance to the fact that the automaker did not solicit your idea and since it is you who went to them of your own free will, you do so on their terms. It does not give the automaker license to steal.

The idea of substituting the lipstick for the lighter was actually received by one company and was given serious consideration. Another considered was a suggestion that the horn blare the name of the car. Both were ultimately rejected as being too gimmicky and, in the latter instance, potentially annoying as well.

Suggestions that have made it over the transom and into production from basement inventors include the mechanical fuel pump as we know it today, power actuation for convertible tops, and a vacuum assist for the manual transmission shift control once featured by Chevrolet. These few hits were scored years ago. More recently, an inventor sold American Motors a seat-belt retraction mechanism that automatically adjusted to the girth of the wearer. The list is not impressive.

Joachim Kolby's "Curved-Bank" suspension system works, but

with only sporadic and limited funds extracted from courageous investors, he has been unable to fully sophisticate the design. His idea, essentially, is to utilize centrifugal force to cause the car to lean into rather than away from a turn, thus transforming the force that causes skidding into one that prevents it. I have driven one of his later prototypes and the system does everything that is claimed for it. Unfortunately, though, it would cost upward of $500 extra to install it on a production car, which leads to the iffy question of how much extra buyers would be willing to pay for superior, safer handling. Detroit, apparently, is unwilling to risk the cost of finding out, so Kolby's invention has been unsalable.

As a private individual and thus lacking intimate contacts within the industry, Kolby faces a further problem not shared by the large original equipment (OE) suppliers. He is not made privy to what Detroit plans to produce two years from now and, you'll remember from previous chapters, two years is the lead time between final design and production. Thus, Kolby's prototypes are two years old at the least when he presents them to potential industry customers. These customers have no interest in anything as ancient as the current model; they're thinking in terms of 1981, not 1979! OE suppliers, on the other hand, maintain Detroit offices whose sole responsibility is to stay abreast of design at the drawing board stage. And the auto industry in turn cooperates with these OE suppliers, but not with the private individual.

Anyone selling Detroit, from within or without, must accept without question the guideline that no matter how meritorious an invention may seem, it must perform its function better than any existing device and do so at the same if not less cost. If the function is a new one, the cost must either be minimal or the device so attractive that the consumer will pay extra for it. Any exceptions today would be in the federal areas—safety, emission control, and fuel economy. Example: a tamper-proof way of relating the concentration of alcohol on a driver's breath to the functioning of the ignition switch. Some keen brains are working on that one, for the idea has every ingredient for success.

The paragraph above could be inserted unaltered into a policy handbook for engineers newly hired by Detroit. It expresses the way engineering committees think. It discourages spending time on concepts that might lead to a dramatic breakthrough in automotive technology, concepts that might be initially costly but which in time could upset the sales charts. In any case, freshly hired engineers aren't put to work designing new concepts; they're assigned to one of the burgeoning staffs which work full-time just to keep up with the latest government regulations. These people outnumber by far those who collectively create new cars.

Only two of the "Big Three" U.S. auto companies have faced engineering decisions of major import in recent times. I speak here of the kind of decision that, if right, might have revolutionized the marketplace; if wrong, it quite possibly could have led to bankruptcy in one instance and serious embarrassment in the other. Both decisions involved fundamental changes in power-plant design and, to put them in perspective, either change would have obsoleted overnight multimillion-dollar investments in existing manufacturing facilities. The first chronologically was Chrysler's decision *not* to mass-produce turbine-powered Plymouths, a move it could have made as early as the 1968 model year.

Back in 1954, Chrysler had startled the automotive world by installing a regenerative gas turbine in an otherwise stock Plymouth passenger car. The regenerative feature was the key to the breakthrough. Earlier turbines as shown by General Motors, Rover,[3] and others were hopelessly uneconomical, as are jet aircraft engines today when they are operated at low altitudes. Most of the heat generated by the power stage is wasted through the exhaust. Regeneration, or recycling the heat back into the combustion process, was known but the absorption units were static and therefore very bulky. One would have filled a trailer larger than the turbine-powered Plymouth towing it. Chrysler's breakthrough was designing an efficient rotating regenerator that in final form was only about two feet in diameter and five inches thick.

The engineer who had dedicated his career at Chrysler to turbine research, George J. Huebner, was understandably enthusiastic. Turbines then and now weren't any more powerful than re-

[3] Now an operating subsidiary of Jaguar, Rover, Triumph, Ltd.

ciprocating engines of a similar size, nor any more or less economical, but they were infinitely smoother in operation, required a far less complicated and therefore cheaper transmission, and, ultimately, routine maintenance could be reduced to a minimum impossible with conventional power plants. Further, the turbine would happily digest cheap and potentially plentiful kerosene or diesel oil and it weighed considerably less than a gasoline engine. On the debit side, some of the materials necessary for the construction of a turbine were scarce and expensive, and there was the problem of obsoleting existing facilities already mentioned. Turbines, for example, require no heavy castings, which meant that there would be no further use for Chrysler's foundries. Also, no existing production line could be adapted to turbine assembly.

Rather than face up to the decision immediately, Chrysler management chose to launch a consumer evaluation program of unprecedented magnitude. Fifty special cars were created in 1963–64, engineered from the tires up to showcase the turbine. Each chassis was built in Detroit, from where it was shipped to Italy for the installation of a handcrafted Ghia body, and then returned to Detroit for distribution to one of 203 "typical consumers" who were selected from among thousands of applicants. These people each used one of the cars as if it were his or her own for a three-month period.[4]

The test lasted from October 1963 to January 1966. A total of 1,111,330 miles was accumulated with an operating time loss due to failure cut to 1 percent by the end of the test. In fact, troubles were almost entirely confined to starting the car, and that was because the procedure was rather dramatic. The volunteer testers became jet pilots for the moment, especially when the inevitable crowds gathered around the cars, and were prone to give repeated demonstrations for which the starting mechanism was not designed. All engines could be and were restored to

[4] Due to U.S. Customs regulations requiring that duty be paid not just on the Italian-built bodies if they were subsequently sold but on each car's share of the multimillion-dollar cost of Chrysler's turbine research program, all but three of the cars have been scrapped. The survivors may be seen at Harrah's Museum in Reno, the Smithsonian, and at the Los Angeles Museum of Science and Industry.

original power between users, or "tuned-up" so to speak, simply by passing a cleaning compound through the intake system. There were no failures of basic engine components.

I had driven turbines on a few occasions, but always with an escort on Chrysler's proving grounds. Then, toward the end of the consumer testing program, I was loaned one of the Ghia-bodied cars with 34,000 miles on the odometer to do with as I wished during a four-day holiday. Operation was simple and fascinating, a fact which I've said accounted for the high incidence of start-up failure. The two-speed automatic transmission was put in the "Park/Start" position and the ignition switched on. Within a few seconds the turbine whirred itself very audibly up to operating speed and ignited with a loud woosh. The inlet temperature gauge read 1,200 degrees F. and the tachometer, 22,000 rpm at "idle." The fun part was to shut off the ignition in a crowded supermarket lot, leave the car, and watch people gather suspiciously around it to hear the turbine whine lazily to a standstill. Neighbors as well as strangers demanded repeated demonstrations!

At first it was ballyhooed that the turbine would run happily on liquid fuels ranging from Nyquil to leaded gasoline. I was warned, however, to stick with kerosene or, in an emergency, diesel fuel. But kerosene is not easy to come by in twenty-gallon lots; I had to take deliveries of my unusual order by appointment with a wholesaler. At cruising speed, with the tachometer reading about 37,000 rpm, the turbine's whine was audible inside the car but not so as to interfere with conversation. Despite its 4,100-pound weight and modest 130 shaft horsepower, the car could reach 60 mph from a standstill in 12 seconds, a performance comparable to the Pontiac GTO or Mustang of those days. And contrary to popular belief, the turbine exercised a braking effect exactly the equivalent of a similarly sized piston engine. Accelerator position controlled a variable nozzle arrangement on the power turbine, giving retardation as demanded. Another notion held by many, that the turbine's exhaust would melt the nylons from the legs of a pedestrian, was of course dispelled by the rotating heat exchanger. You could hold your hand in the exhaust stream at the tailpipe without much discomfort. My overall impression was then, and still is thirteen years later, that the

Chrysler turbine was totally superior to any engine with pistons.

Today, George Huebner has retired from Chrysler disillusioned but not bitter. His proposal to management was to stake everything on the big plunge. Put the turbine in as standard equipment for the volume Plymouth and either become No. 1 U.S. automaker, or sink! Huebner was a siren of a salesman and a skilled manipulator of men, but the closest his management ever came to the big decision was to toy for a while with the idea of offering the turbine as optional equipment for the high-priced, low-volume Imperial. Who knows what would have happened if Chrysler had somehow burst forth from its committee-bred caution and acted. It's too late now. Lagging turbine development programs have not kept pace with federal emission control regulations.

Huebner and his turbine is a classic example of innovation starving from within. It starves from without, too, as witness the case of seventy-five-year-old Dr. Felix Wankel and the rotary engine named after him. Dr. Wankel himself, however, has not exactly starved. General Motors, that fountainhead of NIHism, paid NSU-Wankel A.G. $15 million more than a decade ago for a license to build rotary power plants but has yet to produce the first one for sale. And about thirteen other major corporations throughout the free world have spent additional millions for licenses, but of these only NSU[5] and Japan's Toyo Kogyo Company, Ltd., have actually sold cars powered by the invention.

No power plant in recent times has attracted more vociferous detractors and General Motors was a leader among these until it finally came around begging for a license. A man of normal patience would have told GM to go fill a one-pound paper sack with two pounds of pistons, but for reasons that may possibly be traced to avarice, the good Dr. Wankel forgave his tormentors. Until that point, Detroit as one voice had condemned the Wankel as inefficient, filthy, and incapable of passenger car application.

The pioneering five-year production run of four thousand rotary-engined NSU Prinz Spiders that started in May 1964 perhaps justified Detroit's attitude (and that in England as well),

[5] NSU Motorenwerke, Neckarsulm, West Germany.

but engineers then and now forget that these were all sold to selected customers who were clearly warned of and who accepted the experimental nature of the engine in their cars. It was, in a sense, a cost-free four-thousand-man volunteer testing team. However, NSU never really solved early teething problems with the Wankel, particularly the matter of premature wear from chattering apex seals. The solution to that was found by Toyo Kogyo (Mazda cars), which obtained its license on October 12, 1960, four years before NSU began producing its pilot run of Prinzes.

All Wankel licenses called for uninhibited interchange of technical developments and it was Toyo Kogyo, under the direction of a brilliant engineer named Kenechi Yamamoto, that was destined to solve the seal problem. Unlike most Wankel-NSU licensees (now a Volkswagen holding), Toyo Kogyo from the onset worked toward a goal of mass production at the earliest possible date.

The chatter problem proved to be a combination of apex seal design, induction system design, and seal material in that order of solution. Basically what was happening was that vibrations during the movement of the three-lobed rotor within the troichoidal combustion chamber housings caused the chrome plating on the inner surface to deteriorate. A detailed technical discussion of this isn't necessary; let's just say here that the metallic-carbon seal material that finally worked was the *last one* on the laboratory shelves at Hiroshima that remained to be tested. If it hadn't been tried on that day late in 1964, Toyo Kogyo very probably would have abandoned its rotary engine development program.

Toyo Kogyo has not enjoyed unmixed success with its rotary engined Mazda cars. U.S. distribution starting in 1970 was amateurish at first but, despite this, they sold well and GM emerged from its negativism to buy a license. As I mentioned in a previous chapter, the late Edward N. Cole[6] put the full weight of his GM presidency behind the project and actually advanced it to the point of ordering tooling to build the engines, a $50 million investment at the least. The question of obsoleting existing facili-

---

[6] Ed Cole died in 1977, victim of a crash in the twin-engined plane he was piloting.

ties on a grand scale had yet to be faced because the rotary was slated for use in just one of Chevrolet's many models, a sure sign once again of committees in action.

Meanwhile, superficial evidence mounted that could, if believed, make one think that Ed Cole's enthusiasm for the rotary was ill-founded. NSU had graduated from its experimental Prinzes to serious production of a rotary-engined, luxury sedan called the Ro80. This car was widely acclaimed, named "Car of the Year," and sold well in Europe, but NSU either could not or would not clean it up to meet U.S. emission standards. Much publicized arrangements to import the car died in a maze of litigation that embarrassed rotary proponents here. Actually, the decision to stay out of the U.S. market was due more to the fact that NSU was no longer its own master; a merger with Audi and then Volkswagen was being consummated at that time and the Ro80 conflicted with other offerings planned by the new combine. Then late in 1973 the Environmental Protection Agency published the first of its controversial fuel economy ratings of forthcoming new cars and the Mazda rotary was clobbered. It received a rating in the area of 10 mpg, about on a par with Rolls-Royce and Lincoln and 15 mpg under the average of competitive "economy" imports with conventional piston engines. Mazda sales in the United States, which were 90 percent dependent on its rotary models, plummeted from 119,003 in 1973 to 70,415 in 1974. Mazda promptly protested and finally forced EPA to admit a gross error in its testing procedures. However, the damage was done. Negative publicity is eagerly circulated by competitors, corrections are not, so few car buyers were made aware that the actual economy of the rotary engine as installed in the Mazda RX-3 then current was an acceptable 19 mpg on the city cycle, 28 mpg on the highway, for a 23 mpg combined average.

General Motors, of course, knew the true facts. It also knew that as all the moving parts in a Wankel-type engine rotate rather than reciprocate, that freedom from vibration is uncanny except, perhaps, at idle when there is some imbalance of inertial forces. Anyone who can count will tell you that there are only 20 percent as many moving parts in the rotary to wear out and since engine oil doesn't enter the combustion chambers (except for small amounts metered from the carburetor for seal lubrication and then burned), there is really no need for routine changes. GM knew that rotary engine performance made cars powered by similarly sized piston engines seem like slugs. And most importantly from an economic standpoint, GM knew that increasing the size and power of a rotary engine is accomplished simply by bolting together any number of identical cylinder chambers around a common crankshaft. Thus GM, or anyone else, could produce a low-powered rotary for the Chevette and a high-powered one for the Cadillac, plus versions in-between, all on the same production line and with the same machine tools. The potential savings would more than offset the forced obsoletion of existing tooling used for the manufacture of conventional engines.

Why, then, when GM held the wake for its rotary engine project, did it tell the press that abandonment was forced by being "unable to attain emission standards without incurring too great a penalty in fuel economy"? The technical types making the announcement also stressed that GM engineers couldn't match their rotary engine to a catalytic converter without shortening converter life to an unacceptable degree. Little (relatively) Toyo Kogyo in far-off Japan, a country whose emission standards are stiffer than our own, doesn't even install a catalytic converter on the popular, back-ordered RX-7 sold in the United States today. It meets emission standards with a cheaper, more durable thermo-reactor and economy is actually better than the figures given above for the older, lighter RX-3. And this is despite the fact that the RX-7 is unabashedly a sports car, designed to perform in a league with its principal competitors, the Porsche 924 and the Datsun 280Z.

Answers to embarrassing questions aren't issued by committees, either. GM's technical staff is a hundred times the size of Toyo Kogyo's and somewhere from within it could have some positive solutions to any rotary-engine problem if, indeed, *positive solutions were encouraged by management.* Also, remember that a Wankel license called for uninhibited exchange of technical information on the rotary. Each company in the group, presumably, was continually informed as to the state of the art among the others. GM's announcement that it had elected not to produce the Wankel was made late in Ed Cole's presidency, a few months before his retirement. I can't put words in a dead man's mouth but my guess is that he'd given up the fight. The Wankel was NIH, not invented here!

NIH is a problem created by the system. There is another of equal magnitude, though, imposed from outside the factory gates. It is serious enough that if Henry Ford, W. O. Bentley, or Sir Henry Royce were alive today, designing the cars that bore their names and personally supervising every detail of their construction, they surely would take a second, more cautious look at such direct involvement. The new era of product liability law, the doctrine of strict liability, could well have driven them to take shelter in the anonymity of decision by committee.

It is variously estimated that between 60,000 and 1,000,000 product liability, or tort, suits are filed each year,[7] with those involving automobiles in the majority. Strict liability in its strictest sense means that even a drunk may collect if he's injured in an accident *he caused* when all or part of the car's structure failed to protect him. One recent case involved a Corvette with two occupants who admittedly had been drinking. The car rolled over and the roof collapsed, mangling one man's hand. He sued Chevrolet and an engineer involved in Corvette design testified in court that roll-over tests had not been conducted with that model Corvette. He further testified that such tests would have delayed production so the decision was made to go ahead without them. The plaintiff won the case.

Each recall initiated by the National Highway Traffic Safety Administration (NHTSA) also triggers a rash of related lawsuits. Imagine yourself confined to a wheelchair or in traction after failing to negotiate an unexpected and sharp turn on an unfamiliar road. You're understandably vague as to just what happened to cause the accident but then you read that your model car is being recalled for a possible steering defect. You forget the gnawing knowledge that you'd had a few drinks just before the accident. You sue and there's a chance you'll win, even though

[7] There is no central source of information on this subject. The American Trial Lawyers Association believes even the lower estimate to be high, but then its members are motivated through fear of legislation to hide any dramatic increase.

the defect actually exists in only a small percentage of the cars being recalled. No wonder engineers sleep poorly these days. No wonder trial lawyers are prospering.

If the number of product liability suits continues to multiply, as it certainly will because now instead of suing the other driver in an accident, both parties, or their attorneys, think in terms of suing the manufacturers of the cars involved, few automotive engineers of any stature will escape being dragged into court as expert witnesses. There, of course, they are bound by oath to tell the truth and the truth more often than not is damaging to their employer. With increasing frequency these engineers face the unenviable choice of committing perjury or risking the loss of their jobs. Thus, through fear, even the chairmen of engineering committees will tend more and more to avoid influencing design decisions, to avoid being identified in any way as the instigator of any engineering development that could possibly, from failure of the hardware, be blamed for an accident.

This kind of fear has taken its place alongside government regulations in stifling any innovation in the area of driver control. Driving could be made easier but to make it so would require new responses on the part of the driver to various traffic situations. For example, sometime prior to the formation of NHTSA, I remember Mercury Division experimenting with a pedestal or column control system that eliminated, with the help of an automatic transmission, the need for foot pedals. You pushed forward on the column to accelerate, pulled back on it to brake, and you steered with one or both hands by twisting little knobs on either side of the column. I drove this car for a few days and once I got used to the new motions and reactions demanded, it was indeed simpler to control. But I remember wondering how these new reactions would fare in a sudden emergency. Would I find my right foot pushing instinctively and uselessly against the floorboard where the brake pedal always had been? That, of course, was why Mercury never seriously pursued the innovation. A driver involved in an accident with this or any other new system of control would only have to plead involuntary return to long-conditioned reflexes and the manufacturer would be liable. In the auto industry's adolescence, controls were as varied as the number of makes offered; you learned how to drive your new car through trial and sometimes error. Today there's safety in sameness, for the manufacturer anyway.

Auto industry spokesmen in public bravely accept the new era of government and civil harassment as a "challenge," but internally there's chaos. In the real life world of the drawing board, the engineer must produce cost-effective designs for individual components. That inevitably entails compromise with quality and, quite possibly, safety. Then the package or car, essentially standardized by government regulations, must somehow be made exciting enough to sell. Customers must thirst for the new long before the old wears out or sales will dwindle and the engineers will have no jobs.

Engineers have consciences, too. Imagine the torment of the employee, in the case of *Grimshaw* v. *Ford Motor Company*, who was forced to confirm under oath the existence of that internal memorandum showing his company to have been aware of the fire hazard of Pinto fuel tanks as they were first designed and installed and then, for reasons of cost effectiveness, not incorporating a $10 corrective modification until seven years and nearly two million Pintos later. He told the truth, yes, at the price of his career. However, if he had told Henry Ford II the truth at the time the memo was written, that the design would cost lives and that he, the engineer, wanted no part of it, then his career would have been seven years shorter. I should not like to be faced with a quandary like that.

There is, certainly, room for error even when the designer and his employer put quality and, with it, safety above all other considerations. Automakers must abandon the cost-effectiveness concept forthwith if there's to be any hope of nationwide legislation written to curb the ambulance chasers. An expert witness testifying that as a designer he did his best and failed and his employer testifying that money was no object might be enough to reverse the trend in jury decisions. A penalty might be extracted, perhaps, but not a punitive one.

CHAPTER 7

Behind the Styling Curtain

It has been only recently that a few stylists working for U.S. auto manufacturers have dared to grow beards, and fewer still can be seen in their studios dressed in jeans. This restriction of artistic license extends to more controversial traits as well. While there are undoubtedly some stylists who are gay, these have not come forth to demonstrate against Anita Bryant. Whatever their sexual preferences, though, they are not as a group inclined to grant women much voice in the studios beyond, maybe, selection of upholstery fabrics. Most are men whom you'd swear you've seen before but you can't remember just when or where. That last is the ultimate compliment. Reason: stylists must sell the cigar-chomping president, and sell him so subtly that the president really thinks it was he who designed the car. Every stylist I know who has acquired character or fame, or both, has evaporated from the Detroit scene.

The late Harley Earl was the first stylist. He and his father in the 1920s were building custom automobile bodies for movie stars in Hollywood, and a man named Don Lee had the lucrative Cadillac distributorship for every city and hamlet west of the Rockies. The Earls and Lee naturally knew each other, so when Cadillac decided to offer a medium-priced car, the LaSalle, Lee immediately used his considerable influence with General Motors to forestall the possibility of the new car becoming another box in the image of the four-square, Al Capone school of design one still sees in re-reruns of TV's "Untouchables." Lee sold a sophisticated and demanding market and, indeed, he was embarrassed to even show the "Standard of the World" cloaked in its factory-supplied Fisher coachwork.

At Lee's urgent recommendation, the younger Earl moved to Detroit in 1925 and took over complete design responsibility for the LaSalle. It was to be the first time that a production car was professionally styled, all the way from radiator to taillight. Theretofore, production cars took their shape under the direction of body engineers and the lines fell where they may, with perhaps an assist from on top when the president would superimpose his favorite fender curvature or windshield outline. Although it wasn't the primary purpose, Earl was mostly able to circumvent this during his long career as head of GM styling (the "pregnant" Buick of 1929 being a notable exception) by using his invention of the full-size wood and later clay model as a sales tool with management. Even from the beginning these models were used by diemakers as an accurate representation of finished die shapes. They also served as "bucks" to ensure that draftsmen hadn't miscalculated the space required by components, much less passengers. The basic principles evolved by Earl for the creation of that first LaSalle, in what was then called GM's "Art and Colour" section, are still employed today by automakers the world over.

Earl responded like most stylists to an infinite variety of seemingly unrelated stimuli. His controversial creation of finned rear fenders, first seen on the 1948 Cadillac, stemmed from a wartime admiration for Lockheed's twin-boomed P-38 fighter aircraft. The first Chevrolet Corvette in 1953, a highly unusual venture for that then most staid of GM divisions, resulted from visits to his son at college where he noted the popularity of imported M.G. sportscars. Characteristically, though, Earl was unable to resist incorporating every conceivable item of luxury equipment which pushed up the cost to where that first Corvette and all those which have followed became toys for fathers, not sons. But Earl eschewed automotive nostalgia for his bread-and-butter creations, even though, with one exception, he was the only modern-day stylist in a position of authority who had lived and worked in the so-called "Golden Age" of classic motorcars.

The one exception was Earl's handpicked, carefully schooled successor, William L. Mitchell, who took over as vice-president of GM's Design Staff in 1958 and from that lofty office created the shape of not only GM's offerings but, to a considerable extent, everything else to emanate from Detroit for the next twenty turbulent years. Whereas you may not fully subscribe to former Secretary of Defense "Engine Charley" Wilson's thought that "what's good for General Motors is good for the country,"[1] it certainly is a truism that as GM styling goes, so goes Detroit. Committees may breed sameness but it is the GM committees that lead and the committees at Ford, Chrysler, and American Motors that follow. Competitive stylists who occasionally deviate court disaster, as witness AMC's unpopular, bubble-shaped Pacer. That one's known, in trade jargon, as being "out in left field."

The recently retired Mitchell was the last of a rare breed, a stylist with the clout to set trends and a man big enough to give credit to individuals under him who actually did the work. True, he had to cohabit with committees, but he dominated those with which he was involved and intimidated those which dared to snipe at him from afar. His legacy, however, is a mixed bag. Successive Corvette designs, and he was influential in them all down to the present offering, are widely considered to be works of art. Mitchell's personal favorite, however, is the 1963 Buick Riviera. This was the first GM entrant in a category that came to be known as "personal luxury" cars and although the original Riviera is more highly regarded than any that followed, collectors are not exactly fighting over used specimens today. And, too, whether he styled them personally or not, Mitchell must bear responsibility for the hideously finned 1959–61 Cadillacs, cars universally conceded to represent the nadir of American design efforts. He atoned for this later with the crisply conceived Eldorados and even tauter Sevilles.

Oddly, chief stylists seem to fall victim less to designs that bomb than to internal politics. The reason is a ceremony known

[1] A faux pas to the press by Charles Erwin Wilson, GM president January 6, 1941–January 26, 1953, when he was on "loan" to the government during the Korean War.

as the "executive showing." That is the day between twenty-four and seventeen months prior to initial production when the studio presents its several alternate proposals to management. The cars from a distance, and that is the way they are viewed to measure "road appeal," look real enough to be driven off the stage, but actually they are laboriously hand-fashioned from a special modeling clay and the only items real about them are the wheels and tires. Grilles and bumpers are carved from wood and finished with a chromium paint. Trim of a less permanent nature may be simulated by strips of aluminum foil. The glass areas are also simulated, for there is nothing inside the car but the wood form, or buck, which holds the clay in position. Then to minimize the number of these $200,000 models[2] needed, one side may represent a four-door sedan and the other its two-door sister in the line; or, if a single body style is involved, alternate treatments of the sides may be shown on a single model.

The choices offered management at this key session in the gestation of a car are similar in concept and generally identical in dimensions because the "package" has already been formulated by the product planners and approved by management. It is also already known which if any structural components will be borrowed from existing lines. Engineering has selected engines, transmissions, and other major components from the corporate catalogue. Marketing has projected sales volume and, from that, accountants have figured to a hair how long it will be before the break-even point is reached in the model run. And, too, manufacturing men know in which plants the new car will be built and how much and what kind of new tooling will be needed. This is why such projects are called packages; they are irrevocably outlined before the stylists get into the act. They really have very little to do except to clothe the new baby. And very seldom do packages start with their clothes, Harley Earl's Corvette mentioned earlier being a notable exception. Stylists rarely enjoy opportunities to innovate and thus they usually stay out of trouble. Or put another way, Joan Claybrook of the National Highway Traffic Safety Agency hasn't yet recalled cars because of their looks.

[2] It's not the 6,000 pounds or so of clay at 64 cents per pound but the hundreds of highly skilled man-hours required that runs up the price.

Styling, however, remains a major though lessening factor in the customer's decision to buy a new car as well as, of course, in his choice. Management attaches importance to the executive showings and for better or worse approves the final design because U.S. auto manufacturers are still wedded to the annual model change. Or more accurately, the American car buyer still is, and unfairly so, for he limits this expectation to Detroit products. The same buyer visiting a Mercedes-Benz showroom will ooh and aah over a shape that has been around unchanged for years. Try as it might, Detroit seems unable to break this syndrome of its own creation.[3]

The latest offerings are always billed as "all-new" in advertising and sales literature but internally they are more honestly categorized as carry-overs, face-lifts or, in fact, all-new. Even the latter category almost always includes a significant carry-over content but it is hidden to all but trained eyes. Then superimposed is the interchangeability of parts and structures, again mostly hidden, between different nameplates from the same corporation. The stylist in addition to his esthetic talents, therefore, must have a clearer than average understanding of the complex economics and even more complex manufacturing techniques involved in the mass production of automobiles.

A typical body shell is composed of an inner and outer structure which may be put together from as many as forty separate pieces of sheet metal, or stampings. And bear in mind that the pieces you can't see, such as the cowl structure and floor pan, are far more difficult to shape than the usual visible piece such as a roof or hood. Each stamping, in turn, must be formed by its own, unique die set, called a set because a stamping of any complexity must be formed in stages and at each stage a separate pair of male and female dies is required. A die set in today's money can cost as much as $1 million and most often for a high-volume item several sets may be required at each of several widely separated stamping plants. You can see that in terms of stampings alone the annual model change and, most particularly, the all-new car

---

[3] The concept of the annual model change to stimulate sales was inflicted on Detroit by Alfred P. Sloan, Jr., architect of modern-day General Motors. He was president from May 10, 1923, to May 3, 1937, and chairman from then until his retirement on April 2, 1956.

can be an expensive habit. Carry-over parts, and their interchangeability, obviously are the cost-saving keys to perpetuating this habit. An all-new car is a $300–400 million investment for its manufacturer before the first one comes off the line. The theory, though, is that volume sufficient to pay back this cost is generated by the newness. But major change is possible, even for General Motors, only once every three years or so for a given car line. American Motors, at the other extreme of resources, must make do with an eight- or nine-year cycle.

When I use the term "car line" in the context of the annual model change, I'm speaking of size categories such as compact, intermediate, and standard or full-size, not nameplates. Internally these sizes are given letter designations that are meaningless to an outsider. For example, within General Motors, "C"-bodies are standard-size shells shared by the Buick 225, Olds 98, and Cadillac De Ville. "B"-series are slightly shorter overall but still standard-size bodies used by Chevrolet, Pontiac, the Buick Le Sabre, and Olds 88. The "C" is a stretched version of the basic "B" but both have approximately the same interior dimensions. So, when GM initiated its weight-cutting program with 1977 models in response to government fuel economy regulations, all of the above-mentioned cars appeared as all-new that year. GM intermediates, with their own shared "A"-series bodies, were completely done over for the following year.

The timing of these major changes in not entirely a matter of market demand. Nor is it dictated by any limitation on GM's vast bank account. A major governing factor is the resources available within the tool and die industry, both captive and independent. That industry could not have coped if GM had decided to change both its full-size and intermediate lines the same year. The needs of other automakers must be met as well, which is one reason why GM and Ford don't usually introduce major changes in competing lines at the same time. What may seem like collusion is actually dictated by reality. In any case, each gets its turn at being first with the newest.

The stylist is constantly involved in not only all-new concepts and major changes to existing concepts, but in the routine face-lifts that make the cars appear like they're new for the intervening years. A minor face-lift may involve just a new grille pattern and taillight arrangement. A major face-lift could include most of the exterior sheet metal. A visible clue to the extent of any change may be found in the windshield because that rests in the cowl structure, which cannot be significantly altered without redesigning the entire car. One can also tell which bodies are interchangeable by determining whether or not they share a common windshield.[4] The stylist strives for face-lifts with maximum visual impact, inside and out, at the least possible cost for new tooling, but nevertheless the average one for a high-volume line such as the standard-size Chevrolet or Ford is a $40–50 million proposition. And since these changes are for identification, they are seldom shared by sister divisions. It is this continuing outlay and not the all-new car that is considered wasteful by critics of the annual model change.

There are arguments to support either side of the controversy. Chevrolet never beat Ford in sales until GM's Harley Earl began laying on annual styling changes with skilled hands. Stingy, cantankerous Henry Ford, Sr., was soon forced to follow suit. In post-World War II Europe the annual model change was unnecessary because for many years people there stood in line for every car built. The practice was well accepted by the time a buyer's market returned. In fact, Volkswagen early in 1973 produced Beetle No. 15,007,034 and with it broke the production record for a single basic design held by Ford's Model T. That required just over twenty-seven years to Henry's nearly nineteen but the elves of Wolfsburg continue to milk the Beetle in almost every country of the free world, including a trickle of convertibles still being sold in the United States. It is Daimler-Benz,[5] however, whose policies are lauded by those who think Detroit's annual model change to be extravagant. Mercedes styling, indeed, is changed only in conjunction with significant engineering advances, and even then a strong family resemblance

[4] A local (Southern California) auto glass shop quoted me $148.04 to install a new tinted windshield in either a '78 Chevy Impala four-door or a '77 Cadillac Coupe de Ville, indicating commonality between makes, model years, and body styles. A nearby Chevy dealer quoted $235.00 *plus* installation for the same windshield, a Cadillac dealer $282.00 *plus* installation! All these windshields must meet the same federal standards of optical quality and strength.

[5] Daimler-Benz is the company, Mercedes-Benz the product.

is deliberately retained. But is the Mercedes any less expensive as a result? The bottom-line 280E (or 240 Diesel) is priced in a league with the Cadillac Seville and is much less car; the top-line Model 6.9 can only be afforded by Popes and sheiks. Meanwhile the controversy rages on, with patently suspect arguments used by both sides.

Detroit may be forced to follow the Mercedes precedent by default, whether it fully agrees in principle or not. GM president Elliott M. Estes recently suggested that it might be cheaper for the nation to immediately invest in the development of facilities to mass-produce alternate fuels, such as gasoline derived from shale oil or coal, than to continue with the drastic downsizing of cars to meet the 1985 economy mandate of 27.5 miles per gallon. That program, it will be remembered, costs GM alone $1 billion for each one-half mpg gained. Estes' theory is that the crossover point occurs when it costs more to save a gallon of gasoline than to produce an additional one. He may be warning us that Detroit could run out of money in the attempt to please both the government and the car buyer.

In any case, stylists are busy these days minding not only their own business but that of others, just as they have always been. I first encountered this strange preoccupation with what others were doing in the course of an interview with George Walker, who was Ford's chief stylist back in the mid-1950s. After he'd finished demonstrating for me all the push-button devices in his garish office, he pulled a packet of photographs from his desk drawer. He'd been sipping regularly from a jug he claimed to contain a health drink so I didn't know what to expect. Nude models? No, they were pictures of nude prototype cars being readied for production by his competitors. He was as delighted as a little kid with a collection of bubble gum cards. We trade these at the Detroit Athletic Club, he informed me in confidential tones. At that moment his press agent walked in and he whipped the photos back into the drawer like the same little kid caught looking at a copy of *Playboy* by his mother.

At a lower level there is a formal activity at each automaker charged with collecting what is called "competitive data." It usually reports to product planning but stylists are among the principal beneficiaries. Industrial espionage is a harsh fact of life faced by commercial enterprises ranging from toy makers to ethical drug houses. Agents are planted, premises are trespassed upon in surreptitious searches for plans, and normally loyal employees are fed wine and sometimes even women by the opposition in the hope that they will be momentarily indiscreet.

Tire companies keep the formulae for their latest rubber compounds locked in bank-like vaults with only a few management-level personnel knowing the combination. Lubricant makers actually add expensive ingredients that make detection of the real "miracle" additive through chemical analysis difficult if not impossible. This is especially common when patent protection, for some reason or another, cannot be obtained. In its simplest form, deception even reaches into the field of candy making where the taste secret may be a natural honey (a mixture of dextrose and levulose flavored by the predominant plant native to the source bees' habitat) but its presence is obscured by adding cane sugar (pure dextrose) so that competition will proceed no further in its analysis. Efforts of this type are prompted by the need to stay abreast of competition or, conversely, if ahead, to protect the secret of that leadership. In the auto industry, however, a secret is a secret only for so long as it is kept hidden from prying eyes.

Unlike their counterparts in some other industries, auto "spies" observe a measure of protocol. They seldom trespass. Management almost never hires a stylist or an engineer from another automaker for the primary purpose of obtaining information on that competitor's advanced plans. George Walker showing me pictures of GM's and Chrysler's year-ahead cars was no more than an urge to show off, as basic in every sense as the compulsion of the average man to pull out a picture of his fiancee or new baby. There was little Walker could do at that point in time, whatever competition was doing, to change his own year-ahead cars.

A stylist who has had previous industry experience will invariably and unwittingly disclose some of his former company's thinking in the design portfolio he must show to obtain his new employment. It will also inevitably influence his initial work for his new employer. However, there will be no interrogation as such. It is quite sufficient to include the new man in routine skull sessions held by the styling staff to determine which advanced designs should be presented for management approval. If any of them infringe on a motif known by the new man to be under serious consideration by his former employer, then he is under a moral obligation to voice a warning and he does. Though his action in a sense is a disclosure, the purpose—to prevent inadvertent imitation—allows the warning to be issued with a clear conscience. So, too, would be a warning that the motif departs radically from trends elsewhere. The new stylist is under no duress. Actually an unwritten agreement between auto companies[6] inhibits talent raiding. A stylist (or an engineer) wishing to switch almost always must act on his own initiative.

All four of the domestic auto companies operate elaborate proving grounds, the Big Three in both the Midwest and the Arizona desert. Also, certain public areas are frequently used for testing purposes, such as Florida's Everglades, the neighborhood of Bemidji in northern Minnesota, and the road up Pike's Peak. No protocol prevents spies from photographing test prototypes belonging to their competitors on public roads, and these prototypes are always heavily disguised to guard against that possibility. Thus, actual styling detail is rarely caught but there are clues enough in the photos for the expert. For example, the grille opening would be unaltered, for any change would affect cooling characteristics, that being the probable motive for testing in extreme climates or at high altitude. Also, a switch to front-drive as planned by GM for its 1980-model compacts would be impossible to hide. Climbing trees with a telephoto lens may seem undignified, but you can usually shake a spy or two out of the foliage adjacent to any proving ground. It's simpler and cheaper than hiring an airplane because federal regulations prohibit flying under 1,000 feet without a special permit, and all the companies maintain "air raid" watches at their proving grounds during daylight hours.

Another, more subtle method of gathering information is for the spy to infiltrate the almost continuous technical meetings going on in Detroit or other convention cities. Let's imagine that Chrysler or Ford needed confirmation two years ago of GM's

---

[6] A mutually agreed exception: American Motors can raid but not be raided.

plans to build front-drive compacts. A spy would get himself "invited" to a function attended in force by any of the several manufacturers of a type of universal joint known as Rzeppa which is the constant-velocity kind required in a front-drive application. By midnight at least, in the appropriate hospitality suite, the spy would hear someone bragging about a big GM order forthcoming or, equally usefully, someone else bemoaning the loss of the order. You don't even need to be a spy. I know a native of Detroit who has hardly spent a dime on food or drink in years, and he has no connections whatever with the auto industry. He merely checks the meeting schedules posted in the lobbies of the local hotels, selects a host noted for the good life, pins on his lapel a suitable name badge from his vast collection of forgeries, walks into the private dining room, fills up, and walks out. And being forced to listen to keynote speakers at countless lunches and dinners, he has learned quite a bit about how automobiles are made.

Much like the photographs traded by high-level executives at the DAC, information on the status of orders for the Rzeppa-type universal joint becomes a viable commodity. Let's suppose it was the Chrysler man who ferreted this out in the hospitality suite. He would contact his Ford counterpart and meet for a private lunch in the hopes of exchanging his technical information for a photo of the GM front-drive compact that might be in Ford's possession. (Ford has an enterprising captive photo department, Chrysler does not.) Detroit spies routinely cooperate without ever directly disclosing activities within their own respective companies. Soon, each is able to flesh out a full, illustrated description of competitive plans as much as three years ahead of production, a date which in itself is of considerable interest.

Detroit even spies on you, the customer. You live in a city on the automakers' prototype evaluation circuit (Chicago is one) and are "randomly" selected according to your age, sex, race, and income to attend the showing. In return for free cocktails and dinner, you'll be expected to write down what you think of the car or, alternately, participate in a seminar discussing it. Unknown to the guests, however, the car or cars will be bugged with hidden tape recorders to pick up any comment you may make in supposed privacy. Spies from competing automakers love to infiltrate these gatherings and spike the tapes with their own, hardly objective, commentary. Also, new cars displayed at major auto shows open to the public are frequently bugged, even if somewhat after the fact, because your uninhibited opinions will be useful in the design of future models.

Detroit stylists may be too busy during the next decade to spy on you or anyone else. The big shrink to meet corporate average fuel economy (CAFE) goals is on and about the only secret left of consequence is how to accomplish the downsizing without making the cars *look* smaller. In this, Ford and Chrysler for once seem to have been more successful than GM, particularly in efforts involving full-size cars, but then, they had the advantage of hindsight. GM plunged ahead with its 1977 offerings while the others held back for two years (Lincoln until 1980), rightly suspecting there would be a thriving market for the "last of the big cars."

If ever there was justification for the excesses of which Detroit is so often accused, it is current public acceptance of Lincoln's self-serving advertising slogan quoted above. Despite warnings of impending energy crises and appeals to patriotism, as well as the possibility of a tax on "gas guzzlers," the relatively gargantuan 1979 Mark V Continental, a carry-over design, is projected to handily outsell Cadillac's newly downsized Eldorado. Facts are that the vanity of the American luxury car buyer saved Ford's ass. Lincoln activities would have been in the red for 1979 had Henry II not squeezed another year out of the pre-CAFE body shells used for both the Mark V and the conventional, even heavier Lincoln sedans. Highlighting the charade is the "Collector's Series," specially trimmed Mark Vs complete with tool kits for owners who do their own repairs.

There are several so-called "points of no return" in the gestation of any new car, but corporate dollars start flowing irretrievably out the door the moment management approves the final clay. Stylists move on to other projects and automation takes over. Someday it is envisioned that the entire process of moving from clay model to the first car off the assembly line will be automated but that millennium has not been reached as yet. One problem is that even the most skilled clay modeler cannot achieve an accuracy beyond 0.001 of an inch and therefore dies cannot be machined directly from the clay. Thus, the new car is re-created in plastic and then fed into a machine which translates its contours onto tape. The tape, in turn, operates the milling machines which form the die sets. And in a parallel development, the armies of men who once labored over the detailed design of small pieces have been replaced by automated drafting machines. Throughout, design decisions are pondered over and then made by computers.

Unfortunately, however, this multibillion-dollar investment in numerical control techniques has resulted in little if any reduction in the 24- to 17-month lead time required to put an all-new car design into production. In fact, there are numerous examples on record from pre-automation days, particularly among the struggling independent producers, where a handful of stylists and engineers created all-new and even quite radical designs in half the time required today. Gordon Buehrig's famous "coffin-nose" Cord of 1936 went from penciled sketch to production in slightly less than twelve months, and it remains a highly regarded milestone of its kind still. That, though, was back when most of the industry was short of money but long on ingenuity. And on dedication, too, for Gordon once told me that he was paid all of $350 a month as chief designer for the Auburn-Cord-Duesenberg Corporation. Sadly, he could never afford to buy one of his own classic creations when they were new and still can't, with surviving Cords selling for $30,000 and up.

Then and now, automotive stylists labor under pressures that cook them tender. If a writer creates a work that displeases his publisher, he can find another. The sculptor or the artist is often enriched by controversy. The architect Buckminster Fuller found people willing to live under his geodesic domes but no one bought his futuristic Dymaxion car.[7] Styling studios are fraught with tension because those in them labor to please just one master who collectively is known as management. Management, in turn, must make the decision which either pleases or dis-

---

[7] The Dymaxion (1933–34) was a three-wheeled car of teardrop aerodynamic design built largely of balsa wood and duraluminum to Fuller's geodesic principles. With Ford V-8 power, it achieved 120 mph but only three were built and none sold.

pleases the car-buying public. It can hardly be an objective or even innovative decision because it is made in fear. Neither Ford nor Chrysler has retired a president with full tenure in the past two decades; they've all resigned, or "requested early retirement," which are euphemisms for the axe. This insecurity at the top naturally percolates down into the studios. And sadly, good taste seldom pleases the public. Virgil Exner, who was fired after creating Chrysler's "Forward Look" and "Wedge Shape" and who is therefore a bit cynical, once likened styling to selecting Christmas neckties for one's second cousins.

GM's Bill Mitchell had a game he played with stylists under him. Just when tensions bubbled to the point where a handful of clay was about to be lobbed at his effigy instead of applied to the model, he would come in and order his men back to their sketch boards. Rather than the dreaded "Let's do this one over again," he would say: "Take a week and doodle your own personal dream car—one you'd like to own!" The game sometimes paid off, too. One sketch such as this by an Oldsmobile designer named Dave North evolved directly into the original front-drive Toronado.

It's perhaps best *not* to have your name remembered. Neither the original nor any subsequent Toronado is given much thought on the fourteenth floor of the GM Building in Detroit where the profits are counted. Up there they know which single model year after year sells the most. It is the Chevrolet pickup truck. Who styled it? Not one man in ten thousand, even within GM, would know, except on the fourteenth floor. What car is accorded permanent exhibition as representing the best in design at New York's prestigious Museum of Modern Art? It is the World War II Jeep. Who styled it? No one. It just evolved. It styled itself and thus won over all other contenders as the prime example of functionalism in its category.

CHAPTER 8

Tedium Besets Arthur Z.

Arthur Z. edged slowly along, his bumper sometimes butting the car ahead, waiting to fight his way into the mainstream of traffic out of the vast parking lot and cursing the balky engine that made him hold his left foot on the brake while his right jazzed in just enough gas to keep the tired Chevy from stalling. He popped an upper—the fifth that day, he counted—while steam from hundreds of idling cars rose into the murky, dank twilight settling on the Rouge.

The same fight, every fucking night. Won't be a whitey that'll let me in. Those mothers are checking trunks again. Why they sneak tools in the first place? There's better ways to steal. He shivered and trembled in the car, the benny not acting on him as fast as they used to, and sweat joined the other symptoms. He was worried. They're goin' to catch on to them clocks, too, and soon. It's okay to leave early and have the Club punch you out at three but fakin' overtime, that's stealing. The pill took and he gunned the Chevy into a hole in the line. Whitey ain't got it, he glowed. They're 'fraid of us. He scratches my fender and he knows he's in trouble.

Arthur Z. drove the twelve miles home to Livonia staring through the perpetual drizzle of Michigan winters outside, his black head inside swathed in his own self-created fog of inherited prejudices, vaguely bounded resentments, and sheer fatigue. The fatigue tugged at his guts. It was the distillation of years spent in the hammering noise of the Rouge, the one-two-three and shove-it-home routine of putting a power unit into position in a Ford Mustang at the rate, most of the time, of 70 an hour, 1,715 of them every eight-hour day, 8,575 in a five-day week, but there he stopped his calculating. He wasn't adding overtime or subtracting breaks, and he wasn't exactly sure how many engines he actually touched each week because his crew could keep up with the line one man short. One or the other of them was always in the can, or scoring, or punched out by the Club. Anyway, you couldn't count 'em by the hour. The line kept stopping for someone to disentangle a tool or his foot or a hand. All he knew was he ached, his hair ached, his toes ached, even before he punched in each morning. All he knew was he was sick, that that fine balance between coming up on bennies and down on beer was getting to where he couldn't control it. He wondered if any of the guys could see his problem, or if they had it too. He longed to share it with someone, but Arthur Z. was afraid. He was tired, so tired he didn't have much resistance to his occasional thought that he just might not want to go on living. This way, anyway.

He opened the door to the tidy house that Muriel kept for him and their family. He'd used his GI Bill and Michigan bonus for it when he got back from Korea and him and Muriel had decided to make it together. The builder had lined the street on both sides with three designs of houses, alternating one and then another, and had sold to blacks right from the start. They all had three tiny bedrooms, a shower bath, and a combined living and dining area separated by a counter from the kitchen. For $18,500 they weren't bad in 1955 and one had moved for over $30,000 a couple of doors down just last month. It was a good neighborhood where everybody watched each other's kids but otherwise minded their own business. If you didn't answer your door, they'd understand. And the older kids knew which cars belonged on the street and which didn't, so bill collectors stayed away at night. It was a long way from Second Street in Detroit where him and Muriel had come up.

Arthur Z. was a respected man in his neighborhood, no real close friends but everyone knew he'd kept a good job at Fords' since they could remember and they admired him for making foreman once and then going back on the line of his own. He didn't say much about it himself but people understood that, too. You can't suck whitey's ass without turnin' his color sooner or later and then, man, you ain't got a friend in the plant. Arthur Z. knew where he stood in Livonia, and at the plant. Don't push me, I'se borned here! Nobody was waiting to cause an accident to happen to him. He could turn his back without fear on any man. But when he went in his house, he went straight for the icebox and it wasn't till he was into his second six-pack that he could talk easy with Muriel.

The subject made him more tired before she started in on it. He didn't know any more than her why on a major assembler's wage of $8.335 an hour they couldn't be eatin' steaks that night instead of ribs. Or why he was still payin' $98.35 a month on a ten-year-old Chevy. Shit, how long he'd been payin' that every month for a car and they was never newer than ten years old? His eyes lingered for a moment on his kids in front of the ten-foot Spanish-style genuine walnut veneer stereo console with twenty-five-inch color TV and he thought maybe that was one reason why, but he didn't say so to Muriel. He'd gone along with it two years ago when he was working six ten-hour days a week after a strike so short he'd hardly felt it. Noticing the kids reminded him of those insurance policies Muriel had bought. They ain't gonna die, it's me that's gonna die, he'd protested. But Muriel said that wasn't the idea, that the twelve dollars a week would build up and put the three younger ones through college. The other two had gone their ways before the insurance man came. Arthur Z.'s pride returned and he got another Bud and sat down to dinner with it.

Muriel was an excellent cook and it hurt her feelings when beer and TV took precedent over her dinners, as they most always did. It hurt her too when no one noticed the freshly waxed tile and the new curtains in the kitchen that she'd made. Muriel believed in machines, for her folks never had any, so Muriel got another one every time their Sears account dropped below the $500 limit. She didn't like to admit even to herself that sometimes, like with the power waxer, you had to still do the corners by hand to make it right. Her machines kept her as tired as her husband. They had to earn their way in her house. No one knew, and Arthur Z. didn't care, just which machine they were paying on at the moment.

Both of them went to bed early that night. Arthur Z. was almost always able to leave the couch with dignity, get to the bedroom, hang up his clothes, get under the covers, and then pass out. Muriel would follow a little later, hoping for a little lovin', but it hadn't happened for a long while. She didn't know about the pills which cost nearly as much each month as the insurance, Sears, and car payments combined. Arthur Z. couldn't get it up no more but neither of them knew why. She couldn't see in the dark that sometimes he lay there with his eyes open, the eyeballs rolled up into the corners of their sockets. And when he'd jerk awake in the middle of the night and complain of cramps in his toes and legs, she'd blame it on his standin' all day and turn up his side of the electric blanket. Their love for each other slept under the blanket with them, dormant, hurting, but still very real.

Muriel was up early as was her wont. Arthur Z. slept in, having already gone to the kitchen for a couple of Buds which stayed down this time. Muriel didn't question his layin' there. Though he hadn't told her of his plans, she thought it was another one of those nothin' days off in the middle of the week that the Union got in the last settlement. It was something like that but the UAW had little to do with it. It was Arthur Z.'s turn to be punched in by the Club.

Time Card Clubs flourish in Ford Motor Company plants because, in the interests of efficiency, management installed a new kind of time clock that did away with the old-fashioned time card which had to be individually read at the end of each shift by an army of timekeepers. The new clock recorded comings and goings automatically when the worker inserted his personalized card in the slot. Sized about the same as a charge card (which indeed it was for those in the know), the piece of plastic contained ten holes, nine for the worker's social security number and the tenth one for the number of cards that had been issued to that individual. You could get a replacement if you lost your card, but you weren't supposed to keep the old card and have a friend punch you in with it when you were in fact late or absent.

You also needed the real card to get in and out of the plant gates.

Factory workers everywhere, whether they belong to the UAW or not, acquire the ability to make life easier for themselves, a knack that management everywhere wishes was devoted to increasing productivity. So it wasn't long before Ford workers by the hundreds discovered that any piece of plasticized cardboard of the right size and shape, such as could be cut from a milk carton, that was precisely scored like the card the company issued you would work just fine in the new time clocks. A "Club" consists ideally of a small group of employees working the same job or stations where there is a multiple shift operation, or staggered shifts, or, as in the case of Arthur Z., where less than the assigned number of men can do the job.

Foremen aren't blind or stupid. They knew what was going on but preferred to say nothing because work quotas were not affected by the cheating. The men either got ahead on their work and then disappeared or those on the job covered for the absentees by working harder. And it was a self-disciplining affair. If a member of a Club goofed and failed to punch a fellow member in or out according to the agreed-upon schedule, he was ostracized. He had to work for his living once again.

Management should have known not to turn men and women into numbers. Each job in the plant represented an investment of $40,000 and if management didn't think enough of that expenditure to attach a name and a face to it, the hell with it. I'm just a number and if I ever cared, I don't now. Arthur Z. could even remember when they had to arbitrate to get doors put on the toilet stalls. Nothin' is as precious to a man as his dignity. So it became a game to see what they could get through the inspectors. A couple of sheet-metal screws dropped on the floormat and you had them inspectors huntin' all over the car to find where they belonged. And they didn't belong anywhere, we just put 'em there. The dirtiest trick, an empty Coke bottle behind an upholstery panel, was reserved for a special, a rush job being built for some VIP. Fuck management was an all-consuming goal that united blacks and whites, men and women, and even these with foremen in the sense that the fuckor represented more of an immediate threat to personal welfare than the fuckee way up front in the Green House.

The chief irritant between blacks and whites in the plants really had no basis in the kind of rooted prejudices that today are considered immoral if not illegal. Likes attract likes and superimposed upon such individual friendships as may exist between unlikes, it remains a fact that when integrated crowds gather, as in a plant cafeteria or at the Union Hall, or in neighborhoods, the colors and the sexes tend to separate into clusters. If nothing else, one can talk more freely. You don't have to guard against the unintentional offense or feel you have to get across that you hate Joe's guts not because he's black or white but because you just can't take him, period. Or that Suzie is a bitch, period. Deeper than all this, though, is survival and in that, Suzie's not the threat. Equal Opportunity down in the bowels of the plants where it is more than just lip service is turning whites against blacks just as lack of opportunity had turned blacks against whites less than a generation ago. The same sides, feelings turned full circle. And it surfaces in the parking lots like at the Rouge, and on the streets of Detroit and its environs. The one common denominator, where the divided stand united, is fuck management. And an effective spokesman for these feelings is the United Automobile, Aerospace and Agricultural Implement Workers of America International Union, known familiarly as the UAW, which is perhaps the closest to a dedicated, honest voice the working man has ever possessed.

There are some who still say that if industry had exhibited a social conscience back in the beginning, labor unions would have no reason to exist. I doubt that. Men such as Walter Reuther, who once was a tool and die man at the Rouge, would have fought paternalism just as hard and just as effectively. Walter (the Brotherhood eschews last names) sensed, and rightly so, that dignity of labor was the issue and the cause. Every man and, later, every woman was entitled to a full measure of it for as long as he or she worked at Fords'. His words are in the UAW's quote book: "The working man has but one thing to sell, his labor. Once he loses control of that, he loses everything." Walter rose to foreman and, attending night classes at Wayne University, he completed his high school work and went on to study economics and sociology. That was in 1931, but a year later he was fired for his union activities. That must be on record as one of the costliest mistakes Henry Ford ever made.

Walter and his brother, Victor, went off on a three-year bicycle tour of Europe to study auto workers' unions there and spent nearly two of those years on the assembly line at an auto plant in the Soviet Union. Though he came to like the Russian people and appreciate the problems of their government, the experience made Walter a bitter foe of Communism wherever it surfaced in the American labor movement. He became a UAW organizer in 1946 and formulated, fomented, and led the sitdown tactic that brought union recognition, first by General Motors and Chrysler and, later, Ford. By 1953 when Arthur Z. became a card-carrying member of Ford Local 600, UAW-CIO, Walter had already been president of the Local and had gone on to head both the United Automobile Workers and the Congress of Industrial Organizations.

Arthur Z. had sat with Local 600's delegation at the UAW's national convention one year in Detroit's drafty Masonic Temple, and even as the politicking had swirled above his head he knew that what he was witnessing could not exactly be called democracy in action. One by one, the delegations rose to extol the virtues of the incumbent leadership while Walter beamed approvingly from the platform. "Brother" Arthur went home determined henceforth to stay out of it, just go along, for much the same reasons he later ended his brief flirtation with management. He never actually sat down to figure whether the wages he lost during the sometimes prolonged strikes were ever paid back by the gains. By the time he had connected one set of acronyms, like GAW, SUB, and COLA with dollars in his paycheck, a new batch came along to confuse him. The only beef he'd ever felt a part of was the one where they'd got those doors put on the toilets.

He remembered a conversation he'd had with his oldest boy, Jesse. Jesse said I's goin' to work for Fords' when I's grow'd up. Oh no you ain't, he'd replied. Then he thought, why not? Better'n the Army like you, Jesse persisted, but, as it turned out, Jesse did volunteer because the Army promised him schoolin' in a skilled trade. He'd be an electronic technician and get himself a TV shop when he got out. Arthur Z. hoped he would. When you worked for Fords', you saved a second by doin' your job faster, everybody saved a second, and Fords' saved a million dollars. He'd learned that at foreman's school. But, he reflected, I ain't saved nothin' by that. Arthur Z. could never quite equate the benefits his union had won for him with his personal productivity but he understood the promise of Jesse havin' his own place. He'd set his own pace, he'd be his own boss. Never once in this conversation between father and son did the thought intrude that the customer might be the ultimate dictator, that it was the customer or lack of him which set the pace, that it was the customer who was the real boss over all factories and all TV shops.

For Arthur Z. never once felt any connection or affinity with the Mustangs he'd see on the street or even the rare two-passenger T-birds, collectors' pieces now, that were made at the Rouge back when he started. He couldn't tell which year Mustang was which, though surely the lines of each successive model must be indelibly recorded somewhere in his brain. He'd had a stint as utility man on the line, and goin' around from station to station, a few days at each to replace a man who was sick or who'd quit, there was a lot that was new to him and he'd made mistakes, hundreds of them, and he hadn't reported those that he was aware of. They'd be caught on the sell floor, he'd reason, that's what inspectors are for. No man ever reported mistakes, or chased a car down the line to correct them. So, the thought that his mistakes might be everywhere around him on the streets, maybe lurking uncaught to cause a crash if they were safety related, just never occurred to him. Fords' had made him a robot without care or conscience, but in that he was no more guilty than a management which thinks of inspectors as nonproductive parasites, which treats machines with more consideration than it gives to the men who operate them, and which believes that selling blue jackets with the Ford emblem stitched on them at cost in the company store will motivate the work force.

Arthur Z. had been to Solidarity House, the UAW's International Headquarters on Jefferson Avenue in Detroit, a building which, ironically, was once the mansion where Edsel Ford had lived. While he waited to conduct his business, he saw a man in working clothes walk up to the burly male receptionist and ask to see Walter. Instead of why and who are you, the receptionist dialed a number and the man went straight up. It was, or at least it seemed, as easy as that. And he'd wondered if that man had gone to the Green House and asked to see Henry, how he'd fare. Neither was Arthur Z. surprised when he saw UAW members picketing their own building. They were clerks and stenographers on the headquarters staff who wanted more money and that was the way you went about getting it. Arthur Z. impressed easy. He had no reason to know that the UAW was a big business too, that beyond that gracious marble foyer the old mansion was cut up into a myriad of little cubicles, each inhabited by a college-trained egghead, too soft to have survived in a mill or foundry, too young to have put in time on the line.

Those were the economists and sociologists and degreed liberals from a dozen other disciplines who plotted Walter's strategies to use against management and who supplied him with statistics twisted to fit the need of the moment. About the only difference between Solidarity House and the Green House was that salaries were lower, much lower. The UAW is a clean union, a showpiece of its kind.

It has been said, too, that the UAW ranks with government bureaucrats in adding cost to your new car. Ford claims its last settlement in 1976 would, during the three years of the contract, add $300 to the sticker of each new car. GM claims $500. Walter, if he were alive, would disallow those figures in full, pointing to gains in productivity from the automation he encouraged. His successors, Leonard (Leonard Woodcock) and now Doug (Doug Fraser), haven't deviated from the formula. Close the niches in the guaranteed annual wage, fold in enough cost-of-living allowance to keep up with inflation, extend benefits from the cradle to the grave, retire for time served and not age, and, finally, the not yet reached millennium of the four-day week with five days' pay. Arthur Z. could buy all that but he wondered sometimes where his dignity had went. It wasn't mentioned in the contracts. He still had to fight for it as before, ever reminding himself that he put on his pants the same way as did Henry (Henry Ford II). Did it die with Walter in that little plane up in

Pellston where the labor leader crashed with his wife in the fog and rain or was Walter just talkin'?

One union-inspired program Arthur Z. didn't buy was the hiring of hard-core unemployables off the streets of Detroit. Management from all the auto companies and their major suppliers, of course, eagerly endorsed the idea, for it was cheap public relations. Management in fact had tried it before on its own and knew that very few of these recruits would survive the prework schooling which was mostly drumming home the lesson that, to get paid, you had to show clean and sober and on time every day and stay until the whistle blew. Management, however, made no effort to transport these men from the inner city to the plants and they wouldn't or couldn't cope on their own with Detroit's Rapid Transit System. Nor could they be blamed. The city's not-so-rapid buses had long been ignored by factory workers, so schedules and routes, in turn, ignored the plants. Two hours on the bus each way capped by a long, cold walk to and from the gate made working for a living somewhat more than a drag.

Relative youngsters, most of the candidates were referred by probation authorities or drug rehabilitation centers. It was go or get put away and forgot. There was no meaningful transition provided to give the kids perspective, to let them down gently from the pressures of the streets whence they came, to help them become aware for perhaps the first time that survival the legitimate way would demand certain disciplines foreign to their lifestyles. Instead, they were expected to journey miles from their pads to hear some bull-necked honky outline a pattern for their futures dull enough to turn off a choirboy. It seemed almost as though management had plotted the outcome or, at the least, expected acceptance of the Establishment to well up overnight.

A few dozens at each participating plant did make it out on the floor for on-the-job training and Arthur Z. became a tutor. He resented open display of habits he himself kept concealed. He wasn't used to being called "nigger" by a fellow black. He feared their open defiance of authority would reflect on him. He thought he was cool and they thought they were cool. He couldn't talk their talk and they wouldn't his. In short, there was no communication between these two generations of blacks and more than a few Mustangs, many more than usual, spent a long time getting fixed up on the sell floor at the end of the line each day. He came to equate afros with trouble, personal trouble, for the jobs bungled at his station were blamed on the tutor. Fucked if he did, he figured he'd be less fucked if he didn't, so he refused to train another mother. For that he got three days off without pay and a Record, his first.

Arthur Z.'s short collaboration with management was equally unrewarding. They pleaded with him to take foreman. He'd been utility and knew the line. He was black and if Fords' wanted to sell army trucks, or missile parts, or sedans, or anything else to the government, there had to be a "significant" ratio of minorities in supervision. It felt strange to him to be offered a promotion as his birthright. He didn't fool himself that he was qualified. He had no ambitions with which to dull the pressures, but he agreed to try. It was Selma, Alabama. The men turned their backs. His fellow foremen turned their backs. Only his union agent understood and, before the week was out, he turned to this agent for help. Arthur Z. went back to the line knowing the time had not yet come for blacks to shoulder the white man's burden, at least not at Fords'. But his Record stayed clean, for management was satisfied, even pleased. It had gone through the motions demanded of it by government and could now say I told you so.

Arthur Z. is real. He's still at the Rouge. Him and Muriel are still meetin' their payments and she still don't know why he can't get it up. They got twelve years to go unless the Union folds back retirement minimums. Better maybe not to hurry it. They got no plans, no way of savin', no place but Livonia to call home. They ain't gonna die, it's me that's gonna die, he'd protested, and you know, God willin' and if Walter don't rise again, he's right.

CHAPTER 9

Fall from the Pinnacle

"William C. Newberg, 66, lives in Reno, Nevada, with his wife Dottie and the youngest of their four children. They are both staunch Presbyterians, he being an elder at St. John's, and they own a four-wheel-drive Chevrolet Suburban equipped with a CB radio. 'Life's great,' says he. 'If you ever lived in Reno, you'd throw rocks at Michigan.'" So reads in prosaic detail one of those "Where Are They Now?" columns in the current issue of an automotive industry trade journal.

I put the magazine down and my memory went back twenty years to an evening when Dottie and Bill sat in my Grosse Pointe living room, she damp-eyed and he grim, while I took notes on how it felt to be the ex-president of a major automobile company after only a little over two months in office. As it turned out, there weren't many notes because the interview had hardly started when there was an interruption. The Newbergs' car had been followed, Chrysler Security had notified Public Relations of its destination, and the somewhat embarrassed press agent at my door heralded the end of communications. Why? Because Dottie and Bill were running scared. And I felt for them but I wasn't surprised, then or now, even as I reread those yellowed notes which are still in my files.

Bill: "You work your heart and soul out and all of a sudden they're going to smear and sue you."

Dottie: "Character assassination makes you sick all over.

Worse than something like cancer. People commit suicide for less. You have to hold on to your teeth and have faith."

Bill: "It's difficult to get justice out of a corporation because they're too big."

The Newbergs were running scared because his former cronies on the Chrysler board were suing him, or were threatening to, I forget which, for $450,000, which allegedly represented his financial interests in supplier firms and that, even if you believed the allegations, was the pot calling the kettle black![1] Then I remembered that I'd contacted Dottie later, after the affair had cooled down a bit, to see if she'd co-author with me an article for *McCall's* magazine to be entitled "Fall from the Pinnacle." That effort ended after a few pages of manuscript, too, for the Newbergs by then were planning a book about their shattering experience, which also, as far as I know, was never published. But here is what Dottie started to write, "as told to" me:

"My husband Bill was president of Chrysler for sixty-three-and-one-half days. I'll claim that full half day because even though he called at ten-thirty in the morning from New York to tell me he had resigned, I guess I really didn't believe it until I heard the twelve o'clock newscast.

"Two months later I still wake up thinking it's all a horrible dream. How can a three-minute phone call take away what Bill worked all his life to get? When he was five, he was pailing cows on his family's little Colorado farm. He went to college with one suit, worked summers in lumber camps and on the freighters to Alaska. He came to Detroit with hardly a penny, determined he was going to work for Chrysler, the best company in the world. For twenty-seven years he worked his way up, taking every dog job that came along and turning it to good. Then that phone call, after just sixty-three-and-one-half days on top, and it was all over.

"Judy, our daughter, and I were painting that day at the Arts and Crafts Center. We went downtown to Detroit three times a week for this because we both loved to paint. 'Mrs. Newberg,

---

[1] Chapter 2 details how Newberg was picked as the patsy when Chrysler management was charged by stockholders with conflicts of interest at the highest level. His subsequent fistfight with chairman Colbert in the locker room of a golf club has become a Detroit legend.

please'—the call came over the loudspeaker. I had just prepared my palette and remember being annoyed at the interruption, but then I also remembered that calls weren't put through here unless they were from the family and important. Bill had left straight from the office the day before on the Chrysler plane for a directors' meeting in New York. Funny, the thought crossed my mind, that he didn't tell me one was scheduled until just before he took off.

"As I write it down, our conversation seems too ordinary for so big a moment. 'Dottie'—I thought it was distance that made his voice hollow—'I've just resigned as president.'

"'You're kidding . . .' I knew he wasn't. Bill never could use words for anything but simple statements of facts.

"'No, I've just resigned as president and director . . .' His voice sounded firmer, but I knew that when he added that word 'director' that he was leaving the company completely.

"'Honey, I'm tickled pink.' I said it, and at the time I meant it. I know of no better words to describe executive life in the auto industry than 'rat race.' We'd talked about this the few times we had been able to get away for vacations without a resort full of business associates around. 'Why don't you get out?' I'd ask. 'You've worked so terribly hard. I'd be the happiest wife in the world.' I had a vague idea that Bill could be a consultant or something. I seldom really gave a thought to the $130,000 salary, the stock options and bonuses that bought us our house in Bloomfield Hills, our club memberships, private schools for the children, and the entertaining I loved so much. Bill couldn't do it, though. He'd say that cars were all he knew, and the Chrysler kind were the only ones he cared about.

"I came back to the class from the phone but I didn't tell Judy, except to ask her if she'd mind if we left early. We went right to the car because Bill had told me to catch the noon broadcast. He said that he and the Chrysler people would be meeting the press, and the facts would be reported then.

"'Mother, what's wrong?' The question was put calmly. Judy knew something was so I reached for the radio and let the announcer explain. The minutes he spent talking of the Berlin crisis, a plane crash, and the traffic toll seemed an eternity. Finally he told us what I knew and didn't believe. 'Forty-six-year-old

William C. Newberg today resigned as president of the Chrysler Corporation, just sixty-four days after his appointment.' Sixty-three-and-one-half, I mentally corrected. 'The announcement came after a secret and reportedly stormy board meeting in New York City. Neither Mr. Newberg nor board chairman Lester Lum (Tex) Colbert could be immediately reached by this station for comment.'

"Even when Bill was executive vice-president, he'd had a company airplane and a chauffeur-driven car always waiting for him. I wondered when he'd be back because there was a party at the Vanderkloots—she's Bunky Knudsen's sister—that night. When Judy and I got home, there was a message to call the Chrysler offices. I can't mention the boy's name. He's always been so nice to us, but he had to tell me that Mr. Newberg would be coming into Metropolitan Airport on American Flight 57 and this night his car couldn't be there. Could I meet him?

"All six-feet, two inches of Bill Newberg looked taller as he walked down the ramp of that airplane. There was a crowd of TV and newspapermen waiting too. I thought all they could print was what he said: 'Now I can spend time fishing with the kids—and golf—things I haven't done for twenty-seven years.' Our boys were there with me. They're both adopted and he adores them. On the long drive back to Bloomfield, the boys climbed all over the car, their energy welcoming Daddy home where their tongues couldn't. For once we didn't care about the upholstery. It gave us a kind of privacy when Bill, his eyes never leaving the road, his hands firm on the wheel, said: 'Dottie, I was forced to resign.'

"I wished I were born with a little switch to turn my feelings on and off. I reached for it but it wasn't there when Bill went on to tell me that some of the directors—his best friend Tex Colbert, Alton Jones, Juan Trippe, and Joe Dodge—told him that if he 'didn't talk,' it would all be handled in a 'gentlemanly' manner. Talk about what? Bill didn't hear me because I never voiced the question out loud. He was talking about a promise the directors had made to 'line him up' with Studebaker. It seemed ridiculous, even then, going from the presidency of the ninth [sic] largest corporation in this country to one that anybody knew was in real trouble, but the directors must have had some reason. They wouldn't hurt Bill after all he'd done for them..."

Here our manuscript ended, for in addition to the Newbergs' book commitment and difficulties resulting from Dottie's inability to talk about her fall from the pinnacle for more than a few consecutive minutes without dissolving into tears, John Mack Carter, who edited *McCall's* at the time told me he wanted only "happy" stories in his magazine. Perhaps Carter was right in his judgment, for the poignancy of Dottie's tale, simply told with simple emotions, would hardly have brightened the day for wives of up-and-coming executives, they being the targets of *McCall's* editorial thrust in those days. As it turned out, though, it *was* a happy tale and I could sense this possibility when, at our last meeting, she pressed a copy of *With Christ in the Garden*[2] into my hands. She also gave one to the lawyer who was prosecuting Chrysler's case against her husband. She'd walked right up to him, a stranger on the street, and gave it to him. Crazy woman, he'd muttered, but she'd hoped he'd read it. Maybe he did, for Colbert was demoted by a new management and the Newbergs' legal entanglements just sort of dried up and drifted away. They're happy today in Reno, where they could throw rocks at Detroit if they wished, but they don't.

And nothing has changed on executive row in Detroit. The Semon E. (Bunky) Knudsen referred to by Dottie went on to become executive vice-president of General Motors. Bunky is the son of William S. (Big Bill) Knudsen, World War II production czar and president of GM from 1937 until 1940, when he was tapped by the government to direct industry's war effort. The somewhat embarrassing nickname, bestowed by the father to commemorate their early camping trips together, inaccurately describes the younger Knudsen, who was already a millionaire many times over without his GM salary and bonuses and not the type to bed down for long with any of his fellow executives.[3] In fact, his abrasive independence caused GM's hierarchy to pass him by for the presidency in 1967, that deeply desired capstone

[2] By Lynn James Radcliffe, Abingdon Press, Nashville, 1959.
[3] Others were more fortunate. One Christmas when Knudsen was head of Pontiac Division, he sent all members of the press, male and female, a bedside trinket box inscribed: "Sweet Dreams—Bunky Knudsen."

FALL FROM THE PINNACLE 145

to his career being handed instead to Ed Cole. Bunky promptly resigned and shortly thereafter threw his accumulated GM pension, stock options, and bonus rights out the window by becoming president of Ford Motor Company. That was unprecedented. A few disgruntled GM executives at the topmost level had resigned years ago to form their own automobile companies but none had ever absconded to the competition. You accepted rejection by your peers in dignified, loyal silence, smiling bravely on your way to the bank.[4]

Loyalty, a quality Bunky Knudsen obviously ranked second to ambition, proved the key to what followed. Presidents of major corporations aren't chosen from the pool of unemployed executives without creating bitter resentment among incumbent hopefuls. The loyal incumbent, however, plots revenge against the intruder and not the boss. And as a training ground for corporate infighting, GM ranks as a distant also-ran to Ford. And the sharpest, most loyal student in all of Dearborn was an executive vice-president named Lee A. Iacocca. War was immediately declared between the two and the outcome was never in doubt. One had but to count the soldiers under each. Knudsen had only the dissidents; Iacocca commanded regiments of junior executives whose careers had long been committed to his cause. Of course, none of this could have transpired had not Henry Ford II remained characteristically aloof from the tempest he had stirred until he grew tired of the game and fired Knudsen. The charade lasted just nineteen months. As Henry II explained at the time, ". . . it just didn't work out."

Knudsen's separation settlement could probably have paid for free whitewall tires, or an electric clock, or maybe both, on every Ford produced during the 1970 model run. Or it might have been saved to use a year later to modify those Pinto gas tanks that were to rupture in collisions and burn their owners to a crisp. Or the sum could have been used to distribute Christmas turkeys to the hourly workers. However, the mistakes of the chairman don't appear on the balance sheet. They're only questioned by disgruntled stockholders at the annual meeting who

[4] Detroit thinks it coined the cliche "smiling bravely on your way to the bank" but actually it is attributed to Liberace, the pianist.

are given pat answers and made to look stupid. One wonders what will be said when Henry II and all his past presidents finally come eyeball to eyeball at that last big directors meeting in the sky.

For Lee Iacocca is now a past president too. His ladder was missing a rung, the one labeled heir apparent to the Ford Motor Company. Everybody but Henry II assumed he was. The scenario would be Iacocca as interim chairman until such time as Henry II's son, Edsel II, completed his apprenticeship, which so far has been conducted at outposts of the company far removed from the action. Nobody really knows much about Edsel II, perhaps not even his father. He represents a sort of vacuum in the scheme of things and, of their nature, vacuums are always imperiled by strong pressures from outside. The driving, ambitious Iacocca, however loyal to the father, threatened an orderly succession. There would be a period during which it might be forgotten whose name was on the buildings. And despite 40 percent family control of the company, Henry II's fear of outsiders moving in borders on paranoia.

This fear is deep-rooted. He was recalled from the Navy during World War II to save the family business from a predatory outsider named Harry Bennett who had taken advantage of Edsel Ford's death and of Henry Sr.'s advancing senility to build an empire for himself. The dictatorial Bennett, who some thought insane, bolstered his authority with armed goons who on occasion "arrested" and confined persons, employees and visitors alike, who incurred his displeasure. The Ford plants and lands literally comprised a police state within the city of Dearborn, which also was controlled by Bennett. At one point shortly after World War II's end and cancellation of war contracts, the company was estimated to be losing $3 million a week but no one knew for sure. Bennett allowed very few records to be kept of his activities and, further, he neither knew nor cared about what it took to mass-produce cars and trucks. Ford Motor Company in 1945 was close to total destruction, as much so as if it had been headquartered in bombed-out Tokyo.

Henry II's credentials for his role as savior were unpromising. He had flunked out of Yale after trying both engineering and sociology. His short naval career was routine and shore-based. And he was only twenty-six years old. But he shrewdly kept a low profile for two years until he could prove Bennett's gross abuses and then, with the help of his mother, Mrs. Edsel Ford, and grandmother, Clara Ford, he unseated the tyrant and shunted the latter's protector, grandfather Henry Sr., off to one side as an "adviser." The rest was easy, for the founder had operated the company with relatively little executive help and most of these people, perhaps a thousand in all, followed Bennett into forced retirement.[5]

Next came the task of rebuilding, and the architect of this, more so than Henry II, was the first of many nonfamily presidents, Ernest R. Breech, who had been the chief executive of Bendix Aviation Corporation. Also hired at this time were two future presidents, Robert McNamara and Arjay Miller, along with five other military logistical experts known collectively in Pentagon circles as the "Whiz Kids." From the start Henry II surrounded himself with an army of potential leaders rather than just a few, thus generating the executive turmoil that exists to this day within his company. Ford Motor Company cannot be described as having management in depth; rather, it is tossed about in a stormy sea of giant, patternless waves crashing ambitiously against each other instead of the shore. And Henry II thoroughly enjoys his role in the eye of the hurricane.

It is doubtful if Lee Iacocca, the latest to join the ranks of Ford ex-presidents, will ever allow his biography to be written or even author it himself. He likes to talk of being the first-generation son of Italian immigrants and of his early years in manual jobs but much more is known about his record than about the man himself. He is the circumspect antithesis of his former boss, whose marital problems, sometime penchant for more than just social drinking, illnesses, candor, and associated attacks against the political establishment of both hues, as well as unpredictable actions as chairman of Ford Motor Company, constantly make headlines. In perspective, Henry II's life would pass unreported were he not a Ford but he wears the uncomfortable mantle of

[5] Harry H. Bennett died January 4, 1979, in a California nursing home at the age of eighty-six. He had lived comfortably in his forced retirement on an annuity provided for thirty-four years by Ford Motor Company.

his equally unpredictable grandfather. He has been news since he was born.

Unlike the first time he was bypassed, Iacocca wasted no time moving on. He accepted a widely bruited offer to assume the presidency of Chrysler Corporation on November 2, 1978, and within a few weeks no less than five vice-presidents and one ex-president other than Iacocca found themselves with new assignments. Eugene A. Cafiero was no luckier than Bill Newberg. His sin was being president of Chrysler Corporation at a time when Iacocca was available, so he found himself shunted unceremoniously into the uncertain vice-chairmanship in charge of "planning" and then fired.[6] His qualifications for that planning spot, and also John Riccardo's for retaining his title as chairman and chief executive officer, have been questioned in some quarters because the Corporation managed to lose a record (for any auto company) $247.8 million during the first nine months of 1978. Iacocca understandably sees a future ahead for him at Chrysler; there is no way to go but up!

Bunky Knudsen was not so lucky either. Ten years ago, when it was his turn to be fired by Henry II, he moved almost immediately into the chairmanship of White Motor Company, an ailing, overextended manufacturer of heavy-duty trucks which in some categories compete with Ford products. That company is neither less ailing nor less overextended than when he arrived but, conversely, it might be argued that White would not exist today were it not for Knudsen's ministrations.

Then back at Ford Motor Company, the business press throughout the summer and early fall of 1978 filled its pages with speculation on who was to succeed Iacocca as president. There was general agreement only in that whoever it was, he would face operating problems of unprecedented magnitude. Along with maintaining car and truck sales at a rate that can pay for the multibillion-dollar annual expenditures required to keep up with government emission, safety and fuel economy regulations, profits as well as consumer confidence must be sustained in the wake of government-mandated recalls in 1978 alone involv-

[6] Cafiero has since moved on to become president of De Lorean Motor Company.

ing over 18 million Ford-made vehicles. And Henry II himself faces rather unbelievable charges of personal misconduct (accepting kickbacks from an in-plant food vendor being the most unbelievable) thrown at him in a $50 million stockholder suit filed by one Roy Cohn, the same lawyer it will be remembered who twenty-four years ago set out to purge the government of Communist sympathizers under the irresponsible aegis of the late Senator Joseph McCarthy.

Moreover, Cohn recently amended his lawsuit to accuse Henry II and his Company of paying a $1 million bribe to the Indonesian Government to get a $30 million contract for a Ford subsidiary (Aeroneutronics) and of accepting $2 million from Philippine officials in return for a $50 million investment in a business venture on those islands. But aside from his notorious witch-hunts of the past, Cohn's credibility is marred by the simple fact that no Ford would have any motive to intentionally break or even skirt the law for such relatively piddling sums of money. Henry II is already one of the world's wealthiest men. Corporately, however, there may be some substance to Cohn's allegations. After all, it was quite in style a few years ago for American big business to buy its way into emerging countries. In fact, there was no other way.

This aside and after a suspenseful delay of several months, Henry II picked as his new president the man who was already vice-chairman and, as such, Iacocca's onetime immediate boss, Philip Caldwell. To understand the conflicts that brought about Iacocca's firing, one must remember the improbable "troika" created when he was first elevated to the presidency. There was Henry II as chairman and chief executive officer; Caldwell as vice-chairman and dark-horse heir apparent; and Iacocca as president, chief operating officer, and self-proclaimed heir apparent. All three had a supposedly equal vote in company affairs and though in theory no one of the three had to answer to another, the fact was that Henry II's vote was considerably stronger whenever he chose to exercise that strength than the votes of the other two combined. This peculiar arrangement, though latent with friction, suited Iacocca because in practice he reported directly to Henry II. However, it was not to last. In

June of 1978, Henry II added deputy chief executive officer to Caldwell's title, thus announcing the line of succession, and ordered Iacocca to report to the latter at all times, not just in his, Henry II's, absences. The fact that Caldwell some years before had reported to Iacocca undoubtedly rankled but the clear cause for Iacocca's fully anticipated rebellion was that he obviously was no longer under consideration for the chairmanship upon Henry II's retirement, which, because of uncertain health, could come at any time before the mandatory date in 1982. Iacocca was allowed his dissatisfaction for less than a month and once again there came that explanation: "It just didn't work out."

Aside from complicating my role as a recorder of where they are now, a by-product of constant turmoil on executive row is, of course, loss of corporate image in areas ranging from the financial community on down to the recruitment booths at college campuses. And charged with maintaining this image at Ford as well as at all other large corporations is the public relations department. The function might be compared with that of the fire department of any city except that advice is not often sought on how to prevent fires, particularly at Ford where the man whose name is on the buildings likes to set them. Thus it seems quite appropriate that while Ford PR-men at the working level were busily trying to explain the Iacocca affair in its best light to the press and thus to the public, their director, Walter Murphy of the Iacocca team, was quietly forced into early retirement and his successor was brought in from the outside. Monkey see, monkey do.

There is one automobile company, though, where all that the executives have to worry about is staying in business. This is American Motors, from which no president has ever been fired. George Romney, the most famous of them, led AMC through its shaky metamorphosis into a manufacturer of small cars and then resigned through no pressure other than his own. He wanted to be elected governor of Michigan and was. His chosen successor, a straw-hat-and-cigar-type huckster named Roy Abernethy, was a man with a reputation for being able to sell anything; specifically, more Packard limousines in post-World War II Boston than the total for the country combined, which, by Packard standards, was a lot of limousines. Though his techniques[7] didn't work quite so well with compacts, Abernethy stayed on through an invasion by outsiders that should be described more as a stock manipulation than a stockholder's revolt to retire voluntarily. He, in turn, was succeeded by Roy D. Chapin, Jr., son of the founder of Hudson Motor Company, an AMC predecessor. Then when Chapin moved on to chairman, William V. Luneburg filled the post until his mandatory retirement. It was then occupied by Gerald C. Meyers, who within a few months had moved up to the chairmanship when Chapin retired. All that's expected is for the company to be around and solvent the next morning. All concur that AMC is an exciting, fun place to work.

The more sophisticated business publications such as *Business Week, The Wall Street Journal,* and *Ward's Auto World* are ready at any time to speculate knowledgeably on who is being groomed for the top in any of the automobile companies—who's next—even when all is peaceful as it is at Ford for the moment. The Detroit-based reporters, none of whom has ever held a responsible job in industry,[8] evaluate the candidates' ambitions, political skills, home life, physiognomy,[9] manner of dress, and past assignments as though they, the reporters, were directors of the company concerned. And they're usually quite accurate. Three or four candidates will be presented to readers as finalists and never once have I seen a clean miss. In fact, it is not hard to spot the dead ends in which some vice-presidents find themselves. It is less easy, though, to base judgment on the man's area of expertise. Auto company presidents in recent times have risen through the ranks of finance, manufacturing, engineering, sales, legal, and family and, except at General Motors, most have had some experience in the company's overseas subsidiaries. None

---

[7] During one of AMC's leaner years, the press preview of new models was held in a tent erected on a Wisconsin field occupied only the day before by a herd of cows. Abernethy, on stage, was in the middle of declaring the upholstery in the new Rambler Ambassador to be the equal of any Cadillac when he paused and asked: "What is that I smell?" The suffering press in unison answered, "Bullshit!"

[8] Nor, I must state, have I.

[9] The original *Life* magazine in a piece speculating on the then future GM hierarchy dismissed an executive vice-president named Roger Kyes from consideration on the grounds that he was "too ugly."

yet has come from public relations, advertising, styling, labor relations, dealer relations, consumer relations, or government relations. Those last three berths, in fact, might be called executive doghouses, with Washington being most often the pound from which there is no return.

I find it odd indeed that Detroit should persistently tarnish relations with its dealers by appointing a figurehead to conduct them, usually a former sales vice-president caught more than once with a hundred-day supply of new cars in the pipeline.[10] Incomprehensible best describes sending forth ambassadors without portfolios to deal with either buyers or regulators. From the pervading malcontent of new car buyers[11] sprang the regulators and their regulations which, in turn, have cost Detroit $35 billion to date, a figure that is rising at the rate of perhaps $5 billion annually. This latter sum exceeds by far the combined annual net profits of the four major U.S. auto manufacturers and, of course, new car and truck buyers account for almost all the gross income from which that net is derived.

Detroit employs Gatling guns instead of missiles to defend these vital areas. The name of the vice-president for consumer relations *should* be better known to the public than that of the president or chairman; the fact is, after a brief flurry of appointments some years ago ("Our Man in Detroit"), there is no longer any vice-president responsible *solely* for consumer relations. In further fact, except at the staff level in General Motors where no consumer can reach him, there are not even any vice-presidents for service, only managers, despite that function being the root from which most consumer-related problems have grown. So, lacking strength, purpose, and commitment here, the stature of the titular heads in the Washington offices of the car manufacturers is academic. Richard M. Nixon would be equally frustrated and for the same reason were he to become a lobbyist. Believability would be absent.

Those who fall from the pinnacle in Detroit and then disap-

[10] The "pipeline" is the count of new cars on hand from shipping point to and including the showroom floor. Sixty-days supply is considered workable, forty to fifty days desirable.

[11] A mid-1977 Harris Poll, it will be remembered, showed "more people dissatisfied with car manufacturers . . . than with any other industry . . ."

pear into forced retirement, academia, or the managing of their accumulated bonuses and stock options share one attribute. They are, one and all, nice guys. Their minds were never able to cope with the jackals around them. They lacked ability to react instinctively and instantly when their territories or prerogatives were threatened from within or without. They failed to comprehend the inherent insecurity of the pecking order. As in the animal world, the dominant males of the Detroit tribe are constantly threatened. They relax at their peril. Compassion is unknown.

If the Detroit press corps were to pick its favorite executive, basing the selection on integrity, openness, compassion, and contribution, the unanimous candidate would undoubtedly be Louis G. Seaton, vice-president of personnel for General Motors from 1957 until his retirement in 1970. Few persons outside of the industry and the labor movement have heard of Lou Seaton except, perhaps, Detroit bartenders and waiters, who would surely remember him as the most noble tipper of his generation. But his legacy was greater than that. He represented bellwether management, General Motors, during the period when that bellwether unionist, Walter Reuther, was piecing together, contract by contract, the ultimate wage and benefit package for fellow members of the United Automobile Workers. All the milestone provisions—supplemental unemployment benefits, guaranteed annual wage, cost of living allowance, and cradle-to-grave security—ultimately came from those two men facing each other across the bargaining table. Seaton saw it as his duty to resist excess but to give what was right and just if it could be afforded, most particularly those provisions in each new contract that bolstered the dignity and self-worth of the laboring man.

Seaton and Reuther were an empathetic duo despite the antagonism of negotiations and the impossibility of fraternizing away from them. And of the two, Seaton had the tougher job. Reuther hardly bothered to inform UAW members about what was to be demanded next, the grand strategy; Seaton, however, had to sell his management, not to mention the rest of the industry, every painful inch of the way. Toward the end, he was able to give without permission for he knew better than the chairman and to the finest nuance what would be acceptable to and workable for both sides. More significantly, he was eventually able to resist without permission, which could and sometimes did lead to a costly strike.

Toward the end of each negotiation, bargaining would proceed around the clock until one or the other side approached exhaustion. But Seaton's marathon had only begun. He would slip out a back door, get word to his friends on the press where he could be found, and then host a liquid briefing session of epic proportion. Never once did he disclose a confidential facet of the negotiation; rather, he would explain how it worked, delineate the goals, and point out just where each side had set up its barricades. From that and if they did their homework, the more astute members of the press could report intelligently on the progress or lack of it, even though, as was the practice, they were barred from the negotiating room. Both Reuther and management knew this was going on and neither voiced an objection despite the existence of an official news blackout. As a matter of fact, GM absorbed Lou Seaton's enormous expense account without a murmur, however unpalatable the printed results of his spending might be.

Of the rest, I can think of very few in the modern auto industry who rose to a stature above and beyond their presidencies and chairmanships. George Romney was one, the only one ever, aside from a warped Henry Ford, Sr., who could seriously think of himself as a candidate for the presidency of the United States. Robert McNamara, who has been Secretary of Defense and now is head of the World Bank, was another. Arjay Miller, who is Dean of the Graduate School of Business at Stanford University, is perhaps a third. And to be sure, there are the Ford Foundation, the Sloan Fellowships, and the Sloan-Kettering Institute for Cancer Research, which have channeled money made from the manufacture of automobiles into good works for mankind, but good works late in life have salved many a torn conscience or, as in the case of the Ford Foundation, diverted family finances away from the tax collector. More typical is Frederic G. Donner, who thirteen years after his retirement as chairman still feels compelled to drop in at GM's New York offices every week or so to see how things are going. Who is the more fulfilled, he or the pensioner selling apples in front of the building?

CHAPTER 10

Vice-President, Sales

Newsmen who have covered the automobile industry over a period of years still shudder when reminded of a gentleman named G. Raymond Jones. "Rocket" Jones, as he was called, was sales manager for Oldsmobile Division of General Motors during the mid-fifties and as such hosted the most boring though probably the most expensive new car introductions in memory. Subjecting the press to a two-hour show, complete with a Broadway cast and original music, that was primarily written to fire dealers with enthusiasm, was not uncommon in those days. Some of these shows even managed to be fairly entertaining, particularly when the cast happened to include rising or fading stars of musical comedy who found themselves between roles on the legitimate stage.

The Oldsmobile productions, though, featured Mr. Jones in the lead role and while a salesman he was, an actor and a singer he was not. In fact, he was about the same off stage as on, a sort of Earl Scheib selling cars instead of painting them. It took twenty-one years for my memory to dim sufficiently to buy my first Oldsmobile. And that was despite my wife coming to me from D. P. Brothers' advertising agency where she was secretary to the Oldsmobile account executive. She didn't like the cars either, not incidentally because she was sometimes expected to sit on his lap after hours while he and the rest of the creative staff tipsily composed new verses for "In My Merry Oldsmobile," that hoary tune being the theme for the then current commercials.

At the other extreme during the same era was the $10,500 Lincoln Continental Mark II and its sales manager, Doug McClure. He temporarily transformed the now burned-down Ford Rotunda in Dearborn into an indoor version of a Parisian sidewalk cafe and the introduction of this most expensive of all domestic cars at the time was incidental to fine food, wine, and entertainment. McClure quietly announced early in the evening that orders were on hand for every Continental to be produced that first year, about two thousand in all, and everyone relaxed. I also believe the occasion marked the first time ever that alcoholic beverages had been openly served on Ford Motor Company property, an act that wrote finish to any influence teetotaling Henry Ford, Sr. might still have exerted five years after his death.

The point, however, is that the Oldsmobile was and remains a viable venture while the Mark II went down the tube before its second year was out. Rocket Jones personified, or perhaps burlesqued, the typical new car dealer; the much younger McClure was totally removed from reality. Somewhere between the two lies an approach to selling that would combine success without excess. Detroit has fumbled for this since the automobile was invented.

It is usually quite unfair to judge the excellence of the sales vice-president at any auto manufacturer by the number of units sold in a given year. His performance is largely thwarted, or enhanced, by influences beyond his control. The most independent of these and unpredictable for more than a few months in advance is the state of the national and free-world economies. The world and the United States are really one to the Detroit multinationals. And almost equally independent in its formation is consumer attitude, or "confidence." This is sounded regularly for the industry by the University of Michigan, as well as by captive economists, but who really knows what motivates the consumer? A decision not to buy could stem from rejection the night before in the bedroom as readily as from concern over unrest in Rhodesia or Iran. Consumers as a group are simply not rational. For example, our long-range reaction to the 1973–74 energy crisis was to go out and buy the biggest car possible because, soon, none but relatively small cars would be available.

The sales vice-president is also victimized, or made a hero, by the styling and engineering departments of his company, either separately or collectively. The combined talents of Phineas Taylor Barnum and Earl "Madman" Muntz[1] couldn't sell AMC's Pacer to people who think it's funny-looking. Neither could this duo move the Lincoln Versailles, which costs around $10,500 in today's currency, to buyers who sense it, and correctly so, to be little more than a gussied-up version of the $5,500 Ford Granada. Then outside critics, however unjust, may unpredictably zero in on a particular model, as witness what Ralph Nader single-handedly did to Chevrolet's Corvair.

Safety, in fact, presents as good an illustration as any of the sales vice-president's dilemma. Long experience tells him that safety as such is not a highly motivating feature in the U.S. marketplace. Volvo and Saab have both attempted to transplant Swedish awareness of safety to their products' promotion here with indifferent success. Perhaps forty thousand safety-conscious Americans buy Volvos each year and half that number, Saabs, with either total representing failure by Detroit standards. Buyers take the safety of American products for granted, being shaken in their faith only when a specific nameplate suffers concentrated criticism. Pinto with its proved-to-be-defective gas tank and the Omni/Horizon twins with their allegedly unstable steering are examples of recent attacks which were successfully repulsed, at least to the degree that these models have survived.

Consumer Reports apparently lacks Ralph Nader's clout, even though he is on the board of that publication's parent organization. Its widely publicized condemnation of Omni/Horizon handling by staff testers even failed to impress the National Highway Traffic Safety Agency, which issued a press release pointing out the unlikelihood of owners yanking violently back and forth on the steering wheel and expecting the car to return to its original course of its own accord. However, Richard K. Brown, Chrysler's top sales executive at the time, never knew

[1] Self-styled madman Earl Muntz of Los Angeles was once the world's largest Kaiser dealer.

how many Omni/Horizon sales were lost directly or indirectly from the incident.

Precise definitions, or job descriptions, of sufficient clarity to distinguish the sales function from what are variously called marketing, sales promotion, and merchandising in the auto companies are not to be found. Marketing usually carries a vice-presidency while the other two exist in name at a lower staff level. All three normally report to sales, though it may seem that this stream flows uphill. Let's cite a not-too-fictitious example:

Management prices its line of intermediate-size cars and tells sales that 350,000 must be sold during the model year to realize a reasonable profit. The break-even point is 300,000 cars. Enter now the marketing, sales promotion, and merchandising people, who must do the work. Marketing conducts surveys and finds the sporty models in the line attract youngish professionals on the fringe of affluency; the plusher sedans are profit-poor because they will in the main be discounted to the rental and leasing markets; as many station wagons as ever will still go to families who are convinced they need them to haul a load of grass seed and fertilizer once a year; and, to round out the picture, a trickle of bare-bone sedans will be bought by retirees who have outlived their present cars and by the Bell Telephone Company for use by top executives. From this information marketing decides it must bolster the line's performance image, so secret arrangements are made to subsidize a prominent stock car racing team.

Marketing, however, is troubled by a recurring fact of life in the auto industry. This is that once the introductory hoop-a-la is over, dealers are theoretically free to ignore the line or any model in it. They may in substantial numbers decide to concentrate on the more profitable full-size line from the same maker. After all, suggested retail prices of the two lines overlap substantially and there's a 21 percent spread between the cost to the dealer of a full-size car and its sticker versus 19 percent for the intermediate. One obvious way to solve the problem is to increase the spread for the intermediate by offering secret rebates to dealers who order them in quantities above specified minimums. That, however, can cost $100 a car and unless the dealer passes the rebate on to the retail customer, sales stimulation is zero.

So sales promotion steps in with ideas costing only $20 a car. One is to swamp the morning game shows on TV with free cars for prizes. Another is to paint two thousand cars black and silver exclusively for dealers in Los Angeles County, as they won't know that batches of identical cars were sent on a similarly exclusive basis to the other nine major markets in the country. Still another is to have the governors of the fifty states simultaneously declare Tuesday, March 10, to be "Dodge Day" and award $200 to the parents of all babies born during the twenty-four-hour period. That last is a good one and will predictably cost $240,000, give or take a few babies! At least some of the parents can be expected to put their winnings down on a new Dodge. None of these ideas are original but they will be used again and again, as will some permutation of letting all the adult residents of Spirit, Wisconsin, drive new AMC Spirits free for a week during the introductory period.

Merchandising, meanwhile, has prepared an elaborate guidebook for retail salesmen which explains the "all-new" features incorporated in the line and gives answers to questions that may be anticipated from prospects. And there'll be questions, too, for most of the features are neither new nor unique. So to make the package more palatable, there are included banners for the showroom, handout literature, and mattes and scripts for advertising the product at the local level. All the dealer has to do is to insert his name. Merchandising is an annoyance to management, for it's a nonprofit operation; the dealer buys this stuff at cost if he can be persuaded to buy it at all. What he should be buying is shoe leather, which I'll discuss in a moment.

Unfortunately, however, the luck of the track is such that the new car doesn't win any races. Hertz unexpectedly switches to Ford products. Four-wheel drives have become the new toys of suburbia. Ma Bell embarks on an austerity program to justify a requested rate increase, so its executives are put into compacts. Only the newly engineered turbo-powered sport coupe is selling and there simply aren't enough to go around. At this point midway in the season the sales vice-president realizes once again that marketing, sales promotion, and merchandising, while they may augment good old-fashioned salesmanship, are not a substitute for it. And he is in a quandary because neither he nor his dealers nor their salesmen have ever rung a doorbell in quest of a sale in their working lives. So he gathers unto him his statisticians and sets out to prove in a report to top management why the current economy favors full-size cars, compacts, and light trucks but that intermediates will come into their own next year.

Detroit operates on the theory that sooner or later you and I will need a new car and when that time comes we will go on down to someone's showroom. The entire sales emphasis is on changing the word "need" to "want" and, of course, we are directed to a specific make by constantly exposing us not to the car itself but to pictures of it and words about it. Can you imagine the Fuller Brush Company, Avon, or Shaklee prospering with these techniques? Oddly, top Shaklee sales people are urged on by the incentive of a company Lincoln to use as their own, and the fact is, they could be selling Lincolns, more than have ever been sold before, just by going door to door with one. Or Chevettes, depending on the neighborhood.

I mentioned the difficulty in separating sales and marketing functions and it may just be a matter of semantics. For example, our tale just told, of disaster with intermediates, describes titles and job functions that fit any General Motors car division except that the head of sales at the division level is a manager, not a vice-president. Corporately, though, the sales vice-president reports to the marketing vice-president. American Motors calls it marketing, too; Chrysler and Ford, sales. But whatever it's called, the system relies on the consumer's coming to it rather than its going to the consumer.

Annual inspirational sales exhortations of the type once staged by Rocket Jones, though perhaps more sophisticated, are still relied upon by Detroit, and by the importers as well,[2] to introduce the new cars to dealers, who cheerfully pay their own expenses to attend. Their motive, however, is not to be inspired. The shows offer a rare opportunity, perhaps the only one, to mingle with factory executives. They won't see these executives again that year except in an emergency, so if a dealer wants a more favorable car allotment, or postponement of a "suggestion"

[2] Nearly every key American executive in the import organizations came from the domestic auto industry, a majority from Ford, so techniques vary hardly at all.

that he move his facilities into a new building, or to protest the rumored establishment of a factory-financed minority store in a nearby neighborhood, then is the time to do it. Thus, why should dealers be expected to go to their customers when the factory won't come to them? There is, to be sure, a factory field force in each sales region, but the mission of these people is "dealer development," a term meaning you expand or we'll find another dealer who can. "Sales training" consists of advice on how to close a reluctant pigeon, techniques of finagling high-risk financing from equally reluctant lending institutions, methods of camouflaging the true condition of used cars, and ways to discourage customers from pursuing warranty claims. Again, other than by advertising and promotion, no attention whatever is paid to the cultivation of prospects away from the showroom floor.

It would be interesting if American Motors were to experiment with taking its products to the customer. I suggest AMC because I don't believe the others are capable of an effort sincere enough to measure meaningfully. For the same reasons of *laissez-faire*, I would further suggest limiting AMC's experiment to its passenger cars and not include the Jeeps, which are firmly entrenched as leaders in their field. After all, the proof would lie with meritorious products that are a distant fourth in sales simply because AMC has fewer and smaller showrooms, a relatively minuscule advertising and promotion budget, and, let's face it, the lurking image that it might not be around tomorrow to service what it sells today. Lastly, my suggestion should not be bastardized in its execution by incentives such as the chance to win a trip to Hawaii for two if you just take a demonstration ride. It would mean that AMC's retail salesmen would start knocking on doors or, at the least, telephoning for an appointment to show up, complete with demo, at the prospect's home at a time of the latter's convenience.

What success American Motors enjoys today may very well hinge on its still unique Buyer Protection Plan, a product warranty so simple and complete in its final form, and, incidentally, extendable for a modest fee, that the other manufacturers have been unable or unwilling to imitate it. The Plan, introduced in 1972, focuses on eliminating annoyances and arguments associated with the nonroutine servicing of your new car. Inoperative door handles and bubbles under the paint receive the same priority as a defective transmission. And if the repair requires leaving the car overnight, you are given a free loaner. If it happens away from home, you are recompensed for lodging and meals. In essence, AMC wants you to be happy with your purchase and BPP puts teeth into this wish at the dealer level. The others with their lesser warranties can only hope you're happy, knowing full well that statistical probabilities assure a percentage of you are not. Odd, isn't it, that an effort to keep all owners happy rates as unique?

AMC suffers from another closet image that has troubled its marketing people from the company's formation in 1954. This is that Ramblers and their successors have never enjoyed continuing appeal to the performance-minded, an intangible group also known as the youth market. It's not loss of a sale to an individual hot rodder that hurts, it's the loss of an unknown number of sales due to the influence that kid exerts as the car expert in his neighborhood. When youths of all ages were into four-on-the-floor muscle cars, AMC was late and short with its entries. Now, of course, youths have been driven by usurious insurance premiums into domestic vans and light pickup trucks imported from Japan and again AMC has nothing resembling such currently "in" vehicles to offer. These facts are certainly no revelation to AMC's marketing people. They simply illustrate a dilemma unique to that company and, to a lesser extent, Chrysler. Constriction of offerings bred by shortages of money and resources forces specialization which, in AMC's case, is concentrated on economy cars. That, in turn, establishes an image, for better or worse and, I ask, is stodgy frugality an asset or a cross?[3]

Two major recent movies, each based on best-selling novels,[4] have been made about Detroit and both revolve their plots around a company struggling along fourth in a field of four—ob-

[3] AMC in 1980 will offer four-wheel-drive versions of its current Concord intermediate, to be called the "Eagle," but these are not likely to appeal to the youth market.

[4] *Betsy* by Harold Robbins, Simon & Schuster, New York, 1971; *Wheels* by Arthur Hailey, Doubleday & Company, Garden City, N.Y., 1971.

viously AMC. The scenarios are essentially the same. A dedicated executive vice-president battles from boardroom to bedroom and back against all odds to bring into being a revolutionary car that will dramatically reverse the corporate image. AMC's real-life Roy D. Chapin, Jr., must have squirmed when he saw himself portrayed as a shakily ancient, stubbornly crochety founding patriarch standing four-square against change. He is a patrician in manner and breeding, as his father organized Hudson Motor Company, an AMC predecessor, but that's where the resemblance ends. Nor is or was Gerald C. Meyers, AMC's present chairman but once the executive vice-president, Chapin's son-in-law. Both would love to have a "Betsy" in the line but they were forced to settle on a less flashy, more probable route to survival; namely, stodgily frugal Spirits, Concords, and Pacers, which, no matter how dressed-up, are dumpy cars for dumpy middle-aged America.

Fortunately, there are people passing through middle age all the time and an average of two hundred thousand of them buy AMC's passenger cars annually, just enough for this facet of the company's activities to break even or, at worst, for the loss incurred by car production to be manageable. But the future looks dull despite an agreement with France's Regie Renault to manufacture and market some of that firm's economy cars in this country. It seemed dull enough, in fact, not to make the company's acknowledged marketing whiz and father of the Buyer Protection Plans, William R. McNealy, Jr., too put out when Meyers was chosen over him for the top job at AMC. McNealy, in AMC's first major executive upheaval ever, quietly absconded to the presidency of AMF, a highly diversified and unrelated manufacturer of products ranging from automated bowling alleys to street sweepers.

What keeps AMC in business is the Jeep, a property acquired in the 1960s that somehow survived the late Henry Kaiser's venture into the automobile industry. Unfortunately, however, Jeep's burgeoning output—five to six times the thirty-six thousand units per annum at the time of the acquisition—offers no lessons in salesmanship. Jeeps sell themselves despite intense competition because there is probably no more familiar trademark anywhere in the world.[5] Further, Jeep's reputation and stature haven't been rubbed off on the passenger car lines; for example, AMC's new Spirit is not presented as "a rugged new car by the makers of the world-famous Jeep."

In fact, the acquisition of Jeep Corporation was vigorously opposed by many AMC executives, including Gerry Meyers, who was then in charge of manufacturing. His objections were pragmatic. The single Jeep assembly plant in Toledo, Ohio, was ancient and its equipment was obsolete. Nor could he visualize the totally different Jeep coming down the assembly line interspaced with passenger cars in AMC's other plants. The marketing people were equally unenthusiastic, as a majority of Jeep dealers handled it as a sideline to some other make of passenger car. Shuffling of franchises is an expensive proposition for both factories and dealers and many of the latter could barely justify the necessary new signs, much less stocking service parts. Fortunately, however, poverty precluded changing the Jeep itself beyond switching to AMC-made engines and that, in turn, solved most of the parts problems. The union was indeed fortuitous for both parties but, in terms of marketing, they continue to dine at separate tables.

Reluctance throughout the industry to ring doorbells has its foundation in the sellers' market that prevailed as an aftermath of World War II car shortages. Salesmen just sat around taking orders and when the market was finally satiated in the early fifties, factories and dealers alike began the enticements that would bring you into the showroom. The present generation of car salesmen, whether vice-presidents or trainees at the retail level, knows no other way. There is, admittedly, sincere effort devoted to creating products you say—through surveys—that you want. But in times of emergency, due either to a slowdown in

---

[5] Origin of the name "Jeep" is obscure. Some say it was a convenient acronym for GP (General Purpose) which was the vehicle's official military designation. Then the popular *Popeye* cartoon strip featured a character called Jeep long before the vehicle was designed. However, Willys-Overland Motors successfully claimed its president, Joseph W. Frazer, who was later to be half of Kaiser-Frazer, coined the name in 1942 and was thus able to copyright it. AMC inherited the rights with the acquisition of Kaiser Industries, successor to Willys. Anyone failing to capitalize "Jeep" in his writings will shortly be in receipt of a nasty note from AMC's legal department.

the economy or a backlog of products that are off target, the promotions and eventually the price cutting begin. The closest the industry ever comes to personalized selling is at auto shows, where salesmen willing to man the exhibits are usually the same few who are willing to follow through with a phone call to showgoers who have expressed interest. Unfortunately, though, only about 15 percent of the potential market in a given year will attend auto shows.

I have in front of me a magazine put out by Toyota for its dealers and featured in it are winners of the monthly "Sales Accelerators" contest for December 1978. Their tactics, so pleasing to management, are typical of the industry, as witness the dealer in Georgetown, South Carolina, who captured Eastern honors for his "First Annual Egg Drop." A local disc jockey sat 130 feet in the air atop a rented crane and dropped raw eggs into a crowd of 300 while he broadcast the results live. Catcher of the most unbroken eggs won a cash prize.[6] In the Deep South a Columbus, Mississippi, dealer offered a year's free use of a Corolla for the first person to negotiate a ten-mile course down the nearby Tombigbee River in an innertube. The magazine notes that the dealership's sales staff was on hand to "answer questions and pass out brochures" but that "there was no selling during the race." And finally, first place West went to a dealer who rented Seattle's Kingdome to stage the "World Indoor Paper Airplane Championship." A claimed six thousand participants in the upper deck of the domed stadium aimed airplanes at a new Celica on the turf below, each hoping that one of theirs would be first through the open sunroof to win the car. It was a pretty safe bet for the dealer; no mention was made of anyone winning.

Detroit's concept of a super salesman is one who can think up the biggest and best stunts, which, on rare occasions when they involve the car, can be quite effective. Certainly the cars provided thrill show operators and, seen by millions careening around on two wheels and leaping from ramp to ramp through a ring of fire at state and county fairgrounds, leave a lasting impression of durability and performance for the make involved.

[6] The winning landing pad: a pair of panty hose attached to the frame of a tennis racket.

Chrysler once attempted to break Cadillac's stranglehold on the prestige car market by long-term loans of Imperials to bankers and other influential citizens in communities across the nation. Lincoln until recently got visibility by leasing presidential limousines for a dollar a year to the government and even built a special with a rear-facing, open throne for two days' use by Pope Pius XII when he visited the United States.[7] My favorite stunt, however, didn't sell many cars of record. Promoter Jim (Ice Boxes to Eskimos) Moran, when he was a consultant to Studebaker, outfitted an entire African tribe in cuttings from the upholstery used by that company, and what it proved, not even he could explain.

Many millions are spent annually by Detroit on what might be called goody-gumshoe promotions, much as though the manufacturers were obligated by law like broadcasting networks (which they aren't) to include a specified measure of public service in their messages. All makes vie with each other in cooperation with dealers to provide free cars for high school driver training programs, and the motive, aside from tax write-offs, is obvious. Chevrolet staged a national "Soap Box Derby" for years until cheating by the parents of the kids entered became flagrantly embarrassing. Ford held an annual event at which parents could do nothing but watch, it being the "Punt and Pass" contest with the winners receiving scholarships to colleges of their choice. Plymouth, more on target, tries to relieve the shortage of mechanics with its nationwide "Trouble Shooting" competition, at first restricted to vocational high school students but now including inmates of selected prisons and penitentiaries.

No promotion, though, quite matches in effectiveness or glamor factory participation in professional automobile racing.[8] This reached its height back in 1965–67 when Ford staged an all-out, mostly successful assault on every prestigious world title. And it's expensive, because most titles, such as the Grand Touring championship at Le Mans, require that a specified number of identical cars must be available for sale to the public. Thus, Ford

[7] One waggish magazine editor (me) captioned the handout picture: "Pius trolls for converts."
[8] Paid attendance at auto racing in this country is exceeded only by the horses and would be first if betting were allowed.

found itself briefly in the race car business, having to sell forty replicas of the winning Le Mans cars at $24,000 each, a figure representing but a fraction of what it cost to hand-build them. To satisfy National Association for Stock Car Auto Racing (NASCAR) requirements, at least two thousand duplicates of each engine type or special body style entered had to be available to the public. But winning races did sell a lot of Fords and so, too, did Plymouth's "Super Bird"[9] sell a lot of Plymouths. Having one's nameplate out on the NASCAR tracks, in full view of God and fans and in recognizable form, rubs off on showroom models to give them a pizzazz they might or might not deserve. Factory-subsidized racing teams are still running despite Ralph Nader, the official disapproval of the industry's own Motor Vehicle Manufacturers Association and the precipitous rise in insurance rates that, incidentally, never dropped when the true muscle cars were discontinued.

Today, as always, two purchases loom large in the average family's budget. The largest is the home, but even it can be almost matched by the cumulative total spent on automobiles. For the single person who may live in an apartment, the automobile is the largest. Yet, the atmosphere surrounding a real estate transaction is generally qualitative, while the sale of an automobile is too often quantitative, fraught throughout with mistrust and suspicion on both sides. It is called a "deal" and it lacks dignity. It is a contest of wits during which the baser aspects of each participant's nature emerges. And the entire weight of factory know-how is on the dealer's side. Suggested list prices, itemized on the stickers required by law, are meaningless. The dealer is even reluctant to accept cash because both he and his factory are in the financing and insurance businesses. Some customers may enjoy the flea-market atmosphere fostered by factory pressures, but most don't, as is proved by surveys which consistently rate the industry and its dealers about on a par with fleas.

I've occasionally wished I could afford a Rolls-Royce, not be-

[9] Plymouth in 1969 experienced aerodynamic problems with its stock cars in NASCAR races so a giant spoiler was added to the rear deck along with a nose cone in front. NASCAR rules required that two thousand of these "Super Birds" be sold to the public but there were few takers for the grotesque machines.

cause I like the car or think they're worth the $45,000 and up asked for them, but because of the alternative way they are sold. And it's perhaps significant that at dealerships where Cadillacs or Lincolns are handled in addition to less costly makes, the salesman specializing in the premium car is a breed apart. He and the customer enjoy the instant communication of having both "arrived." There is courtesy, at least to customers who qualify, and sometimes a measure of trust. Haggling is genteel. Your trade-in is "previously owned," not used. You've moved to the top; you "command" a Cadillac. With the Rolls, you're assumed to be already there. You're investing, not spending, your money but you've been taken as surely as if, one day, your heirs opt to display you in a solid copper casket.

Each of these makes I've mentioned has built its reputation on quality of product, but of the three only the Rolls can justify its fat price tag. That justification is handcraftsmanship which, I hasten to note, guarantees nothing of itself except high cost. Lincolns and Cadillacs, on the other hand, are mass-stamped from the same steel, upholstered in the same cloths, and powered by essentially the same engines as Fords and Chevrolets. There is no reason whatever to expect one to serve longer than another in its trek from showroom to junkyard. You've been victimized by a process known in the trade as "upgrading." In fact, it's quite possible to equip a Chevrolet Caprice with all the options already standard on a Cadillac and pay about the same for the cars.

Sales managers for middle-priced makes such as Mercury and Buick spend a major share of their time plotting how to catch you on your way up. Chevrolet and Ford sales managers hope to hold you and, indeed, most of us could spend a car-owning lifetime trading up from Chevette or Fiesta on through the many in-between models to the ultimate Monte Carlo or Thunderbird. You *belong* in a Versailles, says the Lincoln-Mercury salesman to the Monarch owner, it's only $75 more a month. And that seems like peanuts to the average pigeon, so he's moved up. Then he wonders why the legroom is no greater and why the trunk won't hold any more. As I've mentioned, it's because the body shells are interchangeable, identical one to the other in nearly every di-

VICE-PRESIDENT, SALES 169

mension. The salesman had only one thing working for him in this sale—your vanity.

The sales vice-president may exist who is disturbed by the selling techniques in vogue for the past three decades. If so, he keeps his doubts to himself because the system so far has worked. At one end of the period, Americans stood in line to buy cars knowing the price would be padded by unneeded accessories and, in many instances, an under-the-table cash persuader. At the other end, which is now, customers in near record numbers allow their intelligence and sometimes their persons to be insulted and each places himself or herself in this position on the average of once every three years. No degree of malpractice seems able to destroy this nation's love affair with cars. We dutifully lie down on the showroom floor with our legs spread, where perhaps if we kept them crossed, we might find ourselves courted once again.

CHAPTER 11

The Take-Over House

No group of yachtsmen complain more loudly. The automobile dealer hovers forever on the verge of bankruptcy, he would have you think, only to emerge with a bright new franchise and debt on the other side of town. He hasn't rung a doorbell in forty years and thus he couldn't sell a prepaid burial plan if he had exclusive rights for all of Florida. He hates the factory that feeds him, but he has never been known to jeopardize his franchise on behalf of his customers. And he calls these customers pigeons, as we know, though he's hurt when they vote him the least respected businessman in his community. A damning indictment? Not really. The most visible dealers, those who project the image of their fraternity, fit this description quite accurately even if they are, in fact, a minority.

Fifty years ago in any but the largest of cities, there was but one kind of automobile dealership. Pa held the franchise and did the selling, Ma could be found tending the books, and Junior spent his afternoons and school vacations back in the service department under the tutelage of an old-time doctor of motors. And the phone books in each town listed a lot more dealers in domestic makes in those days because, in addition to the usual Ford, Chevrolet, and Plymouth outlets, local citizens derived both a living and respect from representing such then viable nameplates as Hupmobile, Graham, Franklin, and Auburn. Hudson was the No. 4 seller in most places. Studebaker, Nash, and Packard franchises were gilt-edged properties, good for expansion loans at any bank. But most important of all, Pa had to face you, his customer, when he passed you on the sidewalk, saw you at the drugstore, or sat next to you in church. You were a name to him and he to you. If your car wasn't running well, he'd loan you your pick from among the latest trade-ins while yours was fixed. He might even give you his new demo for the weekend, hoping you'd notice the substantial, quite visible improvements made that year, and every year. The only meaningful warranty was Pa's reputation. He was unlikely to dissemble because it wasn't the Fords or Auburns he sold that made you come back, it was Pa.

It would be chauvinistic to suggest that Detroit could return to the selling techniques of 1929, because today a sevenfold increase in volume is handled by a third as many dealers. Instead of thirty or forty new car sales a year, a typical dealer today will see three or four hundred. However, the principles that generated respect for Pa in his community need not have been abandoned. Here again, one would think American Motors would be in the best position to nurture closer, more personal relationships between its relatively small number of passenger-car dealers and their customers, but there apparently is no recognition at the top of any such need. Let me quote Dave Smith, editor of *Ward's Auto World*, interviewing chairman Roy Chapin of AMC in December 1977:

"With concern about AMC's future, how would you characterize your dealer situation? Have you been able to hang on to your good dealers?" asked Smith.

"Bill Luneburg just got back from a week on the East Coast and a week on the West Coast, meeting with dealers," Chapin replied. "He says their attitude is very enthusiastic. Concord seems to be doing what we had hoped it would—bringing in showroom traffic. I just looked at the financial statement, and our dealer profitability is 15 percent higher through September than a year earlier. All in all, the dealer organization is in good shape."

"Have you had much dealer attrition?"

"If you take AMC (passenger car) alone we're down between about fifty and sixty accounts out of a total of sixteen hundred," said Chapin. "Of those, probably half would have been ones that we would've taken out anyway."

"Small ones?" pursued Smith.

"The ones that just weren't getting the job done," came the reply. "If you've got somebody on a five-hundred-car planning potential point and he's selling ninety cars a year, you're better off without him."

"Have you signed up any important dealers in the last year?"

"We just signed up one right here in Southfield, Michigan," Chapin answered. "He's a Honda dealer and now he's also an AMC dealer."

Chapin's side of this exchange seems significant in retrospect. One can hardly argue AMC's need for and concern with volume. Less understandable is the eagerness to dual with an "important" Honda dealer, for the two makes are directly competitive in price and function. In fact, AMC's offerings just might suffer from the side-by-side comparison. And then the meaning of "planning potential" should be probed when no matter how hard the salesman might push a Spirit or a Pacer, the customer is just a few feet and no dollars away from a perhaps more desirable Honda Civic or Accord.

Smith's last question was: "Does that symbolize anything? Honda and AMC under one roof?"[1]

Chapin's answer: "No, I think he's a smart dealer. That's one of the reasons he's so successful."

Not once in this outline of what's expected from the holder of a franchise representing the nation's weakest automaker is there any mention made of the customer, just smart dealers and, by inference, dumb dealers. Volume is king and the tactics used to obtain it are seldom questioned. This now Honda-AMC dealer may, for all I know, enjoy an excellent reputation for fairness and service in his trading area around Southfield, but whether he does or not did not seem to be a primary factor in his appointment. Nor is it cause for lifting a franchise. Dealers are canceled by their factories for but one reason—failure to meet planning potential. Related "faults" leading to termination include uninviting (that is, old) facilities; failure to move with neighborhood

[1] Throughout 1977, rumor had it that AMC and Honda were talking merger.

trends (that is, follow the white middle class to suburbia); refusal to engage in questionable sales tactics (that is, upgrade customers beyond their ability to pay); and, reluctance or unwillingness to help balance factory inventories (that is, reluctance to finance the factory's mistakes). I know of no instance of a factory beating the district attorney to first terminate a dealer for padding service bills, misrepresenting merchandise or placing misleading ads. Tactics bordering on fraud are encouraged, or at least condoned, because they breed volume. And thus was created what is known in the trade as the "Take-Over" house.

The T.O. method of selling relies on constant pressure, moving you through sometimes several echelons of salesmen, each responsible for a step in the procedure that finally finds you sharing a tiny cubicle with the "closer." When you eventually stagger out, you'll probably (no one is supposed to leave without buying) have contracted for much more car than you had intended to buy, at a lot more money than you intended to spend. The difference between your actual resources and what they took you for will be stretched "painlessly" out for forty-eight instead of twelve or twenty-four months. Sometimes half of this total sum will represent interest rates just legally short of usury, overly expensive and excessive insurance coverage, multiple commissions and, possibly, an extended warranty of dubious value. It will be at least a year, due to the small down payment, before your equity in the car catches up with its cash value and, if the market for used cars sours, that may not happen until the last few months of the contract. You have, in short, been had to a degree that varies with the laws of each state.

The District Attorney for the County of Los Angeles hardly altered my definition of a Take-Over house when he closed down the "World's Largest Buick Dealer" in Torrance late in 1978. Among the three dozen or so malpractices relied on by Lyons Buick that offended the authorities was, to quote the charges, ". . . using a sales technique where more than one sales person is introduced during the sales negotiation with the intent of successively increasing the final selling price." It is indeed refreshing to see the law catch up with a free-swinging dealer but it's only the enforcement that's new. T.O. tactics have been around, undergoing constant refinement, for three decades. Lyons Buick was by no means alone. Every factory has franchised its counterpart in every large city.

How does one recognize a T.O. house? Let me quote more of the charges filed against Lyons Buick:

* Using pictures of vehicles which depict options not included in the advertised price.

* Advertising discounts unless the discount is from the manufacturer's suggested retail price and is clearly and conspicuously disclosed.

* Advertising, soliciting, or representing by any means a product for sale if it is intended to entice a customer into a transaction different from that originally represented.

* Advertising demonstrators as "executive cars."

* Charging or attempting to charge customers for services performed prior to delivery without fully disclosing the fact. Also, passing on this charge when, in fact, the dealer was reimbursed by the manufacturer.

* Selling vehicles at prices higher than advertised during the same period of time in which the ad applied, whether or not the purchaser is or has been informed of the lower price.

* Representing that specific equipment is included in the purchase price, without it being installed and operative at that price.

* Failing to give advertised discounts or rebates.

* Offering vehicles at "cost," "above cost," "below cost," or at any sum related to cost, unless the price of the vehicle (to the dealer) is also disclosed.

* Failing to pay off unpaid balances on a vehicle taken in trade, after the dealership has agreed to do so as an inducement to close the deal.

* Requesting purchasers to sign forms that are not completely filled in and/or which contain blanks.

* Misrepresenting the authority, directly or by implication, of a salesperson or other representative of the dealership to negotiate the final terms of a transaction with a customer. (In other words, the whopping discount or trade-in you've been offered by the salesperson will be reneged on at the last moment by the closer.)

That last charge describes a tactic common to many Take-

Over houses. The pigeon, typically of a minority race and, shall we say, not very sharp in the ways of the white man, parks near the lot. He is immediately approached at curbside and injected with new-car (or used-car) fever by a salesman of the same race who *is* sharp. The customer's primary worry is whether or not he can be financed. That question is dismissed as of no concern by this first salesman, who leads his pigeon over to more car than the man can logically afford. He'll end up with even more car than that, for his vanity will be played upon with consummate skill. At this point he enters the first of several cubicles, all of which are bugged, and the original salesman vanishes, as does all semblance of that man's opening promises. The pigeon pleads time for a private discussion with his wife and it too is bugged. By this time, those concerned know all they need about the pigeon's finances, sincerity, and gullibility. He and his wife are ushered to the closing booth and emerge in a bit, clutching a contract they've signed for a car they had no intention of buying at a price that will deprive them and their family of basic necessities for the next four years. The blanks will be filled in later, these being provisions for a chattel mortgage on their personal property in addition to the lien on the car but the property, of course, "must first be inventoried," which is the excuse for the blanks.

So goes the sixteen-hour business day at the Take-Over house; no pigeon, as I've said, is supposed to leave without buying. You may have spotted this store in your neighborhood. Full-page newspaper ads, continued support of old movie reruns on television, impressive multi-acre facilities at a busy intersection, searchlights probing the skies at night, plastic "barrage" balloons hovering by day—the T.O. house must sell a lot of cars to pay for all this. And some are ethical within the limitations of their system. The authorities have tried hard but they've yet to hang a thing on Cal Worthington and his big Dodge and Ford operations in Southern California. Meanwhile, "Ol' Cal" continues his saturation of the tube, occasionally taking righteously indignant pokes at his detractors. And Dodge and Ford do nothing, either, there or anywhere else in the country.

In the middle between Ma and Pa and the Take-Over house stands what is known to the trade as a "quality" dealer. The term is used within the fraternity, not by Detroit, which, of course, likes you to think that all of its dealers qualify. Actually, "quality" describes sales tactics and should not be misconstrued as a guarantee that the dealer's house is in order. Ideally, this kind of dealer is not solely concerned with artificially high volume; instead, he looks upon each phase of his operation as a profit center. Some of the largest dealers eschew T.O. methods but most often the quality dealer will be the one selling between three hundred and eight hundred new cars annually, depending upon the popularity of the make and his so-called planning potential assigned by the factory. That last is simply an optimistic sales quota based on the hoped-for market penetration nationally of the make involved, translated into an equivalent percentage of potential customers within the dealer's trading area. I should note, too, that more than a few dealers who privately abhor T.O. methods are forced into them to protect their franchises and, of course, these are the ones I referred to as ethical within the limitations of the system.

My first move in checking out a dealer for quality (as I understand the word) is to visit his used-car lot. If it's populated by a preponderance of the make for which he's franchised, it tells me his new-car customers are a satisfied group. Then I look at his service department. An impressive array of electronic diagnostic equipment is encouraging, assuming the mechanics know how to operate the machines, but what I seek is evidence of the facilities being patronized by commercial vehicle operators. The best in service costs businessmen far less than a truck or fleet car not earning its keep, which it can't when it's awaiting parts that should have been in stock or when it's back again for repairing previous repairs. The shop catering successfully to fleets is an efficient, reliable shop.

Only then do I enter the showroom, where I hope the salesmen will give me a little time to sit behind the wheel, peer under the hood, slam doors, and kick tires in privacy. I'll give out vibes when I'm ready to deal and when he does approach at a timely moment he'll directly reflect the dealer's way of doing business. Pressure-selling is a skill that's difficult for any but a glib, aggressive individual to master. Others may be trapped into it but they don't stay for long. Associated are faddish dress, cultish mannerisms and, usually, the policy of pairing salesman and customer by ethnic background, which should be of concern only when there's a communication problem. In other words, a quality dealer staffs his showroom with salesmen, whether they be white, black, or green, who know their product; the T.O. house puts priority on the intangibles that may influence a sale.

The quality dealer will appreciate but not insist that you place your financing through him and thus through his bank or sometimes in the case of Ford, GM, and Chrysler, the corporate-owned finance company, because he gets a commission called a reserve which averages around 3 percent on a two-year note. He's also credited indirectly for referred business when he in turn must borrow from that bank. The T.O. house, on the other hand, specializing in high-risk deals, can average a 10.5 percent reserve on three-year notes which when multiplied by their volume can be more significant than the actual profit from car sales. The reserve can climb even higher if an unscrupulous dealer qualifies you as a good risk and sells your note to the lender at a prime 11 percent but *charges you* high-risk interest, his take then being as much as 22 percent over four years. That's what can happen when your only concern is the amount of the monthly payments.

Commissions from insurance placed for you by the dealer when you finance a car through him range from 15 to 20 percent of the premiums for the required collision and comprehensive policies and on up to 40 percent for tempting frills, such as a policy that will pick up your payments if you are sick or injured. These excessively large returns play their part in the juggling that goes on inside the closing cubicles of T.O. houses and, of course, they won't be refused by any dealer.

Factory invoices to the dealer are known as "tissue" in trade jargon and he must pay cash on delivery for his cars. This is usually accomplished by a procedure known as "floor-planning," a sort of floating credit with his bank which enables him to maintain adequate stocks and for which he pays interest at a rate as close to prime as his own credit and the popularity of the car will allow. That is only one of the many costs the dealer must meet to keep his doors open. His needs are obvious, such as other interest payments, the mortgage, utilities, salaries and commissions, amortization of equipment, taxes and advertising. And though all of his ancillary operations, ranging from the service department to daily rentals, are or should be profit centers on their own, the dealer's main source of income stems from the 19 to 25 percent difference between the tissue on his new cars and the suggested retail price itemized on the sticker attached to each of these cars. And, further, since a trade-in is usually involved in a new car sale, the dealer must move the used car and sometimes the trade-in on it before he can pay back the floor-plan loan and realize his profit.

The markup theoretically available within the law[2] ranges from 19 percent for subcompacts like the Chevette to 25 percent for a Cadillac. Most accessories ordered for factory installation are marked up 25 percent on any car while those installed by the dealer command 35 percent. The average customer, bargaining for his new car at "$100 over invoice," fails to realize that the dealer must meet the cost of doing business to stay in business, and it is very much to everyone's advantage for the dealer to be around tomorrow to service what he sells today. A dealer who agrees to such terms is either foolish, philanthropic, or desperate, the latter state usually being precipitated by the bank's withdrawing its floor-planning on cars in stock too long. A dealer must somehow extract from you a price that is at least halfway between tissue and suggested list just to break even unless the particular car you're buying is involved in a factory rebate program. Looked at another way, the dealer must see a reasonable profit in each transaction and he doesn't really care whether it's open and clean in the price you pay for the car or deviously hidden in excessive financing and insurance charges, a deflated trade-in allowance, loading you with accessories, or any combination of these.

General Motors claimed in a recent institutional ad that its dealers, certainly the richest of them all on the average, reported about two cents profit on each dollar of sales in 1978, which, if true, brands them as idiots. Anyone but their accountants would

---

[2] PL 85-506, the "Monrooney Bill" of 1958, requires that the Manufacturer's Suggested Retail Price of each new car and its accessories be affixed to the car. This MSRP is for the customer's information and guidance only; it is not binding on the dealer, who, as an "independent businessman," may raise or lower it at will.

suggest they liquidate their businesses and invest the proceeds in long-term savings certificates, where they could realize 10 percent on their money without ever docking their yachts. But car dealers are not idiots and that two cents on the dollar, while perhaps technically accurate, is entirely misleading to the lay reader at whom the ad was directed. It neglects the dealer's own fat salary[3] and bonus; it omits the "amortization" of his appreciating facilities, the most significant part of which is the dollar value of his franchise; it obscures the fact that cars are a high-ticket item and that 2 percent of 500 cars at $5,000 each is $50,000; and finally, among objections I can think of at the moment, the ad *seems* to be talking about new-car sales, period, so the 2 percent may not reflect substantial profits derived from the dealer's many ancillary activities. In all probability, it proves only that GM dealers are astute businessmen who have no wish to pay a larger corporate income tax than is legally necessary. The high turnover in the dealer body stems from selling out at a handsome profit, not failure. Less than 3 percent each year of this nation's 25,000-plus franchised new-car dealers close their doors for financial reasons and these are readily replaced; the annual fluctuation of the total dealer body is insignificant. No other type of retail business can claim such stability.

My favorite dealership, although unfortunately they don't sell my favorite make, is Thomas Cadillac in the somewhat shabby heart of downtown Los Angeles. This firm, which has been owned by the same family for several generations, operates from an eight-story headquarters built back in the twenties. Above the street-level showroom, four whole floors are devoted to service and another presents selected "pre-owned" Cadillacs. But it's the fifth floor which impresses me because it bespeaks of pride in the product on sale below. It is a museum housing nearly a hundred old Cadillacs, ranging in age from an unrestored 1906 Runabout to a mint 1976 Bicentennial Eldorado convertible. Though the motives of customers who come from all over Southern California may not be nostalgic, it is felt by some that the ghosts of long-gone chauffeurs and their sixteen-cylinder town cars still

---

[3] Later in this chapter I detail the troubles of Chevrolet dealer R. Gordon Butler, who, prior to losing his franchise, paid himself a salary of $275,000 a year!

hover about, reminding the staff of how it was. Perhaps that is why Thomas salesmen wear conservative business suits and sport fresh carnations in their lapels. Harley Earl always did, and this is the same building where, before moving on to Detroit, he and his father designed custom Cadillacs for movie stars. Vicky Thomas, who now heads the organization, is my kind of dealer. I'd pay her full sticker without a quibble, if only she sold four-wheel-drive Land Cruisers or Jeeps. And though I'm certain she'd not allow it, I'd unhesitatingly sign the contract and let her fill in the blanks. A dealership like this can usually be found in any large city, or small town, but not, odds are, in suburbia.

Nowadays if you're black, Chicano, or Cherokee but not, for some reason unknown to me, Chinese or Japanese, it is relatively simple to establish yourself as a franchised new-car dealer. It's even simpler if you're a former professional athlete of any hue. The factories will vie with each other to set you up in what's known as a "company store," and it will probably be located within the trading area of the Ma and Pa or quality dealer whom the factory thinks is not aggressive enough. Your capital investment will be token but you won't be your own boss until the day you buy out. And that won't be easy. Your factory-appointed manager will pour practically all your profits into expansion until, as sometimes happens after a bad year, you're more in debt than when you began. During 1977, according to a publication called *General Motors Public Interest Report,* the number of minority-owned[4] GM car and truck dealerships rose to an all-time high of 128. That's a piddling 1 percent of GM's 11,670 outlets, which is why the headhunters are out in force. The industry has a long way to go and, in my opinion, it's going in the wrong direction. *The minority most trampled on by Detroit is the small businessman.* It is no longer possible, for example, to expand one's gas station into a dealership by selling a dozen new Chevrolets the first year, two dozen the next, and so on. GM will refuse you the franchise and without it you can't get any cars that can be titled as "new."

Another way of becoming a dealer, and from here on in all the ways are hard, is to buy an existing franchise from someone who

[4] Most are not "owned," any more than you own your car until you've made the last payment.

THE TAKE-OVER HOUSE 181

is retiring, or widowed,[5] or in financial difficulties. We're talking here of a point with a 200–300 car planning potential. Most often you'd be buying nothing but inventory, equipment, and that intangible known as "blue sky," for the outgoing dealer would probably wish to lease you his buildings and land. And as to the sky, how blue it is depends entirely on what the community thinks of that dealer. Thus, a deal in financial difficulty is most likely a bum deal with a very murky sky. In any case, the factory would want you to have about $1.00 in cash reserve for every $2.00 you spend or borrow to get into the deal. That means putting $375,000 into a $250,000 operation that consists of nothing but inventory, equipment, and that elusive blue sky. Further, in order to obtain factory approval of the transaction, without which there's no sale, you must somehow have saved this large amount of money by working throughout the early years of your life in the trade, most preferably as a salesman and then manager for someone else or as owner of a used-car lot. Or, of course, you could have a rich aunt or Mafia connections as your hidden source of money but you'd still have to show the experience.

There's a third requirement to obtain factory approval which almost necessitates the rich aunt or some other form of angel. This is that the factory, and GM in particular, will not even look at your application unless you're between thirty and forty years of age. They hope you'll be around for a while despite the obvious strain on one's health from having become half a millionaire before life, as the saying goes, has even begun for you. The only way to waive that one is to become a full millionaire twice over at any age. Then you can establish your own spanking new dealership at a 500-car point for about $1,500,000 plus a $300,000–$500,000 cash reserve plus a bank commitment to floor-plan your inventory. Thus, the root of the social problem between the dealer and his customers becomes apparent; no one can survive in or even enter the business unless he's strongly motivated by avarice.

Ma and Pa would be thoroughly awed if they were to rise

[5] Detroit just recently began begrudgingly to allow widows of dealers six months of grace in which to decide whether to continue operating the franchise themselves or to sell out.

from their graves and tour the facilities of a typical modern dealership. Dozens of employees are needed to keep track of, maintain and sell the 200–300 new cars and 100 or so used cars on hand at all times. There are sales, leasing, business, service, and parts managers, each presiding over a staff of specialists. Mini-computers process orders directly to the factory and internally there really is someone who knows which of the keys fit which of the cars. Where once a mechanic just helped himself to parts as needed, he now must fill out a request and wait for them to be found on the long rows of shelves containing sometimes a $100,000 inventory. A "service salesman" (the automotive equivalent of a knife-happy doctor of medicine) diagnoses your complaint, assigns your car a number, and sends you to the customer lounge, where you are purposely isolated from the mechanic. Actually, mechanics, because, to draw another parallel with medical practice, the man who fixes the brakes won't touch a carburetor. Then when you step to the cashier's window, electronic machines add up labor and material, adjust the running parts inventory, compute commissions, and spew out your final bill while automatically sending reports of each transaction to Detroit. It's all just as impersonal as the dealer himself, who, if he's there at all, is in hiding. I've never known a dealer's office door to be marked, or kept open, or, for some reason, the office itself to have windows facing either in or out. In fact, I've very seldom been in a dealer's office with him there; they are hard men to see. And with good reason, for those customers who seek him out aren't bearing incense and myrrh.

Lyons Buick's losing brush with the law is atypical as yet, representing an unanticipated manifestation of newly strident consumerism in action. Nothing in the charges would have brought more than admonitions from the factory except, perhaps, not paying off the liens on the customers' trade-ins. Franchised dealers are a law-abiding bunch if only because their properties are too valuable to jeopardize by such unimaginative crimes as tax evasion, petty swindling, and knowingly dealing in stolen cars. In fact, most dealers strive to polish their tarnished images by donating cars for driver training, sponsoring Little League teams, and providing transportation for the local beauty queen. It doesn't hurt them financially, however. The factories bear the brunt of the cost for driver-training programs and the rest is tax deductible under the guise of advertising and promotion and, in the case of the yachts and club memberships, the entertainment of important fleet buyers and factory officials. And it is much easier for a civic group to obtain cars from dealers than it is money. What kid, for example, would not be partial to the make in which he earned his first driver's license?

The last really juicy scandal of which I'm aware that involved a franchised new-car dealer was the so-called "Motorgate" affair of 1974. Gordon Butler Chevrolet, Inc., an outlet moving *three thousand units a year* in Lowell, Massachusetts, had aroused factory suspicion by presenting warranty reimbursement claims far in excess of average—about $35,000 worth in January and early February of that year being typical. Chevrolet's area service manager out of Boston, one Frank W. Smith, had been investigating the matter for some time and it might have been forgotten if the dealership had just heeded the warning but instead Smith was found dead one morning floating in the Danver River with a bullet in the back of his skull. During the previous afternoon and evening he had been drinking with two dealership employees, one being the service director, at a local restaurant and the three were seen leaving together. Nevertheless, three weeks went by without an arrest. It was then that the third member of the partying trio, a driver for the dealership and near death himself, told police he had just been stabbed by the service director and another man because he had witnessed the Smith shooting.

In rather odd order, the service director was indicted for fraud against GM, tried and acquitted of the stabbing, and then tried and convicted of "larceny over $100" from GM, for which he was sentenced to three to five years in prison. While in prison, he successfully defended himself against a further charge of "conspiracy to commit larceny." As of the end of 1976, he had yet to be tried for the Smith murder. And somehow in the midst of all his problems, he managed to be accused of an unrelated rape.

The service director was not the only one to end up in court. The conspiracy trial resulted in the dealer himself, a young Columbia Law School graduate whose full name is R. Gordon Butler, being convicted along with another employee, fined $2,500 and sentenced to two years in prison, which he promptly appealed. GM, of course, indignantly canceled Butler's Chevrolet franchise and, in addition, brought suit against him for $600,000, which allegedly represented the actual total of the fraudulent warranty claims. Meanwhile GM descended on its own field offices in the East, firing at least two dozen long-term employees, who admitted under heavy-handed interrogation to as little as accepting Christmas turkeys from dealers. Meanwhile, too, Butler as of 1977 still owned the building from which a new dealer appointed by GM was operating and retained his Toyota dealership, also in Lowell, despite twenty-seven separate counts of mail fraud (sending allegedly false warranty claims through the mail to Toyota Motor Sales U.S.A. Inc.), charges which he denied.

Butler's involvement with Toyota brings to mind an earlier affair which erupted during that importer's rise to the top. The man who directed Toyota's operations in this country from the beginning was a Nisei named Shoji Hattori. The always smiling, suave Hattori, who liked to be called George, couldn't sell Toyota passenger cars at any price until about 1965, when the new Corona model found public favor. Dealers then stood in line clamoring for the franchise which, allegedly, Hattori doled out only to those willing to grease his personal palm. This was an open industry "secret" for about seven years until Hattori, barely one step ahead of the Internal Revenue Service, was summarily yanked back to the parent company's headquarters in Japan for an accounting. He has not been seen in U.S. automotive circles since.

I mention the Hattori affair only to show the two faces of the factory-dealer relationship. It is grounded in suspicion, each for the other. Those who defended R. Gordon Butler in court maintained that padding warranty claims is a practice tolerated by Detroit. Or if that cannot be proved, it is justified by Detroit's arbitrary attitude as to what is and what is not a valid claim. Dealers everywhere unanimously insist they lose money on warranty work, and that argument continues to rage unresolved along with countless other generic disputes involving the franchise system as it exists today. Only one certainty emerges. It is the customer who pays, whether the dealer cheats the factory or the factory cheats the dealer.

CHAPTER 12

The Pitchmen

Time and *Newsweek*, needless to say, have always been hotly competitive publications in every arena in which it is possible for them to compete. They vie with each other for circulation, ad linage, timeliness, depth of coverage and, most importantly, the exclusivity of their cover stories. Of course, certain events and personages have impact that transcends difference for its own sake, examples being the election of a President, the Jonestown Massacre, and Liza Minnelli, but ordinarily even inadvertent duplication of cover stories is unthinkable to either magazine. It does, though, occasionally happen, as witness Ayatollah Ruhollah Khomeini, who made the cover of both on Monday, February 12, 1979. And this too was excusable, for the Ayatollah at that point in time could have triggered a massacre compared to which Jonestown would seem routine. Only once, however, have the two magazines appeared on the same day with cover portraits of the same business executive puffing forth cigar smoke at their readers.

That executive was Lee A. Iacocca, then vice-president of Ford Division, and the occasion was the introduction of the first Mustang on April 17, 1964, an event of importance in the automotive industry and to four individuals in and around it. Of these individuals, two men were painfully embarrassed and disillusioned, while another two were unabashedly delighted, and the story behind this disparity tells as well as any how public, or press, relations works.

Four months prior to the Mustang's debut, *Newsweek*'s bureau chief in Detroit, James C. Jones, was invited to lunch by Iacocca's press agent, Robert W. Hefty, who showed Jones pictures of the new car. It was, Hefty said, the most significant new car to come along in a generation and represented up until that time the largest single investment ever committed by a manufacturer to a new model. Jones and Hefty were personal friends of long standing so when the latter offered exclusivity in return for major space in the magazine, hopefully a cover story, Jones had no reason to doubt Hefty's sincerity. So within a week, Hefty and his boss, Iacocca, were invited to *Newsweek*'s New York City headquarters and the same assurance of exclusivity was extended to the assembled editors of the magazine. But meanwhile, give or take a few days, the publisher of *Time* along with Detroit bureau chief Leon Jaroff were invited by Hefty and Iacocca to the Ford Division offices in Dearborn where they were shown the car and also wooed with a similar guarantee of exclusive rights in return for a major story. So, both magazines, unknown to the other, proceeded to prepare their cover stories on Iacocca and his Mustang for publication simultaneously with the car's first showing to the rest of the nation's press.

Hefty could not have been unaware of the price he would ultimately pay for his double coup, being a former wire service correspondent himself. He would be knighted in his own shop but discredited by the press with whom he worked, the latter not being subscribers to the adage that all's fair in love and war unless they themselves choose to break a release date. For it wasn't just *Time* and *Newsweek* editors who would be mad. The representatives of 120 other publications who attended the preview would feel slighted that they were not singled out for special treatment, but Hefty had no choice. Iacocca's vanity was such that he alone was to be given credit for conceiving the Mustang and the public must know it, whatever the price. Hefty would have been fired if he'd stood on the ethics of the matter, or so he claimed.

Both good and bad guys staff the public relations departments of the four domestic automakers and probably the same could be said of their counterparts among the nation's auto writers. As in any pursuit, talent, integrity, and diligence establish the writer's stature among his peers and it must be said that usually the best will be found in the employ of the most important publications. I use the label "important" rather than "largest" because the press agent's target for his story will vary according to the nature of it. Circulation of any kind is the measure when it's a product of broad appeal to be pushed, so numbers take priority in that instance. But, for example, neither *Better Homes and Gardens* nor the *National Enquirer* would be given much consideration if the project were to promote Iacocca's personal image. He cries for presentation to the "decision makers" who supposedly read *Time, Newsweek,* and *The Wall Street Journal.* The *Journal* and *Business Week,* however, would be first choices if Ford were to announce the acquisition of a majority interest in Toyo Kogyo[1] because favorable comment there reaches those who own, or have been considering buying, large blocks of Ford stock. Then, take the introduction of Ford's late but not lamented $15,000 Italian-built Pantera sports car. The editors of the buff books were courted, particularly those at *Road & Track,* whose affluent readers might buy such an un-Ford-like machine. Finally, if Ford wants something to be seen by GM or Chrysler executives, the auto writers for the Detroit *Free Press* and the Detroit *News* would find themselves sharing a luncheon table with a bevy of press agents in the Company's executive dining room, and the editors of *Road & Track* or the Los Angeles *Times* might never even know what was said unless they happened to read about it.

It is not unusual for Ford or Chrysler to spend $500,000 or more on a national press preview for an important new model or annual model change. GM, which could best afford such extravagance, stages only modest previews these days, as does American Motors, which cannot afford to do otherwise. And, actually, the most elaborate are not all that extravagant when measured against the returns. After each event the PR-man in charge collects his clippings, counts the column inches, and computes what it would have cost to fill the same space with paid advertising.

[1] Ford currently is negotiating for a 20 percent interest in Japan's Toyo Kogyo, which produces Courier light trucks sold here under the Ford name and is a potential supplier of transmissions and transaxles for forthcoming Ford minicars.

He usually comes out ahead, as one can always depend on the "two-hatters" for glowing reviews. The auto writers for all but the largest daily newspapers usually wear two hats—one symbolizing their primary function as ad salesmen and the other their willingness to pass on unedited to their news desks product releases furnished by the host. These show up verbatim in print for weeks to come, especially when that paper runs its annual auto show section.

I became something of a student of the Chrysler previews, having attended at least a dozen of them, first at resorts and then when austerity descended, in more prosaic places such as Atlanta, Dallas, Boston, Cleveland, and San Francisco. My favorites were Miami Beach where the entire 700-room Americana Hotel was commandeered off-season for two years in a row and a bit later, when half of a resort in the Poconos called Tamiment was used *in season*. I was fascinated with the massive logistics involved. Not such obvious tasks as transporting the show cars or putting together big-name entertainment at the main banquet but why, for example, our hosts kept track of the olives and cherries consumed between meals. This was because waiters carried martinis and manhattans around on trays during the various scheduled receptions and it was more accurate to count the garnish than the empty bottles, thus providing a cross-check against the final bill submitted by the hotel. I never found out how highballs were counted but the 6,280 olives to disappear during one year's two-day preview impressed me. That indicated nearly 10 martinis a day for each of the 340 persons, hosts, and guests in attendance!

It along with other equally staggering statistics also impressed Chrysler's accounting department, which began to scrutinize expense accounts submitted by executives of the Corporation covering the days of the previews. Realize before I relate this anecdote that everything was free during the two-day period, for hosts and guests alike, and that both were supposed to be in attendance at every function, not off by themselves in some other bar or restaurant. So it came to pass that the accountants noticed one Ralph Watts, then auto writer for the Detroit *News*, was separately listed as being entertained by thirty-two different Chrysler officials for lunch on *one* day and that same evening the poor guy had apparently been the guest at no less than twenty-nine dinners, not including the banquet staged for everyone by the Corporation. Of course, Ralph hadn't been anywhere except where he was supposed to be and there were some red faces at the Chrysler offices when the guilty vice-presidents wobbled home from Miami Beach. Everybody, it seems, knew Ralph Watts and anyone who has ever filled out an expense account will understand how and why Ralph came to eat so many meals in one day.

The story of Tamiment was not a happy one for the paying guests, who, at upward of fifty dollars a day, were occupying half of this strictly kosher establishment. Chrysler, it will be remembered, was housing its press guests and executives in the other half and also pre-empted prime space in the dining rooms and prime time in the pool and on the golf course. In fact, most everywhere the paying guests went, they were turned away by Chrysler's Pinkerton guards.[2] And it was sad because of a custom peculiar to young, single Jewish ladies from New York City and its environs who would stake a year's savings on vacationing in the Poconos or Catskills in the hope of meeting young, eligible Jewish men. Since the auto industry in those days hired very few Jews and since most of the press were married, the pickings were slim and the ladies were understandably annoyed. Thus it was perhaps not tactful for Chrysler to parade its company-sponsored, sixty-piece Highlander band at sundown. The ladies' faces were stony as they watched. Then when the pipes were finally stilled, one normally sweet young thing standing behind me muttered *"goyim"* to a friend and off they both stomped in the direction of the almost empty bar.

All, however, is not fun and games at these affairs. I've seen top auto executives so drunk that on one occasion the board chairman's face fell forward with a splash into the onion soup he was slurping, while at the same function, a green young reporter from a relatively small paper who got out of hand was sent home to his editor, declared by covering letter to be forever *persona non grata*. That, to my mind, was dirty pool, as was another inci-

[2] The zealous Pinkertons once refused to let Chrysler chairman L. L. Colbert enter the Americana one night quite late after he'd been out on the town without his badge.

dent involving, once again, Ralph Watts. Chevrolet back in early 1961 wished to scotch rumors that it was about to introduce an all-new compact car. Watts was interviewing the Division's then vice-president and general manager, Ed Cole, in the latter's office when the PR director who was present, John Cutter, excused himself. Shortly thereafter, Cole's phone rang and Watts found himself listening to one end of a conversation with a "Holden executive in Australia."[3] Discussed was emergency sourcing in the United States for certain parts to be used in a forthcoming rear-engined Holden car. That afternoon's Detroit *News* headlined a story under Watts's byline, telling readers there would be no Corvair, in this country at least. The caller from "Australia," of course, was Cutter in his office across the hall. Watts's editor didn't think it was much of a joke, either.

The mission of any public relations man should be to present the image of his employer in its best light. Positive ways of achieving this vary with each situation; in fact, PR-men desirous of being accredited by the Public Relations Society of America are given a written examination replete with problems of exactly that kind. And solutions are easy when the boss is imaginary. But all too often in the real business world, however, reactions to problems are negative, ranging from outright lying to PR's own version of the Fifth Amendment—the words "no comment." Perhaps the mostly costly example of PR indecision was GM's response to the consumer advocate Ralph Nader when he first appeared on the automotive scene. As I've already detailed in Chapter 1, GM's vice-president for public relations, Tony DeLorenzo, was issuing a stream of "no comments" at a time when private detectives hired by the Corporation were shadowing Nader and then got caught in the act. Resulting from the public outcry on Nader's behalf that followed, it will be remembered, was the formation of the National Highway Traffic Safety Agency and, with it, government intervention into the design of automobiles which has cost the industry and, thus, car buyers $35 billion to date.

DeLorenzo is still employed in the same capacity as the Cor-

[3] General Motors-Holden's Limited, a GM subsidiary, manufactures Holden vehicles in Australia. This make has never been imported to the United States.

poration's top PR-man so it must be assumed that GM's actions did not reflect his advice or else that he was kept unaware of what was going on until it was too late. I'm only sure if one were to ask him which was true, he would answer, "No comment!" However, one mistake of this magnitude should surely forestall others, but it didn't, as I also mentioned in the same chapter. This was GM's lame reaction to the disclosure that it was installing Chevrolet engines in Buicks and Oldsmobiles. The mishandling only cost the Corporation $60 million to rectify but the initial response was, once again, "No comment." And Ford PR was no more helpful while the press was unraveling the engineering intricacies of the fiery Pinto gas tanks. Why is it press agents have never learned to utter those four simple, honest words, "We've made a mistake," and then go on to outline the positive action planned to correct the mistake? The answer, most probably, is they are hired to hide mistakes and have no ready answers when they fail. And that, in turn, is because management is not willing to admit mistakes, even to its own PR department.

Thus can be seen the essence of the conflict between press and press agents. Cooperation from the public relations department is exemplary when some auto writer wishes to "test" a new vehicle; nowadays, the companies don't even ask to read your report before it is printed. They're also quite helpful when you are assigned to profile a noncontroversial executive; in short, the New York *Times*'s recently abandoned watchwords, "All the News That's Fit to Print," also fit the PR-man's mission with only slight reinterpretation. But when a writer zeros in on something negative, all of PR's manpower and expertise is directed toward blocking the story.

I remember experiencing this when editor of *Motor Trend* magazine. I was covering the Union/Pure Oil Performance Trials in Daytona Beach and it was much like being assigned to watch grass grow. These Trials did not rate as a spectator sport but they were taken seriously by the factory teams entered, which mostly were staffed by professional racing types hired for the month-long effort. And, too, I knew that beating the rules was and is a game to racing mechanics everywhere. Each tries to outcheat the other and they take as much pride in detecting their fellows as in the perpetration. Thus, the Pontiac team was unable to hide that they'd won their class in the economy contest by installing beer cans prefilled with gasoline into the fuel systems of their cars. National Association for Stock Car Auto Racing (NASCAR) officials who monitored the event discovered the illegal modification, issued a press release disqualifying the Pontiac team, and everybody enjoyed a good laugh at the offender's expense. It was really no big deal, and not even very clever, but when Pontiac's then vice-president and general manager, John De Lorean, heard I'd mentioned the incident in my coverage for *Motor Trend,* he instructed his public relations department to contact my publisher with an offer to buy the entire issue, already in print but not yet in readers' hands. That would have been about 600,000 magazines at 75 cents each and, of course, the offer was rejected despite Pontiac's being an important advertising client.

The automakers' public relations staffs range in size from perhaps one hundred professionals at General Motors and its divisions to barely twenty at American Motors. If one is to count related functions such as civic and government affairs and employee communications, the figures should be increased by half again. But somehow, the tiny AMC group manages to garner almost as much ink as its much larger competitors in addition to performing all the other necessary functions of PR such as speech-writing, staging previews and press conferences, locating lost executive luggage, and accompanying the chairman and president everywhere they travel. Perhaps this is because AMC people have lived with negative situations long enough to know that any answer is better than none at all.

Of all the automotive PR-men I've dealt with, there are two among whom I'd split the title of being most creative. The indefatigable Frank Wylie of Chrysler accumulated his score in my books by a succession of small triumphs, while Tom Tierney, formerly of Ford but now operating his own investment firm in Dallas, climbed to the top on the strength of one unforgettable event he staged.

A close student of comic strips might spot an example of how Wylie operates. Have you ever noticed when there is a car in the sequence, how it always seems to resemble a current Chrysler product? That's not surprising. Each year, Wylie furnishes all active cartoonists a photo album showing corporation products coming and going from every angle. Wylie, however, is on my black list for another of his schemes. He sends *free* weekly car columns to a list of over two hundred newspapers, thus making it difficult for free-lance writers to *sell* similar columns. And a typical editor removed from the Detroit scene would never guess the origin of these columns, which are mailed in plain envelopes; promotion is soft key, incidental to the useful information contained therein.

Tierney, in turn, will be forever remembered in automotive circles for a press preview of new Ford models he orchestrated in Flora, Illinois. This town of 5,500 or so souls had until then but one claim to fame, it being the human habitation closest to the exact geographical center of the U.S. population, but soon after Tierney's arrival every family with a licensed driver was into a brand-new, all-white Ford car or a bright blue light truck, 1,538 in all. In fact, the vehicles were so new, it would be a month or more before any were to be seen elsewhere in the country. Another problem Tierney solved with one imaginative phone call concerned housing his guests who numbered over three hundred executives, technicians, and members of the press. Flora had only about thirty-five motel rooms so Tierney ordered up a train to be parked for the duration. It was the longest all-Pullman train ever assembled by the Atcheson, Topeka and Santa Fe, mainly because he insisted on drawing rooms rather than roomettes. Then, because Flora is not the coolest place to be in mid-September, he added several baggage cars which were converted, with the aid of the Flora Fire Department's No. 1 pumper hooked in tandem between the cars and a distant hydrant, into shower baths. It was, I must admit, a unique experience to spend two nights on a train going nowhere and finding your shoes freshly shined each morning. I forgot to ask Tierney what connection there was between the country's center of population and new Ford cars.

Perhaps the grossest ploy Ford ever used to hopefully guarantee ink from a new car preview was to have each newspaper invited send along a teenage "reporter" in addition to the regular staffer assigned. All expenses were paid, scholarships would be awarded for the best stories, and the chances were good that many would be the sons or daughters of the editors who, naturally, would give prominent display to their stories. But instead of being respectfully awed, the young men and women asked far sharper questions than their chaperons dared and some of them filed copy about which Ford was strangely silent. They questioned, in essence, what the fuss was about. How can new cars be news when their older brothers were dying in Vietnam, when crops were sprayed with DDT, and when lumbermen were allowed to scalp the tops of mountains? It was a good lesson in sanity for us all!

The tactics used at news conferences have never ceased to annoy me. PR-men go about planting questions they want asked among the more gullible "reporters" and there are other questions they can be sure will be asked anyway, and they know by whom. Thus PR shapes the content of the stories that result without actually writing them. It is my observation that the true professionals among the newsmen present seldom ask a question in open forum, for what good is the answer when it is heard by all? These men and women flesh out their files before and after the conference in private confrontation with the source. PR, in turn, has us all down as either "safe" or "dangerous," the latter being taken as a compliment by those so labeled.

Every new car season entails two sets of previews, one being the kind I've described for daily newspapers and the other, downright austere testing sessions for long-lead buff magazines. "Uncle" Tom McCahill was the man who started the testing business shortly after World War II. At first, the auto companies would have no part of this gargantuan, balding upstart who wrote such things as "the car corners like a pig on roller skates," but Tom came to be accepted and then even wooed. In fact, he achieved such stature that he was given his own private preview ahead of the magazines. In his heyday, few factory engineers would ride with him on the test track more than once because to Tom the purpose of car testing was to see how fast the machine would travel around a long, sweeping turn without upsetting. And so it is to all his imitators, but there's a slight problem which renders the expensive testing apparatus and carefully evolved techniques used by the bigger magazines rather meaningless. In order to obtain a representative acceleration time or fuel economy figure, engineers concur that at least ten like vehicles should be tested under identical conditions. Tolerances allowed in mass production can cause data obtained from two supposedly identical cars of the same make to vary to a greater degree than those from two similar cars of different makes. That, however, didn't bother Uncle Tom, whose only testing equipment ever was a stopwatch and the seat of his pants.

Car testing is a precarious occupation in more ways than one. The buff magazines compete hotly to be the first to test the latest and newest and sometimes, as I was once, they are trapped by their own eagerness. I was a young, green tester for *Motor Trend* back in 1955 when the first Ford Thunderbird, the now classic two-seater, appeared and in our eagerness to scoop competition, we committed ourselves to a cover story at a time when the only object resembling a T-Bird in existence was a single clay model. A picture of this inoperative model was taken and we printed covers by the hundred thousands, complete with blurbs announcing the "1st Complete Test!!!" Copy was due several weeks later but still, in all of Dearborn, there was no operable car. Thus, I "tested" the clay model with the help of Ford engineers who already knew the performance figures, commented eruditely on the handling and comfort, and not a single reader complained. Nor, in fact, did Ford, for under the circumstances I couldn't justify griping about much other than the ashtray being stuck shut.

I remember, too, the invention of "Car of the Year" awards, now a dubious charade but originally well-intentioned and honest. Walt Woron, then editor of *Motor Trend,* got the idea and chose the 1952 Cadillac as his first winner and the compact, short-lived Willys Aero as runner-up. The cover of the issue announcing the award showed the lucky Cadillac sailing over a railroad crossing, all four wheels airborne. Willys was delighted, coming out with ads[4] headlined "Hats Off to Cadillac!" Cadillac, however, thought the picture was undignified, hardly what an owner would do in his Cadillac, and refused to attend the award ceremony. But within a few years, "Car of the Year"

[4] Willys in those days sponsored the Metropolitan Opera on radio and took every opportunity to needle its Cadillac-owning audience with news of its second-place award.

awards as well as "Import Car of the Year," "Truck of the Year," ad nauseum, from all the magazines that jumped into the act, went to the highest bidder. To be sure, winners can generally be justified on technical grounds, but so too can some of the losers. It became a matter of which manufacturer would plug the magazine and its award the hardest on TV and billboards and, most importantly, which would commit to the biggest advertising schedule in the donor's magazine. Only *Road & Track*, bless its stuffy integrity, stayed consistently aloof.

Unlike some industries, Detroit in modern times has never to my knowledge indulged in any practices deserving to be labeled as payola. Christmas at auto writers' homes seldom sees gifts from manufacturers that can't be "eaten up, smoked up, or drunk up in one day."[5] If the gift isn't perishable, it is hardly ever worth more than the $25 acceptable to the Internal Revenue Service. Admittedly, auto writers are seldom without one or more sets of "loaner" wheels in their driveways, but that can be justified on the basis of familiarizing them with the product. And there are frequent junkets to faraway places; once there, however, the guests tour auto plants and not the Louvre or the Left Bank. Nor is there such a thing as "company poker" played by press agents in the all-night games that are a feature of every hospitality suite. I have seen more than a few underpaid, addictive writers sorely wounded at these tables yet, oddly, PR planners avoid Las Vegas as a site for previews on the theory that the press can't afford it.

It is, I suppose, convenient to have a phone number one can call to get quick answers to routine questions, set up noncontroversial interviews, and to find a hotel room for you in Chicago during the Democratic Convention. Nevertheless, there are newsmen assigned to Detroit who would not mourn if the function of public or press relations was eliminated at the auto companies. The basic conflict between those who must ferret out news, good or bad, and those who are paid to push or hide it, whichever is called for, becomes the more painful when you know that practically all PR-men once worked the other side. They absconded to the enemy because the pay was better,

---

[5] A pronouncement by a GM president years ago that became accepted as a guideline to gift-giving throughout the industry.

something like double the salary of the average United Press bureau chief for starters. Once there, they became inoculated like their bosses with the idea, as I've suggested in Chapter 1, that no odor will arise when they go to the toilet. If they resist, they won't last for long.

One exception was the late Warren Jollymore, who took genuine pride in his employment by General Motors without ever marrying his job. Jolly was, in fact, one of the few who ever became a confidant of Frederic G. Donner, a man who liked everyone to think he was totally without emotion during his tenure as chairman. But we saw Donner through Jolly's eyes. Thus, rather than criticizing him as the crochety crank he delighted in being, we would praise his startlingly detailed knowledge of the most obscure workings of the Corporation, repeatedly note in our stories that it really wasn't Donner who said "there's no slice of pie too small for my finger" and, in general, do our best to humanize our subject—all thanks to Jolly. And somehow this jovial ex-boxing champion who had such a great name for a press agent always found time to pop for a wet lunch when things weren't going well for a friend and, as he had legions of both, this charity may well have led to his premature death at his desk from a stroke. GM ceased functioning for a couple of hours the day of his funeral; the entire executive staff was in attendance, along with most of the press. Fittingly, Jolly, who would never drive anything but a Cadillac, took his last ride in one.

CHAPTER 13

"Call Us Toll-Free"

Even the most basic of modern passenger cars is composed of about fifteen thousand separate parts and if you attempted to assemble your own by buying all of these parts one by one from a dealer, what sells for $4,000 in his showroom would cost you nearly $24,000 without counting the man-hours you'd spend putting the car together. Granted, auto parts retailed by car manufacturers through their franchised dealers are grossly overpriced[1] and all aspects of the system are currently being scrutinized by various government agencies. However, the sixfold spread between what is asked for a factory-fresh new car and what it would cost to take the parts for one home in baskets meaningfully illustrates the advantage of mass production.

Now, realize what's involved when you or a dealer attempt to repair a car. Whether the failure is mechanical or caused by accident damage, you must first reach the offending part by undoing in sequence what has been accomplished on an automated assembly line, replace the part, and then put it all back together again essentially by hand. And unfortunately most processes developed to speed the pace of assembly lines cannot be readily duplicated by hand methods. For example, the car is painted before the trim and glass are installed so there is no need for mask-

---

[1] In Chapter 7, I cite the example of identical replacement windshield glass ranging in price from $235 to $282 plus installation at dealers in different GM makes whereas the same windshield can be purchased at an independent auto glass shop for $148, including installation.

ing. And if you've ever seen what is normally the lower half of your mechanic protruding out from under the hood, legs flailing, while he struggles to replace, say, a set of spark plugs, realize that the engine was not yet in the car when the original set was installed at the factory.

The attention designers pay to facilitating service in the field is as yet only token. I can't see much evidence of progress. They've done away with a few formerly necessary routines such as periodic adjustment of the brakes and putting water in the battery. They've extended lubrication intervals with the result that service stations and dealers now charge a "rack fee" whereas, before, the slight labor involved was included in the price of the oil. On some but not all new cars, you can change a bulb in the instrument panel by unfastening a couple of screws and pulling out the cluster. Headlights can now be aimed without removing the trim surrounding them, and electronic ignition systems have doubled the length of time you can drive between tune-ups that cost twice as much. But that's about it as of 1979 models and it isn't impressive when compared with our capability of putting men on the moon.

The reasons for this cannot be traced to lack of talent in the auto industry. It stems from unwillingness to sacrifice or even compromise in two areas, the most pertinent being convenience on the assembly line. And lurking unacknowledged in the background is reluctance to seriously threaten profits from the sale of service and parts. Thus we see very real advances in durability negated by the skyrocketing cost of routine maintenance and minor repair. Then, compounding the problem is the complexity introduced by mandated emission controls and, to a lesser extent, safety equipment.

Actuarial statistics on the automobile, unlike those on humans, have not changed significantly in the last thirty years. A car's average life span was thirteen years or 125,000 miles, whichever came first, in 1950 and it's about the same today. There have been changes, though, in the nature of the terminal illness. In 1950 it was total engine failure. In 1960 it was the cancer of corrosion. In 1970 it was a spreading paralysis of the secondary systems such as power steering pumps, vacuum brake boosters, and electric windows. As the decade ends, it is a general sclerosis of such nerve centers as ignition and carburetion and by 1990 there will be automotive euthanasia. All vehicles in use which can't pass stringent annual emission tests will be ruled off the roads. And note the trend. The decision on life or death has passed from the owner to the mechanic. In 1950 any car could be restored to life if you were willing to pay the price; today and tomorrow, degeneration of a single complex component can relegate a car to the junkyard.

No individual mechanic can possibly learn all he needs to know about even a single new model in a manufacturer's line before that model is obsoleted and a new, very different model takes its place. Thus the trade has been split into specialties, and those who view the trees, to turn an old saying around, fail to see the forest. For example, there are carburetion specialists and automatic transmission specialists at opposite ends of the shop. A customer arrives, complaining that his transmission shifts sluggishly and erratically. The service salesman knows the problem could be in the carburetor because the carburetor signals the transmission when to shift, or it could be that the transmission isn't listening, or it could be that the transmission hears the signals but can't respond. What to do? It's possible the customer will get the full treatment, driving out many hours and dollars later with both components replaced. No attempt will be made to find the partially plugged or leaky vacuum line or loose electrical connection, which could be the minor cause or causes of the problem, unless the car still does not operate properly after the rebuilt components have been installed. And you won't be offered a refund for those even though they weren't needed.

I don't say this happens all the time, only that it could and does happen. Nor do I say that the service departments of franchised new car dealers are all crooked or stupid. But however conscientious and honest the majority may be, they are simply overwhelmed by the complexity of the modern automobile in its almost infinite variety. A variety, I should emphasize, that exists within any single manufacturer's line, even most imports. To illustrate, Chevrolet has computed that it could theoretically build 2 million cars in a model year without one being the exact duplicate of another. And as may be imagined, independent garages, which attempt to service all makes, are at an even greater disadvantage because their people are not invited to attend service schools conducted by the manufacturers. If, as I noted in Chapter 6, there is no single engineer currently in the employ of auto companies who has ever had the opportunity to single-handedly design an entire car, how can one expect a mechanic to know all there is to know about fixing one? Thus, the trend to specialization.

A possible solution to the problem is to construct the car in modules, so designed that related components are mounted in a drawer, so to speak, which can be pulled out for easy access to the offending part. Perhaps the closest approach to this was Volkswagen's Beetle from which the entire engine and transaxle assembly could be removed, with a little practice, in about twenty minutes. Remember, however, that Dr. Ferdinand Porsche created the Beetle for the Nazis back in 1938 and he was under strict instructions to keep it simple. Also, the car came before the factory in which it was later mass-produced.[2] Dr. Porsche didn't have to proselytize his design to existing manufacturing facilities. The Beetle may have its faults but complexity of maintenance is not one of them. Nonetheless, the concept rebounded to the consumer's disadvantage. It fostered a brisk trade in rebuilt components and assemblies; instead of diagnosis and repair of, say, a burned valve in the engine, mechanics would replace the entire engine on the theory that it was faster and therefore cheaper. This practice spread to all makes, with the result that today mechanics do very little repairing of any complex component. In fact, many of the new generation of mechanics know no other way.

Another approach to simplifying repairs, also pioneered by Volkswagen, was to route as many systems as possible through a kind of intelligence center mounted on the car which in turn could be plugged into a computerized diagnostic machine at the dealership. The machines cost each dealer about $50,000 and worked well if, of course, you were willing to be wedded to the local Volkswagen franchise. The machines have not been made

[2] Volkswagen's original plant at Wolfsburg, Germany, produced only a few passenger cars before and during World War II. Approximately fifty thousand military vehicles were built, but civilian production of the Beetle did not begin in any quantity until 1949.

available to independent garages by the few automakers who have adopted the technique. And, oddly, the installation will be found only on relatively simple cars like VWs and Chevettes, not on the Cadillacs and Lincolns that most need it.

As a matter of fact, automakers, whether domestic or foreign, are even reluctant to make factory-authorized maintenance manuals readily available to independent garages, not to mention owners. This absurd secrecy, prompted by the desire to "protect" franchised dealers, has created a significant trade in unauthorized, privately printed guides which, if they're to be accurate and complete, obviously must painstakingly duplicate the contents of the real thing. And with somewhat but not much more legitimacy, a similar exercise in proprietary rights has encouraged a proliferation of specialized tools to service specific models and components. Each new car spawns about $2,000–$3,000 worth of these, without which some maintenance jobs simply cannot be performed in the field. So, once again the customer is pressured to patronize the franchised dealer because no independent garage can justify investing in more than a few of these single-purpose aids. The need for these tools, I might note too, is another good example of assembly-line convenience receiving precedence over ease of repair. A car *can* be designed so that it may be repaired with tools commonly available in the field.

So far, I've talked about maintenance or repairs for which you are willing to pay to have performed. Those which come "under warranty" and are supposedly free have caused infinitely more animosity between customers, factories, and dealers. To realize why, take the owners manual out of the glove compartment of your car and read it carefully, searching for a sentence telling you that, while not recommended, you will *not* necessarily void the warranty by having the required routine service done by your neighborhood gasoline station or, for that matter, by yourself. The implication will be there, but nowhere is it clearly stated. Nor are you clearly informed of the exact procedure to follow, should you not patronize the franchised dealer for your warranty service, to establish proof that the work has been done. Those coupons in the book cannot be filled out by any Joe Blow and mailed off to Detroit, attention of the records department.

They must be fed properly into the system and the only access to that system is through the franchised dealer.

Nobody will check on you unless you have occasion to file a claim amounting to more than a few dollars. Or, more particularly, if one month or a thousand miles after the warranty has expired, your cooling system ruptures without warning and the resultant overheating damages your engine beyond repair. That one is the "sticky" as the English call a cinnamon bun. Technically, you are not covered because the warranty is quite specific about dates and mileage. You feel, however, that the car should have lasted just a little longer than it did and that therefore the dealer should fix it without charge or, at the least, at a drastically reduced charge. And to get even more technical, as the dealer surely will, the warranty, had it been in force, would only cover the failed radiator and not the related damage. You should, he will say, have foreseen the consequences and stopped immediately, in the fast lane of the freeway if necessary. Thus, your claim falls into a gray area known in the trade as "corporate policy" on two counts.

First, it is the unadvertised policy of domestic automakers to honor claims for major failures of components that can reasonably be expected to function more than just a few days or miles after the warranty has expired. Then, more recently, rising consumerism and the relatively new legal doctrine of strict liability I discussed in Chapter 6 have prompted Detroit to consider fairly if not favorably claims involving a sequence of events. So at this point, a search is made for your "required maintenance" records, of which there are none in the manufacturer's possession because you had the work performed by other than a franchised dealer. Your own receipts for routine inspections at your neighborhood gasoline station matter little. The man was not factory-trained and, by implication, was incompetent. You are whistling against the wind despite what may be said in the owners manual.

Under the rules that existed before the doctrine of strict liability began being enforced by the courts, your brakes could fail due to a defect in material or workmanship and, in turn, force you to evade a pregnant lady pushing a baby carriage by crashing into a storefront. The pregnant lady is hysterical, your car is demolished, and the storekeeper claims you have damaged thousands of dollars' worth of his merchandise. Even if your car was under warranty, the manufacturer would have been obligated to do no more than to reimburse you for what it would have cost to fix the brakes had none of the subsequent events occurred. The rest, had you pursued it in court, would have been a matter to be subrogated between the manufacturer's insurer and yours. As automakers are self-insured in matters of product liability, it's probable *your* insurance company would have paid and that *you* would experience some difficulty when the time came to renew your policy.

Automakers maintain large and competent legal staffs and, in the past, have won all but the most spectacular cases against them by default. Few individual owners were able or willing to do battle against the Detroit giants; that is, until the National Highway Traffic Safety Agency began forcing the recall of cars to correct defects that could or did cause accidents, injuries, and deaths. There are four important differences between defects corrected by recall and those that might be noticed and corrected under warranty: 1) recalls involve only safety-related items; 2) recalls are not subject to time or mileage limitations; 3) owners of record are notified of recalls whereas other defects known to the manufacturer may be unpublicized; and 4) *all* the potentially defective parts involved are replaced under recall, while under warranty terms the part must actually have failed. Today the man whose brakes quit, the storekeeper, and even the pregnant lady stand a fair chance of being compensated for their misfortunes by the manufacturer of the car, which is as it should be.

However, let's for the moment play devil's advocate. The average car, as I've said, contains about fifteen thousand different parts which must continue to function separately and in harmony under all conditions for at least the one year or twelve thousand miles of the warranty. "All conditions" include temperatures ranging from a minus-60-degree wind-chill factor in northern Minnesota to the plus-160 degrees not uncommonly endured by a locked car soaking up the sun in a Florida parking lot. These parts must stay glued together for the farmer who does most of his driving on poorly maintained dirt roads. They must resist the attack of the corrosive chemicals used to melt ice and snow. They must withstand the generally nonchalant American attitude toward routine maintenance typified, contrary to popular opinion, by the "little old lady from Pasadena" who expects her car to unfailingly start once a week and putter about on her errands, while hardly ever in its lifetime warming up to proper operating temperatures. Far happier is the life of a car driven three hundred fast, hard miles a day by a traveling salesman.

The devil must be given his due. Today's car is essentially more reliable than the far less complicated television set sitting warm and undisturbed in my home. Most components in a car will function less erratically than the toaster in my kitchen. The seats show less sag from more sitting than the sofa in my living room. To be specific, each piston in my car will reciprocate 17,082,000,000 times, not counting hours spent idling at traffic lights, before it or some other crucial part expires and I have the whole car crunched into a cube and sent over to Japan to became a new Toyota or Datsun. That's a lot of ups and downs!

Why is it, then, that today's cars are more cursed than praised? One reason is the statistical probability that one car in every ten thousand or so from any single manufacturer, whether it be Ford or Cadillac, will combine so many assorted, minor ailments, right from the day it is delivered to its unfortunate owner, that attempts to fix it defy the law of diminishing returns. Such a car is known to trade and public alike as a "lemon" and each example becomes highly visible, it not being unknown for persons victimized by such a purchase to paint signs on the car labeling it a lemon. One irate owner in recent times even set fire to his new Lincoln Continental on the front lawn of Ford's Los Angeles assembly plant.

Each manufacturer is fully aware that a lemon will roll off the end of the assembly line at predictable intervals, but despite the most conscientious effort at quality control, and despite a multitude of final inspections, that lemon will not be exposed until it begins service in the hands of its owner. And with greater statistical probability, there will be partial lemons; that is, otherwise excellent specimens with chronically malfunctioning engines, or transmissions, or windshield wipers. These last get fixed, sooner or later, under warranty, but usually not until the owner becomes thoroughly disillusioned with the make and all the people who represent it. The true or total lemon, as I've said, can never be fixed. Once recognized, it should be replaced without charge or question, but that, the manufacturer stubbornly refuses to do. Statistical probabilities are ignored; it just can't happen. It's your fault. You have somehow abused the car.

What causes a lemon? The reason is the tolerances, or variances in fits, that must be allowed to permit economical mass assembly of machines as complex as today's automobile.[3] You don't have to be technically minded to visualize that if, say, assembly specifications permit a variance of from 0.0007 to 0.0027 inches in the clearance between connecting-rod bearings and the crankshaft (these being actual figures allowed on a popular Chevrolet engine), that in the course of a day's production the law of averages will see to it that there will be "tight" engines and "loose" engines and a few ideal engines. And because this particular tolerance is only one of hundreds that must be allowed throughout the complete car, the course of a week's production will see one or two very loose cars or very tight cars. The mating point of practically every moving part in these fortunately rare cars will be at one or the other extreme of tolerance. Both extremes define a lemon just as the equally rare chance of perfect fits throughout defines the "ideal" or, as engineers call it, the "happy" car. The only way to ensure nothing but happy cars, within the limits of human error, is to hand-hone *every* moving part to a perfect fit. None but Rolls-Royce and Ferrari can afford to do this, and even they have been known to produce an occasional lemon.

All of these reasons, however valid, as to why a lemon escapes the factory are of very little solace to the buyer who is stuck with one. Communication, of course, would help—not from the pages of this book or from the National Highway Traffic Safety Agency but from the factory responsible. To further this aim, Chrysler Corporation some years ago pioneered the concept of "Our Man in Detroit." Byron Nichols, a vice-president who hap-

---

[3] Henry Ford is erroneously credited with being the father of mass production. Actually it was Henry Leland, who won the prestigious Dewar Trophy in 1909 for proving to Britain's Royal Automobile Club that three of his contemporary one-cylinder Cadillacs could be completely dismantled, the parts mixed at random, and then reassembled and run for five hundred miles without malfunction.

pened to be available, was, according to the press release, installed in an office behind a battery of toll-free telephones ready to speak personally with any owners who called. Whether Mr. Nichols actually answered the first few calls to come in, I do not know. He retired shortly thereafter, but the concept, in theory, remained. Here, from two opposite ends of the nation, are examples of how it works today:

Bill Logan of Sun Valley, California, purchased a Dodge van in May 1977 with which he planned to tow a fifteen-foot travel trailer. An unusual number of problems developed and when he went to his dealer to have them resolved under warranty, the work was not performed to his satisfaction. He then turned to the Chrysler customer service organization for assistance, contacting them first by mail. In about thirty days he in turn was contacted by phone from Detroit and assured that a field representative would meet with him and see that the vehicle was properly repaired. An appointment was made, Logan took time away from his work to attend the meeting, but the factory man did not appear as promised.

Between then and December 1977, Logan made numerous phone calls to Detroit which he claims were never returned. He then had his attorney write Chrysler a letter which did result in a phone call and once again he was promised that the Los Angeles zone office would take care of his problems. This time arrangements were made for the necessary repairs; however, despite the van being in the shop for a month, it was returned with the original howl in the rear end, the same unpredictable tendency for the brakes to fail completely, a still inaccurate gas gauge, a loose headliner, and no explanation for an unfavorable discrepancy between the advertised payload and the useful payload.

Logan continued unsuccessfully in his attempts to obtain assistance from Chrysler's zone representatives. He was ignored. So, too, were more phone calls by him to "Our Man in Detroit." Then after two years of fruitless effort within prescribed channels, he requested help from the "Action Line" staff of a popular recreational vehicle magazine. Although the magazine was able to contact various factory officials in Los Angeles and Detroit on Logan's behalf, the run-around continued. "Action Line" found it impossible to talk with anyone in Detroit who would admit responsibility for establishing policies and procedures in the area of customer service. Chrysler told the magazine that the "corporation" established all policies and procedures. As the magazine put it when reporting Logan's troubles to its readers, "By this time we thought we were beginning to discern a pattern in the way Chrysler's Detroit and zone representatives handled customer complaints." Meanwhile Logan, who followed all the rules prior to requesting help from the magazine, still had his lemon, another victim of Detroit's persistent refusal to acknowledge the law of averages. And Chrysler Corporation, in turn, is now the villain in an adverse story concerning its products and service policies which has been seen by the magazine's several hundred thousand readers.

Harold Litoff of Providence, Rhode Island, also spent about two years attempting to persuade Chrysler to perform warranty work on his 1977 Aspen station wagon, purchased new in November 1976. His problems were persistent hard starting and stalling, a fender which had cracked along the hood line, and a rocker panel that would not retain paint. Although patient for about the same length of time as Logan and similarly unsuccessful in the channels of protest open to him, Litoff has just begun to fight. He is currently enlisting support for a class action lawsuit through advertisements in the New York *Times* and the Boston *Globe* which solicit similar experiences from other Aspen (Dodge) and Volare (Plymouth) owners. As of January 1979 he claims to have had correspondence and phone conversations with over sixty like-minded respondents. Here, too, certainly, the advertisements which have undoubtedly been seen by many more persons who may have been thinking about the purchase of a Chrysler product, can hardly help the corporate image.

Messrs. Logan and Litoff may or may not be aware of the statistical probability that one in ten thousand new car buyers will end up with a lemon, whatever make they may buy. There is no reason to expect them to know this. Every consumer, not just nine thousand, nine hundred and ninety-nine, is entitled to complete satisfaction with his purchase. Logan and Litoff, in fact, are exceptions who protested publicly. Most buyers stuck with a lemon merely unload it on some unsuspecting dealer or private buyers, swallow their loss, and avoid that make in the future. Communications is the problem, not the inexorable law of averages.

"Our Man in Detroit" is obviously more fiction than fact, not only at Chrysler but his equivalents at the other manufacturers, domestic and foreign. The circuitous run-around that lands complaining customers right back at the doorstep of the dealer where the problem started, or else in court, seems no different today than it was back in 1965–66 when I was editor of *Motor Trend* and lent a sympathetic ear almost daily to readers who had reached the limit of their patience and had come to the magazine as their last hope for help. If there was a trend apparent then, it was not a specific manufacturer whose products failed more frequently but, rather, almost total lack of communication from any of them. And it didn't make me feel any better to know that I, as a member of the press, could bypass the tape by calling the public relations department and generally get some action whereas the consumer, on his own, was denied this resource.

One would think automakers would be concerned with their financial stake in maintaining quality control and thus avoiding customer dissatisfaction, because here is an actual example of what can happen when a car *is* fixed under warranty: A certain small but vital engine part (a freeze plug) costs 4 cents to install initially. If the work is done improperly, it can be corrected at the engine plant for a labor cost of $4.00. If the defect is not discovered until after the engine is installed in a car, factory costs to fix it rise to $36. But if the car gets into the hands of an owner and repairs must be made by the dealer under warranty, the car's maker is out of pocket $200!

But here is the problem: Let's guess that of the fifteen thousand parts in a car, perhaps ten thousand of them can be classified as components; that is, they perform some function that is essential to the continuing, safe operation of the car. Now, if each of these components is built to a reliability factor of 99.999 percent (which is highly unlikely), the overall reliability of the car can mathematically be only 91.200 percent. In other words, if every part could be built to this purer-than-Ivory (soap) reliability standard, one car out of every ten still could be expected to give its owner some trouble. However, according to the same mathematics of probability, if the reliability of the components drops to 99.000 percent, only one car out of every hundred will *not* give its owner some trouble. Fortunately, industry achievement falls somewhere closer to the first figure.

Customer satisfaction, or the lack of it, starts with a new car that either gives trouble-free service during the period of its warranty or does not. As we have just calculated, odds are it will not be perfect. At this point, goodwill remains if the trouble is promptly corrected with a minimum of inconvenience to the customer. But let's assume that problems arise, that the car is not fixed properly the first time it is returned to the dealer, or the dealer feels the problem was caused by neglect or abuse. Here looms the importance of clear and sincere communications if the goodwill of the customer is to be retained. Unfortunately, communication between factory, dealer, and customer is not clear and sincere, and *therein lies the single greatest problem facing the automobile industry, domestic and foreign, today!*

For starters, the industry could explain in simple language, much as I have done above, the very real difficulty—in fact, impossibility—of producing nothing but "perfect" cars, and why. If the industry, or any single company in it, could bring itself to admit that it can and does make mistakes and show its customers, through institutional advertisements, that expectation of perfection is unreal, I suspect much of the present animosity and, with it, the miserable industry image, would begin to evaporate. Then it might dry up completely and blow away if the same basic standards of honesty and concern were exhibited in every contact, at all levels, between dealer, customer, and factory throughout the duration of the warranty. Letters should be acknowledged, phone calls returned, and the buck should stop on the factory's doorstep.

General Motors obviously does not remember that famous sign on Harry Truman's White House desk. Instead, it has evolved test programs in the San Francisco Bay, Minneapolis-St. Paul, and metropolitan Buffalo areas which use voluntary arbitration to settle unresolved vehicle complaints. Better Business Bureaus in those localities cooperate by maintaining pools of volunteer arbitrators chosen from all segments of the community. The parties involved agree on an arbitrator and may testify themselves as well as call in expert witnesses. In the San Francisco test, which is the latest of the continuing series, the decision will be nonbinding on the customer but binding on General Motors. Arbitration is limited to "current disagreements which involve the interpretation or performance of the written warranty for new (GM) vehicles" and specifically excludes complaints involving alleged fraud or violations of the law, or complaints involving damage or personal injury in which product liability issues or insurance claims are involved. While the standard GM vehicle warranty (12 months or 12,000 miles) remains unaltered, the press release announcing the San Francisco test stated that disputes concerning the "manufacturer's responsibility for any GM vehicle that has not passed its third year in service or 36,000 miles" would be covered. This is the first official acknowledgment I've seen by any automaker of the so-called "corporate responsibility" policy mentioned earlier in this chapter.

Now to zero in on a specific area of the communications gap, and also to explain why I primarily blame the factories for its existence, we should examine why dealers generally tend to evade making repairs under warranty. The reason goes no deeper than dollars and cents. The factories reimburse the dealer $12.50 an hour for labor and charge back the parts used at cost. Normally, dealers bill customers $16.50 to $22.50 an hour for labor, depending on the level of local rates or union scales, and sell parts at a 35 to 40 percent markup. In other words, the factories force dealers to tie up shop space and mechanics' time to do work from which no profit is derived. In fact, some dealers claim they lose money on warranty work. Not being their accountant, I can't prove or disprove that last claim but it does seem inequitable to expect the dealer to correct the factory's mistakes without being adequately compensated for his efforts. And certainly this is why the practice of padding warranty claims is so widespread. However, and however the controversy is resolved, it is the customer who suffers.

As to how to avoid a lemon or how best to communicate with the factory should you be unlucky enough to land one, I have but one suggestion. It is to make full use of your city's or state's "Office of Consumer Affairs" where it exists. I have in California and the resulting action was amazingly prompt. The dealer paid me back in part for two successive valve jobs that, between them, didn't last for 5,000 miles. And sometimes the problems are simple. The last car purchased in my family was a 1978 Mercury Zephyr with "Z-7" option. We had it for a week before we noticed there was no way to raise or lower the window in the right front door, or any evidence that a way was intended. Unblemished upholstery covered the spot where the crank should have been attached. Later, quite by accident, we found the crank lying under the front seat. Today, 10,000 miles and no problems later, we consider ourselves lucky.

CHAPTER 14

The Experimental Affordable Vehicle

Perhaps I'm too easily muddled by the numbers that issue forth from the Bureau of Labor Statistics but here is what muddles me. In the two decades that will shortly have passed between 1960 and 1980, the Bureau's Consumer Price Index as a whole has risen 135.8 percent but one of its components, new cars (retail), has gone up only 50.8 percent.[1] Yet, my own personal index tells me that the least expensive new domestic car on the market in 1960 was selling for an amount very close to $2,000 while today, as we enter the 1980 model season, its equivalent costs almost $4,000. According to the way I figure, this is approximately a 100 percent increase in price. And today's least expensive offering is not even an equivalent. It's significantly smaller inside and out, it has less power, and I don't see a single feature essential for getting me from Point A to Point B on it that wasn't standard equipment twenty years ago. Both the new and the old will stop, start, and go, and will keep me warm and dry while they're doing it.

I am, of course, aware of "adjustments" that are made to the Index which, in effect, hide the fact that today's cars cost twice as much to buy as they did in 1960. And these adjustments are paradoxical. Specifically, the Index does not reflect product costs

[1] Based on 0 percent CPI, December 1959.

passed on to the consumer for improvements in quality, safety, reliability, performance, durability, economy, carrying capacity, maneuverability, and/or comfort and convenience. The list would seem to include every possible area of improvement except, perhaps, changes in styling and appearance which are specifically excluded from the adjustments allowed, this being why, of course, cars show favorably on the Index as compared to, say, medical care services and home ownership. What's paradoxical can be seen in the history of Henry Ford's Model T, the car that "put America on wheels." The first one in 1908 sold for $825; by 1925, a vastly improved version could be bought for $260! And Ford was not alone. Practically the entire auto industry in its formative years had only one formula for success—a better car at a lower price. But today, as each new model season dawns, it's a better car at a higher price. In other words, it has become accepted practice in the industry to soak its customers for progress whereas in the past a better car was the only kind that could be successfully sold at any price.

I'm further aware that the Model T's threefold and more drop in price was due primarily to Henry Ford's invention of the assembly line. The more cars he built, the less it cost to build each one and thus his outlay for constant improvement was easily absorbed. And so it was with his major competitors, who quickly adopted Ford's better idea until sometime around 1927 when the prices of all cars began to rise again. Why? One reason, of course, was inflation. A Model T at its lowest-priced heyday in 1925 retailed for about 16 cents a pound. Today's nearest equivalent, the Ford Pinto, costs you $1.50 a pound, which is almost a tenfold increase. And when equated to wages then and now, we again see approximately a tenfold increase for, you'll remember, we must compare Arthur Z.'s $8.335 an hour or $66.680 a day with the $5.00 a day paid to his grandfather back in 1925. Then, lastly, although I don't have the then and now costs of materials readily at hand, we can, I think, fairly assume the same tenfold increase for them in raw form per pound.

At first glance, inflated wages lend substance to industry's argument that you can buy today's car for the same or slightly less cost in terms of the man-hours you work to pay for it. In fact, the average price of a new car actually declined from about 50 percent of the median annual family income to 35 percent between 1959 and 1973. It's easily calculated. The Ford worker in 1925 had to set aside forty-eight-days' gross pay to buy a new Model T but his gross was also his net. There were no taxes or fringes taken out of his envelope. Arthur Z., who can save only what he sees in his check each week, would have to work about ninety days to get his Pinto. The difference, however, isn't all that substantial because we're talking about ten-hour days then and eight-hour days now. So, it would almost appear as though the industry deserves praise for holding the line on prices, perhaps slipping a bit here and there but in general satisfying its stockholders while staying within the various guidelines set by a succession of administrations, Democratic and Republican.

Nevertheless, I persist with the nagging thought that cars don't have to cost as much as they do. They compete for my *spendable* income, not my man-hours of work, and somehow I seem to end up with less to spend each passing year. And more to spend it on. Cars today vie with video entertainment centers, swimming pools, college educations, and globe-circling vacations as much as they do with each other. Thus, to keep my transportation expense in perspective, I habitually buy used rather than new cars. Call it perverseness if you will but I'm with the majority. Approximately two used cars change hands for every new one that is sold. A good used car might even be called the prototype "experimental affordable vehicle." Still, the thought lingers. Why can't new cars cost less instead of more? I'd certainly prefer one that does.

The answer lies hidden three paragraphs above. Though human ingenuity might not have kept cars, like hamburger, from costing tenfold more per pound between 1925 and now, engineers, perhaps, could have designed a Pinto weighing the same 1,650 pounds as the Model T instead of the 2,594 it lugs around today. At least then we might have a $2,475 Pinto and with it Detroit would be making a positive contribution to the cost of living by aiming a resoundingly negative blow at the Consumer Price Index. And it also might help Pinto sales.

Unfortunately, however, fat cars share the experience of fat people. It's cheap and easy to gain weight but expensive and difficult to get rid of it, especially if you attempt the transformation on a crash basis. Furthermore, most consumers still think fat is beautiful. The marketplace on its own has given U.S. automakers no incentive to watch weight other than that 15–20 percent share allotted by default to the imports. And while lust for a chunk of the imports' business undoubtedly influenced GM's decision to create the Chevette, which was the first of the domestic minicars, it was by no means the primary motivation. At the onset a cautious hedge against probable ramifications of the 1973–74 energy crisis and then a compelling necessity, the Chevette and the Omni/Horizon from Chrysler that followed owe their existence to CAFE, the corporate average fuel economy mandated by law that dictates 27.5 miles to the gallon by 1985. Lighter, smaller cars across the board are the only way to meet that mandate. But what disturbs me is that the Chevette is not cheap. It's an "affordable vehicle" only in the sense that it costs less to operate. It does not fully reflect the logic that the 1,994-pound Chevette should be priced significantly lower than the 3,084-pound Nova, the latter currently being the next step up in the Chevrolet line. The 1,090-pound difference results in only $761 less cost. Put another way, the Chevette costs about $1.80 per pound and the Nova, $1.40 per pound.[2] If we were talking ground round instead of hamburger, the per-pound difference would be understandable but there is nothing to suggest that the Chevette is constructed from better materials, or with more care, than the Nova.

Detroit's seeming inability to remove cost from its product in direct ratio to reduced weight is best reflected in pricing policies for the new generation of full-size and intermediate cars. These weigh 700 pounds less than their predecessors on the average but cost more. General Motors, in fact, calls attention to the increase by publicly stating it must spend $1 billion to achieve each ½-mpg reduction in CAFE. Why? The hard facts of the matter can be found once again in history. As I've stated, the volume leaders of the industry did not start passing the cost of product improvement on to the customer until 1927 or thereabouts and in so doing they disowned the origin of this volume.

[2] These calculations are based on suggested retail prices current on March 1, 1979, and do not include destination charges, taxes, and license.

Specifically, it originated in making new cars more rather than less affordable. Thus, a return to the thinking that built the industry would require a single manufacturer to price an entirely new line solely on the basis of labor, material, and fixed overhead. The cost of the research, engineering, styling, and tooling required to create this new line must be gambled one time, in the hope that volume generated by realistic pricing would pay back the gamble, as it did so munificently for Henry Ford.

In 1925, however, Henry Ford was the sole holder of Ford Motor Company stock. He had no one to answer to if he failed but himself. And his influence was such that stockholders and management of competing auto companies thought Ford's way to be the right way. Failure could be sudden but so too was success. Imagine yourself, though, as chairman of General Motors or, for that matter, Henry Ford II today. Could you justify to your stockholders a decision to gamble the $2.7 billion tooling and development costs of bringing GM's new front-drive "X" cars (Chevrolet Citation, Buick Skylark, Pontiac Phoenix, and Oldsmobile Omega) to market?[3] Could you assure these stockholders that 3 million could be sold in one year at $3,500 each to reach the break-even point as against 1 million for each of three years at $4,500? Could you be certain that much higher volume at the $3,500 level would be maintained for two additional years of glorious profits? The answers are unpredictable because no living chairmen and few living stockholders in GM, much less a majority, have ever been faced with such questions.

I trust by now I have clarified two possible ways of creating the "affordable vehicle." One way doesn't even require the construction of a prototype. It consists solely of a return to the competitive pricing policies of yesteryear. The other, obviously, lays in a search for cheaper and/or lighter equivalent materials and components. There are two more ways, too, one which I am reluctant to include because the American car buyer has historically refused to accept it. This is to re-create the Model T, allowing newer, more durable design but restricting creature comforts to the standards of the original. Volkswagen, for example, tried

---

[3] Publicly introduced on April 19, 1979. Suggested list prices were not established at this writing.

such an approach with "The Thing" but never sold more than a few ten thousands in this country. The Thing and its ilk have their place on the back roads of Ghana and the Philippines but not, it would seem, here. It doesn't, in fact, sell well in Mexico, where it is made. The fourth approach, a partial one and also highly unlikely, is that the various government agencies involved in the design of cars fold up their tents and thus allow manufacturers to remove about $600 worth of useless or at least unproved and controversial equipment, mandated by these agencies over the years.

I wouldn't suggest that anyone hold his breath while awaiting a purely economic solution either. Today's management is not free to be bold even if it possessed the necessary vision and courage. That unfortunate but realistic condemnation leaves us with cheaper or lighter equivalent materials and components, around which many prototypes have been constructed and none produced. However, before we explore the gains to be expected from substitute materials and components, we should first look at their role in the costing of a car as it is done by industry today.

GM's $4,500 "X" cars will be sold to dealers for a minimum of $3,645; that is, at a 19 percent discount.[4] The most basic car in Chevrolet Citation form should cost $3,264 to manufacture, which leaves the Division and ultimately the Corporation a $381 profit per car *if*, and only if, the four divisions involved sell a combined total of 1 million "X" cars for each of three years. Broken down, the costs per car include: materials, $2,346; direct labor, $127; transportation, $186; manufacturing overhead, $83; advertising and promotion, $57; warranty, $40; design, $5; engineering, $47; and miscellaneous costs, including amortization of special tooling, $373. If significantly less than 1 million cars are sold for each of the three years, material costs could increase somewhat, amortization of special tooling would climb drastically (at the expense of profit), and the others, excepting minor

[4] It should be remembered that $4,500 is not an "out-the-door" price. It does not include distribution charges and the mandatory equipment required by some states. Thus, the most basic Chevrolet Nova (old-style Citation) delivered for $5,065.95 in California as of March 1979. Add to that applicable taxes and license fees.

adjustments in advertising, design, and engineering, would remain relatively unaffected.

It can be seen that the cost of materials represents the greatest single expense and should be the area, presumably, on which it would be the most rewarding to concentrate. Using the 1975 Ford Country Squire station wagon as an example because it is typical of the now almost extinct era of the automotive dinosaurs, material usage breaks down as follows: steel, 3,368 lbs.; iron, 761 lbs.; rubber, 132 lbs.; plastics, 120 lbs.; glass, 115 lbs.; aluminum, 65 lbs.; zinc, 58 lbs.; copper, 36 lbs.; lead, 32 lbs.; and nickel, 2 lbs. Add in approximately 160 lbs. of miscellaneous materials such as fabrics, insulation, and paint, and we reach a dry weight of 4,849 lbs. for the complete car. The 1979 Ford LTD (Country Squire) on a seven-inch shorter (114.4-inch) wheelbase, the first of this company's new generation of "full-size" cars, weighs only 3,845 pounds in station wagon form. Inexplicably, however, you pay $1,175 more for 1,004 less pounds of car. The 1975 model sold for $6,115; the 1979 equivalent, $7,290.

Thus, all apparent avenues leading toward the affordable vehicle seem closed and we, the consumers, seem destined to pay $400–$600 more for our cars with each passing year. By 1989 at this rate, the cheapest domestic car on the market will have a sticker price of $6,590! That forecast, incidentally, is based on today's $3,580 Chevette "Scooter," an austere minimodel that in standard form doesn't even offer a rear seat. And it would be more like a $7,200 Scooter in 1989 when you add in all the charges you must pay to get it out the dealer's door. Obviously, a technological breakthrough bordering on the miraculous must occur to reverse the trend. Or, on the other hand, should we, the consumers, re-evaluate our attitude toward personal transportation and encourage automakers to revive the Model T?

Let's look at what's on the technological horizon first, keeping in mind that Detroit predicates its thinking on continuing a potpourri of models to suit everyone's taste and pocketbook. Further, for the purposes of this exercise, we must acknowledge that government-mandated goals already enunciated in the areas of fuel economy, emission control, and safety will in essence remain laws of the land. We'll start with the engine.

The gasoline-fueled piston engine has remained Detroit's darling since the invention of the automobile simply because no alternate form of propulsion has been found, with one exception, that to the industry's thinking is either superior in performance *and* economy or that is equivalent and cheaper to manufacture. The one exception, and only a partial one at that, is the diesel, which in modern passenger-car form gives somewhat inferior performance and costs more to manufacture but which is accepted despite its deficiencies because of superior economy.

Electrics have been around since the dawn of the automobile and so too has steam propulsion. The most modern electric carries about nine hundred pounds of batteries which can propel it no further than fifty miles at an average speed of thirty miles per hour, at which time the batteries must be recharged. Attempts to find longer-lasting batteries than the conventional lead-acid type have so far floundered on cost. The penalty extracted by batteries available today is not so much their weight as their bulk. Their installation encroaches severely on passenger and cargo space, making the electric practical so far only as an in-town car or light delivery truck. Electrics can be easily made to go faster but only at the expense of the total time they can travel between rechargings. Obviously, to be considered as an all-purpose substitute for the gasoline-powered automobile, they must at least quadruple their mileage potential at double their present speed. And, too, the recharging process must be accomplished in ten minutes rather than the present ten hours. Should this millennium ever be reached, the electric offers many advantages, primary among which are silent, smooth operation with very little pollution of the atmosphere for exceptionally long lifetimes.

No one in the industry seriously envisions the electric as the car of the reasonably near future except, possibly, in so-called hybrid form. This consists of a complete electric car *plus* a relatively small gasoline- or diesel-fueled engine which can be operated whenever necessary to recharge the batteries, or to provide current directly to the electric motor(s) as in a railway locomotive, or to both charge the batteries and provide the primary source of propulsion under light-load, cruising conditions. In any one of these forms, the hybrid is more complicated and thus more expensive to produce than the conventional automobile. Also, of course, the advantages of silent, smooth running and a near pollution-free exhaust would be lost. Some thought, too, has been given to hybrid cars which, like trolley buses, could be connected to a central source of power on certain main arteries, but again such ideas have floundered against the combined cost of manufacture and provision for the power source in or above the highway.

The steam car is another ancient turkey that existed even before Nikolaus August Otto and E. Langen produced the forerunner of today's gasoline engine in 1877. In fact, one Solomon de Caous back in 1595 attempted to build a steam carriage and aroused so much alarm among French authorities that he was put in a lunatic asylum. A steam carriage built by Nicolas Joseph Cugnot was running with reasonable success in 1770 and it was this machine, designed for the French Army, which is credited with being the first self-propelled vehicle anywhere, on or off rails and on land or water. Certainly the best known American steam car was the Stanley, produced with considerable success commercially between 1897 and 1927. A Model 735 Stanley of 1920 would cruise comfortably at 45 mph, out-accelerate most cars, and last for about a hundred miles between stops for water. The end was in sight by 1914, however, when Charles Kettering invented the self-starter for gasoline engines, as even the last of the Stanleys required a half hour or so to build up a head of steam. The ultimate American steamer, that built by Abner Doble between 1924 and 1932 in Emeryville, California, would start in a minute and a half, go 1,500 miles on 24 gallons of water, and generally outperform most cars of its day. However, the chassis alone cost $8,000 and therefore very few were sold.

Steam power has been experimented with periodically in modern times by Detroit's Big Three, most notably by General Motors, which usually has an operating prototype or two at its laboratories and proving grounds. Another intrepid steam fan was William P. Lear, Sr., inventor of the car radio, eight-track stereo, and builder of the Lear Jet, who sank $5.5 million of his personal fortune into an effort to produce a practical steam-powered automobile. The unsolved problem that besets them all is that water remains as the best working fluid known for vapor engines, and water freezes. Lear claimed to have invented a superior fluid which he called "Learium" but later admitted that it too was no match for water.

As late as 1969, GM said: "Whether a practical steam engine automobile can be realized in the future is still an unanswered question. However, new engineering materials and technology, along with the possibility of new fluids replacing water as the working medium in the cycle, make the steam engine a contender among proposed low-emission power plants." No further statement has been issued by that company in the decade since. Lear, about the same time, said: "I've been billed as the champion of the steam car. I'm not really the champion and I've got 5.5 million reasons why I'm not." But none of these problems seemed to bother Stanley and Doble owners. On cold nights, they simply kept the pilot light burning under the boiler and the next morning steamed merrily off about their business.

My own thought is that it's not technology but the complexity that defeats a revival of steam. The necessary componentry made GM's state-of-the-art steam engine about 450 pounds heavier than the piston engine it replaced and it produced but half the horsepower. Installation required a seven-inch extension to the engine compartment of the otherwise conventional car. True, from time to time, various inventors claim to have designed steam engines that are both small and extremely powerful (Bill Lear was even planning to enter a steam race car in the Indianapolis 500) but nothing seems to come of these projects. One acknowledged advantage of steam is a relatively low emission output; however, HC, CO, and NO_x are no lower than could be expected from an essentially simpler gas turbine. Another is use of potentially more plentiful fuels such as kerosene or diesel oil.[5] Summarizing, the most optimistic projection for steam would be its possible use in trucks and buses and then only if the conventional diesel engine failed to meet future emission standards. Steam engine research at present is not a high priority project, either in Detroit or elsewhere.

Any discussion of steam necessitates brief exploration of the most improbable power plant of all, which might be called "Dr.

---

[5] Approximately 15 to 30 percent more product could be obtained from each barrel (42 gallons) of crude if refineries were reprogrammed to primarily produce light oils rather than gasoline.

Duryea's steam turbine atomobile." The idea, broached in some academic circles, is to harness the heat from a tiny nuclear reactor to create steam and thus power the car or, alternately, tap radioisotopes to create electrical power. Once built, if that were possible, the first kind would indeed be economical to operate because the fission capabilities of the reactor would probably outlive its owner—even though the vehicle would weigh at least twenty tons because of the three-foot thick concrete housing needed to shield occupants and pedestrians from lethal radiation. It would not, however, be an affordable vehicle to buy and certainly it would not be welcomed by the "Greenpeace" cult. Known available radioisotopes, on the other hand, have a half life of from three to eighty years and the cost for the initial and each subsequent fueling would range from $100,000 to $2.7 million! For this price, the buyer would get a 6.7-horsepower car.[6]

The so-called external combustion or Stirling engine has been extensively investigated by both General Motors and Ford, the latter optimistically reporting in 1975 that mass production might be possible by 1985. The Stirling, invented in 1816 by a Scottish minister named Robert Stirling, is what might be described as a "closed-circuit" vapor (or steam) engine, although today organic fluids such as Freon are preferred to hydrogen and helium or the water of the original. The working fluid or gas is permanent and the heat source is external, fired by any conventional fuel such as kerosene or diesel oil. The Stirling is extremely efficient in modern form, being capable of producing 200 horsepower from just one cubic foot of engine.[7] It is virtually inaudible a few feet away and produces emissions far below any standards yet envisioned by the federal government. It is, however, complex and difficult to mass-produce, but despite this it is considered one of the more promising alternates to the piston engine.

The word "alternate" is the industry's, not mine. I feel, and history has generally proven, that any invention may be simplified to the degree that it is readily producible (witness

[6] Data in this paragraph were reported by General Motors Research Laboratories on May 7, 1969.
[7] Necessary componentry such as the regenerator tends to minimize the size advantage of the Stirling engine.

synthetic rubber and the atomic bomb) if the incentive exists. Detroit, apparently, does not as yet acknowledge the necessity of looking beyond some adaptation of the conventional piston engine for the immediate future. An incentive did exist for the motorhome industry. Plagued by complaints of noisy auxillary power generators disturbing the peace of campgrounds, Winnebago[8] recently announced availability of an optional Stirling installation to supply air conditioning, heat, and interior lighting for that firm's coaches. Admittedly, however, the Stirling's potential superiority does not seem to embrace a unit production cost lower than that of the piston engine, assuming that both devices advance in this direction.

I discussed the near coming of the automotive gas turbine in Chapter 6 when its leading proponent, George J. Huebner of Chrysler Corporation, persuaded management to at least entertain his proposal that the engine be made standard equipment in the volume Plymouth line by the end of the 1960s. If you can visualize two household-type fan blades facing each other, one motorized and the second connected to whatever apparatus you wish to drive, then you understand essentially how a gas turbine works in a ground vehicle application. In an aircraft, of course, you need only the powered blade to produce the driving jet force. In the actual engine, the power turbine is revolved by the blast of jet fuel burning in compressed air and directed against its blades. And the ease with which one can visualize the operation of the engine is its attraction. Unfortunately, however, automotive applications have always been burdened by the scarcity and thus cost of materials that will withstand combustion temperatures as high as 2,500 degrees Fahrenheit, more so than by problems of fabrication and assembly. With jet aircraft engines, it's cost be damned so progress in that field is seldom transferable.

When I mentioned the atomic bomb, I did not do so facetiously. There was a very real incentive, however horrible, to first develop and then produce this bomb in useful quantities and the seemingly impossible job got done. True, the gas turbine may

[8] Winnebago Industries of Forest City, Iowa, is the largest U.S. manufacturer of Class A motorhomes.

never be more fuel-efficient than a piston engine but that deficiency must be equated to the type of fuel used. The lower the grade of fuel, the potentially greater the supply, and a turbine can be designed to digest household heating oil. Thus, it might actually save fuel. Its capability of accepting emission control actually starts from a higher base than did the piston engine but nowhere near an equivalent amount of effort has been expended to explore this capability. The turbine, in fact, languishes for the very reason that it is the most promising alternate engine for the experimental affordable vehicle.

Williams Research Corporation[9] of Walled Lake, Michigan, has produced a prototype turbine compact and light enough to be held in both hands and powerful enough to propel a Jeep at freeway speeds. And unlike electric cars, the turbine excites prospective buyers. Given the impetus of all-out, dedicated effort, material problems could be surmounted but the turbine continues to languish because Detroit insists on saddling it with the costs of obsoleting billions of dollars' worth of manufacturing facilities—old and new foundries, machine tools, and assembly lines unique to the piston engine—that cannot be adapted to turbine production. This reluctance to change is understandable; the men who must make the decision are comfortable in their lifetime association with the old way. They'd have to go back to school!

No discussion of alternate engines can be complete without mention of the Wankel rotary. Problems that have delayed more widespread use of this design were also detailed in Chapter 6 but I reiterate here my belief that domestic production of the Wankel, if not killed, has been indefinitely postponed by the entrenched inertia of piston-oriented Detroit engineers. While not an avenue of itself toward the creation of the affordable vehicle, Wankel-type engines can be made in a range of power outputs on one set of machine tools, or "transfer line" as the assemblage is called. This would effect major manufacturing savings because a single basic engine design could meet the varying needs of each automaker. To increase power, as I pointed out in Chapter

[9] Sam Williams, founder of Williams Research, was the engineer on Huebner's staff who developed the rotary heat exchanger, key breakthrough in turbine application to the automobile.

6, you simply add additional "cylinders," or rotors and their housings, around a common crankshaft. Adoption of the Wankel would be a step, at least, in the direction of more affordable power plants.

I trust you, the reader, have survived this necessarily technical discussion of alternate engines for it leads to a rather nontechnical conclusion. An alternate engine design can do little to further our search for the experimental affordable vehicle unless it contributes simplicity. And as any engine is but one component, albeit a major one, of a vehicle, the goal of simplicity must be expanded to include every part of that vehicle on down to the lowliest fastener. The truly simple car is not an impossibility. Those that qualify are abundant in history, the Model T just being the best known example. A better illustration for my thesis, also from the same maker, would be Ford's first eight-cylinder car of 1932. Here was a 70-horsepower package of utilitarian driving excitement that weighed only 2,000 pounds in roadster form and sold for $460, only $10 more than the stodgy, four-cylinder Model A which it replaced. It was adequately sized and comfortable, but hardly luxurious. It also, with a touch of modern engineering, could meet a CAFE of 27.5 miles to the gallon. This particular roadster is the most desirable of all Fords in the eyes of collectors today, bringing $25,000 and more in restored or excellent original form. Why? That premium price is predicated on excellence and esthetic appeal, not rarity.

In seeming defiance of logic, let's project this exercise of forty-seven years ago as our target affordable vehicle of the immediate future. We are wedded to a car that with the most elementary updating could produce one horsepower for each twenty pounds of its weight, not necessarily the concept of eight cylinders. If power were by turbine, we could have a simple two-speed, clutchless planetary transmission. Let styling be dictated by function; for example, the car in sedan form could have the right rear door and glass interchangeable with the left front and the bumpers, front and rear, could be identical as could the roof panel for both two- and four-door versions.[10] If the car weighed but 2,000 pounds, there would be no need for power assists. Nor

---

[10] American Motors built just such a concept car over ten years ago.

need it be tiny for space of itself weighs nothing, only the structure surrounding it, which, Detroit has proved, can be lightened significantly.

We the customers for this affordable vehicle, in turn, must reevaluate our conviction that personal transportation is but an extension of our living rooms. Do we really need reclining bucket seats, stylized indications of speed and engine function, automatic windows, stereo music, perhaps even air conditioning, and all the other accouterments which, though maybe not specified by you for your present car, must be allowed for in its design? And most important of all, must this package be reshaped and retrimmed each model year, changing it only for the sake of change?

We have a clear choice and if you, like me, continue to buy used instead of new cars until our choice is made available, Detroit will quickly get the message. If, on the other hand, we accept without murmur the needless extravagance, the blatant excesses that are built into our cars in the name of progress year after year, then no profit-oriented organization on earth would be foolish enough to re-create the affordable vehicle. Motorcycles aren't the answer and neither are Volkswagen Beetles, although the latter came closer—two more wheels closer, at any rate. We must, in essence, *distinguish between needs and wants*, recognizing that least expensive function fulfills the one and price be damned gratification the other.

CHAPTER 15

The Solution

Against the wall in the room where I'm writing this is a bookcase and in it is a copy of *My Years with General Motors*[1] by Alfred P. Sloan, Jr. This book, more than any other I've read, presents the case for Bigness and though it is clearly labeled an autobiography and thus a history of the man and the creature he gestated, I've no doubt it was intended as a guide for future generations of young executives, particularly those already employed by the creature. If I were a librarian, I'd find a slot for it on the shelf with other how-to's, in the same section, say, as a book on how to restore and refinish antique furniture or, more appropriately perhaps, one on how to lay out a steam-era model railroad complete with sidings leading to miniature industries in quantity and variety sufficient to ensure that railroad's model prosperity.

And much as we might someday revive steam, Mr. Sloan's book, first bought only by those who felt obligated to read it, has been rediscovered. It's in a belated second printing as a required text for students seeking their masters in business management. In it, right at the beginning, they will find this: "Management has been my specialization. On many occasions when I was chief executive officer I had individual responsibility for initiating policy. However, it is doctrine in General Motors that, while policy may originate anywhere, it must be appraised and approved by

[1] Doubleday & Company, Inc., Garden City, N.Y., 1964.

committees before being administered by individuals. In other words, General Motors has been a group management comprised of very competent individuals. And so I shall often say 'we' instead of 'I' and sometimes when I say 'I', I may mean 'we'."

Then on January 9, 1931, chief executive Sloan addressed a memo to the Operations Committee. It read in part: ". . . I think, notwithstanding that we have a reputation of a fact-finding organization, that we do not get the facts, even now, as completely as we should. We sit around and discuss things without the facts. I think we should break ourselves of that and not permit any member of the Committee to have an important problem determined upon without all members of the Committee have [sic] the facts before them and are placed in a position to exercise their own individual judgement, otherwise the Committee is not fair to itself and to the Corporation because it is not discharging its full responsibility to same." Mr. Sloan was beginning to realize, as someone at Ford expressed it years later, that "a camel is a horse designed by committee."

I said Mr. Sloan created General Motors. That is true, as we know the enterprise today. He came to an existing corporation founded in 1908 by William Crapo Durant who, between that year and November 30, 1920, when he (Durant) was forced to resign for the second and last time, brought together at least forty acquisitions in the auto and related industries around his original base, which was the Buick Motor Company, then the nation's No. 1 producer of automobiles. Mr. Sloan, meanwhile, was the president and, with his father, the principal owner of the Hyatt Roller Bearing Company when it was bought by Durant in 1916 to become a part of United Motors, which in turn was enveloped by the colossus two years later. Sloan didn't exactly start at the bottom in GM; his entry level was as vice-president, director, and member of the Executive Committee. And within another two years, an overextended General Motors found itself without the cash to meet its payroll.[2] All the major car-producing divisions except Buick and Cadillac had almost ceased production and those two were operating at reduced rates. It was during this period of economic panic that Sloan formulated his prin-

[2] This, of course, is what led to founder Durant's second and final resignation.

ciple of decentralized operating divisions managed and succored by central committees.

In so doing, he created a business enterprise that not only survived but prospered on an unprecedented scale. Between late 1917, which was the year the "old" General Motors Company became the "new" General Motors Corporation, and December 31, 1962, when Sloan was compiling statistics for his book, employment increased from 25,000 to over 600,000; dollar sales rose from $270 million to $14.6 billion; and total assets grew from $134 million to $9.2 billion. Never once during this period, which included violent fluctuations in the national and world economies, did GM miss paying dividends to shareholders (whose numbers went from three thousand to more than a million) although there were years when dividends paid far exceeded net income. As Sloan notes: "This is a measure of the significance of General Motors as an institution in American economic life."

I said in Chapter 1 that it was not my purpose to condemn or even to question the vertical evolvement of the automobile industry. Certainly, Wall Street and widows alike have reason to bless GM and, to a lesser extent, the other three survivors. However, now that the industry has evolved, and stagnated in terms of new entries, I think these blessings should be re-examined in terms of their future contribution. We should probe into the present, lopsided division of the automotive marketplace, the forbidding problems of entry, the high-handed practices that nurtured a vast and unnecessary expansion of government, and ask if it is still the way to go. The answer may be distasteful. The solution could require creation of one last, hopefully temporary bureaucracy—that charged with divestiture. So, let the trial begin.

A cogent argument for Bigness is the talent it attracts to its factories, research laboratories, and proving grounds. And to its committees too, for while strong management may not guarantee excellence of product, it is the surest warrantor of corporate prosperity and thus the best hope for higher salaries and eventual retirement. The history of the U.S. automobile industry has proved this approximately 2,500 times, as there have been that many failures. Then of equal importance, Bigness assures a reservoir of plant, facilities, and finance to expedite action once a decision is taken. But the aspiring young automotive engineer or executive today has little choice other than the Big Four. Would he or she prefer challenge to security if it were available?

In any critique of the remaining automakers, separately or collectively, one must acknowledge that the design and production of a full line of cars, covering all size and price ranges and each with its fifteen thousand parts, lies beyond the means of all but a handful of U.S. corporations. A single model can be assembled in limited facilities and with narrow resources, specialized units like the Checker taxicab for a market too small to interest the Big Four, but major components must be bought from existing sources, which of course are the same Big Four. When Henry J. Kaiser, whose Kaiser Industries was a big corporation by any standard, announced plans in 1944 to enter the automobile industry, he bragged he was "prepared to commit as much as $50 million." A knowledgeable observer at the time commented: "That's not bad for openers!" Today, openers leading to mass production would run closer to $500 million, for which you would get one basic model in one body style, produced in one plant. Henry Ford II claimed in 1960 to have dropped $250 million on the Edsel, which in its two versions was nothing more than a variation on existing Ford products. It differed only in its exterior styling and trim, yet its failure after but two years of manufacture severely wounded the nation's third largest industrial corporation.

Contrary to popular assumption, neither General Motors, Ford, nor Chrysler has done anything illegal in modern times to in any way interfere with or restrict the entry of a new producer. They didn't have to. This was in effect accomplished, painlessly and legally, by the sheer size of the incumbents. Nor, for that matter, have they seen fit to prevent imports from moving in and selling through their existing dealer organizations. Currently, about 1,800 dealers handle a noncaptive import[3] in addition to their domestic lines. The legend that Detroit put the squeeze on Preston Tucker and his then revolutionary rear-engined "Torpedo" back in 1948 has no basis whatever in fact. Tucker never claimed that. He simply ran afoul of the Securities Exchange

[3] The term "captive" means imports produced by overseas subsidiaries of American automakers.

Commission in his attempt to finance production, and though he was later vindicated on charges of fraud, the legal battle wiped him out. Then, much more recently, we find Chrysler delighted to sell an unused plant in Pennsylvania to Volkswagen for domestic production of the Rabbit.

There are examples, too, of the Big Three (AMC makes it a "Big Four" when I must use that term) moving into a specialized area once the exclusive purview of independents without disturbing anyone's position. Today's burgeoning market for four-wheel-drive utility vehicles is a good illustration. The Jeep, made under various aegises for the civilian market since World War II, and then International's Scout had the field to themselves, except for a trickle of imports, until 1967 when Ford introduced the Bronco and, more significantly, 1969, with the addition of Chevrolet's Blazer. "We welcome the competition," stated Kaiser and International bravely at the time, but to their considerable surprise, competition greatly expanded the market and to everyone's benefit, including Chrysler's, which followed along several years later. Jeep is still No. 1 and International sells more Scouts than ever.

Another specialty is the large, truck-type station wagon. Not too long ago, these were sold only to industry as personnel transports and the sole suppliers, except for sporadic flirtations by Dodge, were Chevrolet and International. Then these vehicles were "discovered" as the ideal prime mover for full-time trailerites, those who follow the sun for work or pleasure. Jeep moved in with its Wagoneer, now No. 1 in the field, International's Travelall (now Traveler) still does well as does Chevrolet's Suburban, and the others jumped ahead by inventing the maxivan which, when equipped with seats and windows, can carry several families, tow the heaviest trailer and, during the work week, double as an ideal commuting jitney. Then when supplied in cab and chassis form, maxivans are the basis for thousands of Class B motorhomes whose bodies are manufactured by at least a hundred independent firms.

The heavy-duty truck, those giants with a gross vehicle weight of 33,000 pounds or over, is a field by no means dominated by Detroit. International out of Fort Wayne, Indiana, is No. 1, Mack from Allentown, Pennsylvania, is No. 3, and other independents from Ohio, Washington, and California fill the fifth through eighth slots. Though Ford is No. 2 and GMC No. 4, Chevrolet comes in a distant ninth. Chrysler, in turn, gave up completely[4] in this lucrative market. AMC hasn't, however. Few people outside the industry are aware that its AMC General Division is the world's largest builder of heavy-duty military trucks. But specialty builders don't have to be big to prosper. FWD Corporation of Clintonville and the Oshkosh Truck Corporation, also in Wisconsin, have survived for years, each with an annual volume of less than five hundred units.

Bigness is sometimes thwarted by its grandiose approach to modest projects. General Motors Truck & Coach Division decided around 1970 to manufacture complete Class A motorhomes. Theretofore, truck makers including GMC had been content to supply assembled chassis to the many independent body builders in the recreational vehicle field; in fact, prudence dictated not competing with one's customers. But, once approved by committee, GMC's project set out to swallow itself. A totally new chassis with air suspension was engineered around the front-wheel-drive powerpack from the Oldsmobile Toronado for GMC's exclusive use, thus obsoleting the modified, cart-sprung school-bus chassis the Division still offered to the trade. GM Styling designed a body so curvaceously streamlined that living space inside was seriously curtailed, a problem further aggravated by the mandatory choice of overstuffed, "decorator" interiors. Technically, the coach was superb but practical it was not, and it bombed. Obviously, nobody involved had ever spent a month on the road in a motorhome, for how else can you explain a lavatory so arranged that one must sit on the toilet to take a shower? Or, assuming customer acceptance of this misdirected bidet, no provision to waterproof the toilet-tissue dispenser?

Does this motorhome that failed support the case for bigness? General Motors dropped maybe $20 million on the project, an amount that would put all but the top two or three independent

[4] Chrysler Corporation flatly stated it was government safety regulations, existing and anticipated and particularly the one involving anti-skid braking, that triggered the firm's unexpected abandonment of medium- and heavy-duty truck manufacture.

recreational vehicle manufacturers out of business overnight. A factory would close, two hundred or so employees would be out of jobs, investors would lose, the economy of some small town would be disrupted, and existing owners of the coaches would find themselves with unwarranted orphans whose resale value had dropped by half. GM, however, still honors the warranty, stocks spare parts, was unruffled by the $20 million loss, and the employees involved were assigned to building vans in the same plant space. Inherent in bigness is the capability of absorbing minor errors, and the occasional major one as well. But, on the other hand, inherent in a small, specialized, and more directly experienced organization would be the unlikelihood of this particular error occurring.

More pertinent to our discussion, perhaps, is the Corvette. As I mentioned in Chapter 7, this pioneer and now only modern-day American sportscar started life as one of GM stylist Harley Earl's rare personal projects (the Italian-bodied Cadillac Eldorado Brougham of 1957–58 was another) and evolved from a one-of-a-kind 1953 Motorama show car to a tentative production run of three hundred units late that year. What automaker other than General Motors could afford to measure public acceptance by producing three hundred cars essentially hand-built of the then new and untried plastic, fiberglass? The original intent was to move on to a steel-bodied Corvette, the sheet metal for which would be stamped out by relatively inexpensive Kirksite dies. Production would be limited, maybe 6,000 Corvettes a year at most, because Kirksite was too soft to permit longer runs. However, and contrary to expectations, engineers found a way to partially automate the molding of fiberglass bodies and, despite early problems with uneven surfaces, the material continues to be used today in over 40,000 Corvettes annually.

Could an independent have persevered with a similar experiment? We have only Kaiser to draw a comparison. That company, also in 1953 and coincidental with the Corvette, introduced the Darrin-styled KD-161 sportscar. This car, too, had a fiberglass body and in some respects was more imaginative and advanced than its competitor. However, Kaiser-Frazer was a dying enterprise at the time, as were most of its dealers, and by 1955 had collapsed, leaving only the Jeep as a viable survivor. If

THE SOLUTION

one could find a Kaiser dealer, one could buy a KD-161, but those few hundred customers that did so knew there was no future for the car. There was room in the market, however, as Ford later proved with its popular two-seater Thunderbird, circa 1955–57. And there have been serious attempts since, notably the Canadian-built Bricklin, of which about 2,000 were sold, and the forthcoming De Lorean DMC-12, which at this writing will be built in Northern Ireland. Carroll Shelby made money for a few years with his adaptations of AC Cobras and, later, Ford Mustangs, and even American Motors tried with its Nash-Healey, though not very vigorously. I mention these specialty nameplates, among which only the Shelby and the later Corvettes could be considered true sportscars, because neophyte automakers in recent times have invariably chosen this port of entry. And it is perhaps the most illogical, as legends such as Porsche, Jaguar, Triumph, and M.G. must be unseated in the minds of enthusiast buyers, not Detroit. But it can be done for the Porsche itself is a post-World War II creation, not entering series production until 1950 and still made in quantities of less than 50,000 vehicles annually. Rolls-Royce, it might be noted while speaking of legends, makes about 2,000 cars a year and does so profitably.

I could go on looking into niches, occupied and vacant, but the comings and goings in the suburbs of the industry do little to upset the market penetration statistics of the four incumbents. Though significant change is possible, even feasible and desirable, there's no chance with the present alignment that it can ever again be instigated by a newcomer to the industry. Nor can redistribution of penetration be achieved by foreign automakers establishing plants here. Volkswagen already has one, Nissan (Datsun) has optioned land, Toyota and Toyo Kogyo (Mazda) are narrowing their search for sites, Volvo has temporarily abandoned its plans, and American Motors will probably assemble certain new Renault designs suitable for the U.S. market. However, all these efforts except the latter are or were intended as a hedge against currency fluctuations and the resulting products will simply replace equivalent cars currently being imported. While beneficial to the U.S. economy and to the domestic labor force, these cars are not likely to meaningfully affect sales of

Chevrolets and Fords. They will feed off their own, just as a "Made in U.S.A." label has not helped the Volkswagen Rabbit to date.

The key question to be asked is: "What justification exists for breaking up General Motors, Ford, and possibly though not probably Chrysler into smaller though still self-sufficient entities?" The answer does not lie in academic interpretation of antitrust law. Monopoly is not the issue. *Justification exists because Bigness, whether monopolistic or not, has bred and continues to breed a woeful, burdensome, multibillion-dollar multiplication of government!* The arrogance of Bigness has created a bureaucracy dedicated to its control and inevitably, as has already started to happen, your and my freedom is disappearing into the same maw as that of General Motors and Ford. We as individuals certainly can't afford this and neither, for that matter, can Chrysler or American Motors. The industry is being regulated beyond its capacity to cope and, as a result, its products are priced beyond our reach. Who was at fault, where the blame lies, is no longer of concern.

If you think the plague is confined to its point of origin, Detroit, let me quote J. W. Marriott, Jr., president of the worldwide Marriott hotel chain:

"It is becoming more and more popular to tear down the free enterprise system, the system that made this country the most productive with the highest standard of living in the history of the world.

"We're letting government run away with the football! In our democracy I thought government was supposed to be an impartial referee. But somehow they're in there trying to change the rules and calling the plays, as the special interests cheer for more points to be scored against business.

"And so I suggest a revolt. A taxpayers' and business leaders' revolt against far more government than we need. Or deserve. Or want. Or will stand for. Or will pay for.

"When you think of how government has grown, consider this: the average taxpayer has to work until May to pay his taxes.

"If that's not madness, I don't know what it is . . ."

Divestiture of a part of the automobile industry (and the oil industry) would not be "tearing down free enterprise." It would be allowing free enterprise to re-create itself, at least in that sector of the economy for which Detroit is responsible, a sector that generates more than 18 percent of the country's Gross National Product and provides jobs for some 14 million Americans—one out of every five workers. And concurrent to this divestiture of industry must come a demobilization of bureaucracy, that vast army of civil servants in auto-related government agencies who rotate their time between composing forms to be filled out and filing those returned. These forms, reports, audits, and information searches are estimated to cost all industry $116 billion annually; Detroit's 18 percent share amounts to $20.9 billion. And that doesn't include the cost to support the bureaucracies. On a per car basis, the cost of regulation and the often superfluous equipment or modifications generated by these regulations will reach $1,000 by 1985, and that's in 1979 dollars!

If Chevrolet were spun off from General Motors, it would still comprise an organization about nine times the present size of American Motors and the plight of the latter illustrates how divestiture would work. An AMC executive, appearing recently before the Senate Committee on Commerce, Science and Transportation, pleaded for a "careful relaxation of federal constraints to permit industry-wide cooperation on basic research efforts," he believing that to be the most productive and cost-effective way to develop new automotive technologies quickly. He was actually pleading AMC's dilemma; his company lacks the resources to meet current and pending federal regulations, whether measured in talent, time, or money. More pertinently, his company cannot "re-invent the car" as called for by transportation Secretary Brock Adams in a recent speech. And that is how it should be. Place the entire industry in a situation where no segment of it is large enough to independently afford the luxury of regulation, *then dare government to shut the whole down!*

I do not pretend to have the detailed knowlege of industry resources that would permit me to block out the exact composition of the newly independent car producers that would emerge from divestiture. Obviously, each entity must have the facilities to manufacture and assemble engines, captive or shared facilities to manufacture stampings and assemble these into bodies, and then a plant to put it all together in the form of finished cars. Transmissions, axles, and other major components could be bought from newly independent suppliers spun off the corporate tree; for example, GM has three separate facilities for the manufacture of automatic transmissions. Its AC Spark Plug Division is larger than any existing independent producer of ignition components and so too is the Harrison Radiator Division in its field. And, Fisher Body could be independent again, as it once was.

Chevrolet Division alone embraces six car lines out of a total of nine that each sell in volume equal to or greater than the combined registrations of American Motors' three lines;[5] that is, 250,000 or more units a year, which is the commonly conceded dividing point between profit and loss for a "lean and hungry" independent. In addition, there is Chevrolet truck, which is the single largest seller in that Division's stable. Chevrolet, in other words, could be divided into seven separate producing companies. Applying the same rule-of-thumb to Ford Division, we find another six lines, plus the truck, which in this case too is the single largest seller.

Could these newly independent producers afford the research, planning, marketing counsel, styling, and plant engineering formerly provided at least in part by GM's central staff? I believe so because much of this staff activity is redundant, or if not, it could be categorized as theoretical and thus many man-hours away from practical application. The vast GM Technical Center, for example, is a "think tank" and it does not ordinarily create hardware ready for instant production. GM Styling is presently divided into self-sufficient "studios" which parochially serve each Division with as much secrecy as if they were indeed separate entities. About the only measurable loss would be access to the corporate vault. The newly independent producers would have to borrow money on the open market. A measurable gain would be reduction in overhead. I know from my own experience in the magazine field that a property with a circulation of around 100,000 copies a month can be quite profitable for the four or five people involved in its production, but once the title is bought by a large publisher, circulation must triple to meet its

---

[5] AMC's Jeep is not included, it being counted as a truck in production and registration totals.

share of the cost to support that publisher's central staff of vice-presidents and assorted experts. Central staffs tend to be a burden in most organizations. They cut productivity by creating nonproductive work for themselves and also for those they are supposed to advise.

Divestiture of the auto industry, I'm sure, would be a tremendously complicated financial transaction. The wail of existing GM and Ford stockholders would waft across the land, at least until they realized taxes might drop faster than dividends if, indeed, there were any loss. Automobile dealers would cry out in pain too until they found they were wanted and appreciated by their newly independent factories. They just might reach the sales vice-president on the phone for the first time in most of their lives. And customers would approve of having car salesmen knock on their doors once again. Service might not be instantly perfect but it would be less complicated because of the deproliferation of models.

I'm certain morale would bloom at the factories. The talented men and women at the divisions now administering policies decreed by committees would create their own and enjoy the rewards attendant on the birth of any thing one conceives, whether it be babies or ideas. Communication between assembly line workers and top management would be only the length of the building away. And this same newly aware management might listen when the union asks for a seat on the board or doors on the toilets, rights that those who never leave the "Green House" find hard to understand. Then, in turn, the union would listen when management explains why a strike could cost everyone his job. "What happens to me?" lament those on the committees. "Compete with your junior for a job in the plant," comes the answer. "Your mature judgment might be valuable when tempered by swing-shift reality!"

The day of divestiture may never come. Aligned against it is an oddly assorted but powerful group, even odder because those allied don't recognize the nature of their alliance. We have the chieftains of industry whom the stockholders elect. The chieftains then commit wrongs against their customers, wrongs of great magnitude, wrongs of commission and omission, and the customers, who are the people, rebel. They rebel by approving a proliferation of government to control the chieftains and then the stockholders, who pay for this proliferation, wonder where their dividends went and blame the government. Somewhere in all of this, there may be sanity, but I fail to see it.